INSPIRED LIVING

SUPERPOWERS FOR HEALTH, LOVE, AND BUSINESS

CAROLYN McGEE

FEATURING: SUNSHINE BEESON, KATHY BOYER, MARIBETH COYE DECKER, LESLIE FRASER, JUDY GIOVANGELO, REBECCA LYN GOLD, TERRI HAWKE, DEBORAH HODIAK-KNOX, SHARON JOSEF, JACQUELINE M. KANE, KELLY KARIUS, DR. SONIA LUCKEY, BIRGIT LUEDERS, RENEE MORITZ, DONNA O'TOOLE, ANNA PEREIRA, JIM PHILLIPS, MARK PORTEOUS, REV. JOY RESOR, KYE SUN ROSE, DAWN SIMPSON, DENISE M. SIMPSON, CHRIS STONER, JANETTE STUART

INSPIRED LIVING

SUPERPOWERS FOR HEALTH, LOVE AND BUSINESS

CAROLYN McGEE

FEATURING: SUNSHINE BEESON, KATHY BOYER, MARIBETH COYE DECKER, LESLIE FRASER, JUDY GIOVANGELO, REBECCA LYN GOLD, TERRI HAWKE, DEBORAH HODIAK-KNOX, SHARON JOSEF, JACQUELINE M. KANE, KELLY KARIUS, DR. SONIA LUCKEY, BIRGIT LUEDERS, RENEE MORITZ, DONNA O'TOOLE, ANNA PEREIRA, JIM PHILLIPS, MARK PORTEOUS, REV. JOY RESOR, KYE SUN ROSE, DAWN SIMPSON, DENISE M. SIMPSON, CHRIS STONER, JANETTE STUART

Inspired Living

Superpowers for Health, Love, and Business

Carolyn McGee

©Copyright 2022 Carolyn McGee

Published by Brave Healer Productions

Paperback ISBN: 978-1-954047-65-5

eBook ISBN: 978-1-954047-64-8

Definition of "Inspired" from vocabulary.com

"If something is so extraordinary that it's worthy of being described as inspired, you might think that the gods had something to do with its creation. In fact, inspired originally meant "directly inspired by God or gods." It comes from the Latin in-"in" and spirare "to breathe." Maybe such supernatural power did breathe life into something truly excellent. Or maybe the humans just worked very hard and had a great idea."

DEDICATION

What is an Inspired Life? It is living authentically, openly, and powerfully in whatever brings you joy.

This book is dedicated to all who desire to live an Inspired Life—to the people who've overcome a challenge to live fully in their power and be seen as their truest self.

The Hero's Journey, according to Joseph Campbell, is the path from struggle to success. We all have our unique version of the Hero's Journey—some are perilous and some more calm. They all are powerful in creating our unique path toward living our soul's purpose. We choose this life to evolve our souls and make this world a happier, more loving space. This is inspirational.

As we live in our unique truth, we allow others to step into theirs.

By my side, as I stepped into my authentic self and lived my joyful, inspired life were my children. Sarah and Kyle inspire me every single day. I'm so proud of them for the lives they're creating and the lives they will touch.

DISCLAIMER

This book offers health and nutritional information and is designed for educational purposes only. You should not rely on this information as a substitute for, nor does it replace professional medical advice, diagnosis, or treatment. If you have any concerns or questions about your health, you should always consult with a physician or other healthcare professional. Do not disregard, avoid, or delay obtaining medical or health-related advice from your healthcare professional because of something you may have read here. The use of any information provided in this book is solely at your own risk.

Developments in medical research may impact the health, fitness, and nutritional advice that appears here. No assurances can be given that the information contained in this book will always include the most relevant findings or developments with respect to the particular material.

Having said all that, know that the experts here have shared their tools, practices, and knowledge with you with a sincere and generous intent to assist you on your health and wellness journey. Please contact them with any questions you may have about the techniques or information they provided. They will be happy to assist you further!

TABLE OF CONTENTS

INTRODUCTION | i

CHAPTER 1

TRUST IN TRUTH | 1

THE JOURNEY TO EASE AND FLOW IN
EVERY AREA OF YOUR LIFE

By Carolyn McGee, The Decision Queen, Sacred Haven Living Guide

---

CHAPTER 2

THE ENERGETIC GREEN SMOOTHIE
FOR YOUR ANIMALS | 11

SO YOU CAN CONNECT WITH THEM ANYWHERE AND ANYTIME

By Maribeth Coye Decker, Animal Communicator,
Medical Intuitive, Healer

CHAPTER 3

HEALING AFTER THE DEATH OF YOUR PET | 19

A SIMPLE TECHNIQUE TO EASE END-OF-LIFE TRAUMA

By Kathy Boyer, Animal Communicator, Energy Healer

CHAPTER 4

MY JOURNEY INTO MEDICAL INTUITION | 29
CLOSING THE GAP BETWEEN WHO YOU ARE AND WHO YOU DESIRE TO BECOME

By Sharon Joseph PhD., Channeler,
Medical Intuitive, Animal Communicator, Healer

———————————

CHAPTER 5

JOY BEYOND GRIEF | 37
HEAL YOUR HEART AFTER LOSS

By Judy Giovangelo, Founder of Ben Speaks,
Advanced Grief Recovery Specialist

———————————

CHAPTER 6

AT FIRST AWARE, THEN FULLY ALIVE | 47
ENGAGING YOUR SUPERPOWER FOR A LIFE WELL-LIVED

By Jim Phillips, Certified LIFE Strategist and LIFE Coach

———————————

CHAPTER 7

SHINE YOUR AUTHENTIC LIGHT | 57
CULTIVATING YOUR SUPERPOWER USING JOYFUL SELF-CARE

By Janette Stuart, Angelic Practitioner

———————————

CHAPTER 8

CONQUERING FEAR TO LIVE YOUR LIFE ON PURPOSE | 66
HOW TO MAKE A GIGANTIC LEAP TOWARD YOUR DREAM!

By Kye Sun Rose, Energy Healer, Spiritual Coach

———————————

CHAPTER 9

GOLDEN EARTH ENERGY MEDITATION | 75
MAKING SURE GRIEF DOESN'T MAKE YOU SICK
By Renee Moritz, Shaman, Medical Intuitive,
Energy Medicine Practitioner, Animal Communicator

CHAPTER 10

ACTIVE INNER STILLNESS | 85
REDIRECTING STRESS FOR NEXT-LEVEL FOCUS AND ENERGY
By Dr. Sonia Luckey, DNP, MA, FNP-BC, PMHNP-BC

CHAPTER 11

THE BREAKDOWN
BEFORE THE BREAKTHROUGH | 95
ACHIEVING UNTOUCHED LEVELS
By Chris Stoner, The Fascia Performance Coach

CHAPTER 12

SPILLING THE TEA | 105
AN EXTRAORDINARY ACT OF REBELLION
By Deborah Hodiak-Knox, Transformational Coach, Designer

CHAPTER 13

FEAR TO FREEDOM | 113
THROUGH COURAGE AND DIVINE TRUST
By Sunshine Beeson, Iridologist, Hypnotherapist, Retreat Facilitator

CHAPTER 14

ACCESSING YOUR INNER TRUTH | 122
HOW TO EXPERIENCE LIFE-CHANGING
SPIRITUAL GROWTH THROUGH MEDITATION

By Donna O'Toole, RN, B.Ed., Massage Therapist, Druid Priestess

---

CHAPTER 15

DIAMONDS AND SAWDUST | 133
CREATIVE EXPRESSION FOR JOY AND MANIFESTING

By Anna Pereira, CEO and Head Goddess of The Wellness Universe

---

CHAPTER 16

HEAL YOUR INNER SABOTEUR | 144
IGNITE YOUR ABILITY TO ATTRACT GREATER ABUNDANCE

By Jacqueline M. Kane, R.T., LMT, EFT, Master Energetic Healer

---

CHAPTER 17

ACTUALIZING YOUR IDEAL LIFE | 155
MANIFESTATION STRATEGIES TO HELP YOU
ACHIEVE PERSONAL FULFILLMENT

By Leslie Fraser, LMT, JFB MFR Expert

CHAPTER 18

A MOTHER'S HEART | 165
EMBODYING YOUR INNER NURTURER

By Dawn Simpson, Intuitive Spiritual Life Coach, Energy Healing Guide

CHAPTER 19

THE DEPTH AND BREADTH OF LOVE | 173
AN UNEXPECTED JOURNEY
By Rev. Joy Resor, Spiritual Mentor, Joy Bringer

CHAPTER 20

SEEKING SOLACE | 186
FINDING HEALING AND JOY IN NATURE
By Terri Hawke, Naturalist, Animal Communicator, Energy Healer

CHAPTER 21

THE POWER OF YOUR STORIES | 195
A YOGIC PATH FOR WRITING TO HEAL
By Rebecca Lyn Gold, E-RYT, Founder of Yogic Writing™

CHAPTER 22

REBOOT, RESTORE, AND HEAL YOUR BODY | 203
HOW TO DETOX THE RIGHT WAY
By Birgit Lueders, MH, CCII

CHAPTER 23

BALANCED THINKING | 213
HOW TO LOVE UNCONDITIONALLY
By Kelly Karius BSW, RSW, Mediator

CHAPTER 24

LEADING WITH SOUL | 221

A SIMPLE PRACTICE TO THRIVE IN YOUR DIVINE PURPOSE

By Mark Porteous

CHAPTER 25

MAKING FRIENDS WITH THE
DARK NIGHT OF THE SOUL | 231

DISCOVERING INNER VOICES TO TRANSFORM DEPRESSION

By Denise M. Simpson, MEd

CLOSING | 241

MY GRATITUDE | 242

ABOUT CAROLYN MCGEE | 244

INTRODUCTION

My mother is one of six children. The four girls were teachers and came home to Mother with their kids every summer. I grew up with the joy of seven cousins and my sister playing together on my grandparents' seven acres with a river babbling down a hill. The aunts would pair up with two keeping track of all the kids so the other two could relax and chat.

It was a beautiful way to grow up. We each had jobs and lived as a community. When an aunt said, "Go help with the dishes," we did it even if we did dishes the day before. All the adults were treated the same. We helped weed the gardens, set the table, cook, and clean.

We were outside playing from breakfast to dinner, and the big rules were, "Stay with a buddy and don't go in the river." We did plays, were gods and goddesses, wrote books, explored, and watched the clouds shift into shapes. My love for community and collaboration was born there.

My favorite part was going on adventures and journeys with my grandmother. She was an avid gardener and naturalist who seemed to know every plant that existed. "Look at the pretty pink lady slipper! They are rare, so we don't pick them." We would go on hikes with a picnic lunch and explore. "I love the orange of the paintbrush flowers. What would you paint that color?" I used my imagination when I was with her, and she encouraged curiosity about plants, animals, history, and mythology.

My quest for magic and community continues in this book. My intention for Inspired Living was to gather and create a community that supports each other in the moment and beyond. This group of 25 authors accomplished this beyond my wildest dreams. Each experts' Hero's Journey story is powerful, vulnerable, and enlightening.

I'm touched by their personal and professional awareness; they open their hearts and share their stories to invite you to open your hearts to possibilities. The tools these brilliant authors offer are powerful gifts for expanding awareness and global healing. Just as there are the ripples on the front cover art flowing out from the person's heart, these authors, with their stories and tools, create a ripple effect of inspiration from their hearts.

This ripple of inspiration creates its own energetic system within our Inspired Living author group, which then ripples out to all of you, the readers. As the magic and inspiration changes your life, it ripples out from you to your friends, families, and communities. This is how we raise the consciousness of the world!

Please join us in the Inspired Living Superpowers Community on Facebook to meet the authors and see what magic we continue to create.

https://www.facebook.com/groups/inspiredlivingsuperpowerscommunity/

CHAPTER 1

TRUST IN TRUTH

THE JOURNEY TO EASE AND FLOW IN EVERY AREA OF YOUR LIFE

Carolyn McGee,
The Decision Queen, Sacred Haven Living Guide

MY STORY

You are moving to North Carolina and will be there by Thanksgiving!

For years I felt like I didn't belong anywhere. At times, I didn't even feel like I belonged to me. It seemed like everyone was against me. I couldn't trust anyone, including me. Life was one struggle after another. Making a decision and taking action was challenging.

In July 2020, I woke up to my angel guide voice saying: *You are moving to North Carolina and will be there by Thanksgiving.* **"WHAT!?"** The world was in a pandemic. I signed my apartment lease for another year the day before. I owned a local business I was in the process of rebuilding after the shutdown. *How could I move?*

Then, I remembered trust. Taking three deep centering breaths, I asked my guides: *Please make the process and move easy.* And I started making plans and taking action to move.

The journey to trusting this voice and taking action to bring that statement into reality took enormous trust in my relationship with myself, my intuition, and my spirit guides.

It was not always that way for me. For many years I was taught to validate information outside myself. *What would Jesus do? I should call Amy and ask her what she thinks. Will the family approve?*

My dad was an alcoholic, and as a child, he would be lying on the couch in my play area, and I'd say, "Mommy, something's wrong with Daddy. He won't wake up to play." Her reply, "Carolyn, he's just sleeping," felt wrong. I knew it was more than that but didn't know what it was and learned not to ask or trust what I noticed.

When he moved to California to try a "geographical fix" to his drinking, it was never discussed. "Daddy's helping Uncle Bob, and we don't know when he will be home." Mom never acknowledged to my sister and me that she was angry and upset. I knew there was something more to the story that wasn't shared, but after constantly being told that everything was good, it led me to not trust myself or my senses and moved me further into that continual loop of outside validation over my feelings.

As I started dating, I developed the same pattern of believing what my boyfriends thought was best for me versus what I felt deep inside was right for me. When I married, the pattern continued, with me believing my husband over what I knew to be right for me. This caused an imbalance in our relationship and eventually a divorce.

I came to the point where I didn't know who to trust. I certainly didn't trust me. And I couldn't understand or reconcile the energy difference between what I was feeling, what I was sensing, what I knew, and what everyone around me was telling me to do.

Realizing I wasn't modeling a healthy, balanced marriage to my kids gave me the courage to leave my husband and learn to set boundaries to determine who I was and what was important to me. I moved to a little town in MetroWest Boston with my two children and started the path back into me.

Most positive memories from my childhood were of my grandparents' home. My grandma's flower garden was a safe and vibrant place for solitude and reflection. Every color of the rainbow grew in this hillside acre. The magic of the river tinkling below, the gentle breeze caressing my hair, and the sweet floral scents soothed my soul. The stone well surrounded by purple lilacs, enchanted me.

I recreated gardens with shoots from my grandma's garden in my new home and allowed the flowers to nurture me. A wishing well fountain brought tinkling, flowing water and beautiful memories to my yard. I created a soothing and supportive home using my intuition to add what felt inviting and release what felt heavy.

My children and I grew up in the safety and nurturing of that home. They grew to be healthy young adults, and I grew back into myself. *I am remembering who I am.*

Another step in my journey—rediscovering that I can communicate with angels, spirit guides, and other celestial beings as well as animals— allowed me to remember my soul's purpose: to be me, to be authentic, to be loving, to create community, connection, and collaboration.

I love to create not only art but also systems. So, I played to all my strengths and started my dog walking business and my intuitive coaching business, which led me back to myself and deeper into what I'm here to teach.

It took many years of deep personal development work and regaining and remembering my divine abilities before I recognized my own truth. When I did this, my relationship with everything and everyone improved. *I am confident and comfortable in who I am. I know what I have to offer the world.* I trusted me, my truth, and my choices.

From one to almost seven, I lived in Durham, North Carolina. Then we moved back to northern New York, where my parents were from. After college, I moved to Massachusetts. I would joke, "I'm a southern gal stuck in the north." I never felt at home in the north. The energy was powerful, but it wasn't supportive of me. I felt like I was walking against the tide with every step. My mantra became: "As soon as my kids are out of college, I'm moving to North Carolina!" I was heading home.

When my youngest decided to go to The Ohio State, my intuition said: *It's time to start the process of moving from Massachusetts. Trust that the right place will arrive in the right time.* I sold my home and moved into a beautiful townhouse apartment. This was the first step in acting on my guidance.

I felt completely nurtured, safe, and cared for in a way I'd never been before. There were maintenance and support people, so I didn't have to do it all myself. I was taken care of and allowed to flourish and focus on me for the first time ever. I still had my gardens and fountains supporting me energetically and of course, my animal companions.

In March 2020, I closed my in-person business like the rest of the world. I used the time for introspection and creativity. I started writing again. Designated the logical and analytical one in the family narrowed my perspective and abilities to make a difference. Saying yes to Laura Di Franco to write in *The Ultimate Guide to Self-Healing Techniques* opened a portal to my soul that allowed me to recognize that I can be both.

Writing a chapter in that collaboration opened my creative flow, which also expanded into my businesses. A few short months later, I was able to reopen the business with a completely restructured and simplified method of managing it.

This will make it easier for me to have someone manage it or maybe even sell it when I move. The simplification opened more energy for me to do my intuitive work, my heart's desire. I was the best of both worlds.

I just signed my lease for another year, thinking: *I am not moving during a pandemic,* when I woke up to that angel voice stating, *you are moving to North Carolina.*

You've got to be kidding me; you couldn't have told me this yesterday?

Then I remembered all the lessons I learned and what I taught about patterns in relationships, trusting in guides, and in ourselves. I knew this was the right thing for me to do and in the right timing, so I just asked: *Please make it easy and guide me each step of the way.*

The move was easy but not effortless. I let go of belongings that would not make the trip and searched for my new home from 1000 miles away. The only times I ran into obstacles were when I started pushing, when I didn't trust my intuition, or when I started doing instead of being and receiving.

A friend and I traveled to North Carolina in October and found the perfect little place for me. The moment I stepped into the house, I knew: *I am home.* I didn't realize I was further stepping into my life's purpose with this property.

About four years prior, I went on a guided journey into a sacred temple to create my one-year, five-year, and 10-year vision. My ten-year vision was to create Sacred Haven, a community and way of living and learning from life's experiences to tap into spiritual and earth guidance.

I didn't know exactly what Sacred Haven would look like or be. After I moved, while walking in my backyard, I realized: *Oh, here I am. This is my Sacred Haven.* In one corner is the Grandmother tree to heal my matriarchal line and those of my clients. The Grandfather tree is the center, and the Sacred Ceremony tree graces the communication corner of my property. These three trees tower over all the houses, filled with chattering squirrels and chirping birds.

As I walked my backyard, the entire layout of Sacred Haven unfolded. I wandered barefoot in the grass with the breeze on my skin, feeling the winter sun and knowing where each magical element would be.

The garden with my grandma's plants will be in the center. I need to grow medicinal herbs.

A dragon emerging from a fire pit yet to be built will clear away old patterns and beliefs.

My wishing-well fountain is where manifestation happens.

I am happy I followed my intuition to keep that wrought iron table; it's where I will write.

Every place I looked became a portal or a key to healing. That vision of Sacred Haven came alive for my clients and me.

Having the faith to trust that angel voice when it really didn't make sense allowed me to step fully into my life purpose and see the plan for how all my tools and energies come together. It was easy for me to refine my workshops and clearly explain what I do. The energy that held it all together is relationships because how we show up in one area of our lives is how we show up everywhere.

- If there is never enough support in your life, what is blocking receiving in every area?
- If you have unhealed wounds from your family, how is that coloring your intimate and business relationships?

- Do you have enough/not enough in family, friends, money, and health?

I have always loved puzzles and rising above to see the big picture from all the components. Understanding the Sacred Haven concept and how it affects all our relationships, and how each of these energies can support our transformation was enlightening and life-altering.

This journey of trusting myself, living in my truth, and allowing experiences to heal is what I came here to learn and teach.

A journey into the sacred temple is my gift to you. My five-year vision was to write a best-selling book, and now I'm an author in seven! Enjoy the journey and expect miracles.

THE TOOL

PREPARATION

Locate the directions so you know where north, east, south, and west are. There are apps on your phone if you don't have a compass. You will create a grid around you before you journey. Have your journal and pen handy.

Gather something that represents the four elements. Examples are:

1. Crystal for Earth in the north
2. Feather for air in the east
3. Candle for fire in the south
4. A small bowl of water in the west

PURPOSE

In your journal, write down a question or pattern you want answers to. Are you starting to notice patterns in how you interact with people or respond to situations? Do you know you need to make a change but don't know how?

JOURNEY

Sit in a comfortable chair with your feet on the ground or directly on the ground. Set up your grid around you. Keep your spine straight. The journey is optimal sitting versus lying down.

Take three deeps breaths in through your nose and out your mouth.

Imagine you are in a bubble of energy, like a soap bubble, that surrounds your body. If there is any energy that is not yours or is not of love, ask it to leave. Call back any energy of yours that was left with other people or events. Envision a blue light surrounding the bubble protecting you and your energy.

Focus on the energy of your heart chakra—the spot in the center of your chest.

Imagine a pillar of white light that starts in your heart and extends past your throat through your head and out the top of your head into your own personal star, 36 inches above your head. This is your connection to the divine masculine, the source of spiritual guidance and inspiration.

Now bring your awareness back to your heart and see that pillar of white light extend from your heart, past your solar plexus (just below your diaphragm), your sacral, (between your belly button and hips), and through your root (at your hips through your feet) and out of your body into the earth. Feel that pillar of light moving through the earth, down into that molten lava heartbeat of Mother Earth. This is your connection to the divine feminine.

Feel the energy move through your divine heart, connecting you to the divine feminine and the divine masculine, your connection to all that is and all that ever will be.

Now, bring your inner vision and awareness to a path; you intuitively know that this path is bringing you on a sacred journey.

You realize that you are expansive and present—feeling your body and spirit.

As you walk down this path, notice there is a beautiful temple all built of stone. It's off in the distance, and we're going to walk by an enormous crystal blue lake, and the temple is reflected in this lake.

You notice this temple against the sky and in the reflection of the lake, within and without, outside and inside.

Walk by the lake and approach the steps to the temple. As you see the steps, you notice a guide. Don't analyze what the guide looks like; just allow the loving support.

As you and your guide start to slowly walk up the stone stairs, feel your soul as a separate energy. You see it stand next to you, magnificent in its brilliance. I invite you to see your soul as tangible because it is.

Walk into the center of the temple, and notice other energies here; they are more spirit guides.

Notice there is an opening in the ceiling of this temple, a big circle with a white pillar of light coming from beyond the beyond, through the center of that temple, shining through the ceiling, creating a light circle on the stone floor.

Walk to the edge of the circle of light with your guides and ask your question. See and feel the support of all your guides. They stand behind you, supporting your quest.

Listen or sense deeply for the answer. You will remember it all when you return.

Celebrate receiving the answer. You asked and now know.

See how your soul shines even brighter as you gain this insight.

Acknowledge your guides and thank them for being there to support you.

I invite you to ask your soul to become even more defined and present for you.

Really see your soul and ask your soul if there is anything else you need to know now.

What is your next right step? What is possible for you? Your soul knows, so listen to the voice of your soul.

And now, thank your soul and invite your soul to step back into your body.

Perhaps move your body a little bit to feel that integration again.

Feel the alignment: your soul's head with your head, hips with hips, and toes with toes.

Thank all the guides who showed up for you.

Notice that pillar of light starting to fade away, and the support team fading away.

Walk down the stairs, out of the temple, and thank your guide.

Walk past that beautiful lake again, noticing that the reflection outside is also inside.

Continue down the path, and as you reach the end of the path, start to feel your awareness coming back into your body.

Feel your fingers and toes. Feel your body in the chair or on the ground.

Slowly open your eyes and write your experience in your journal.

I would love to hear about your experiences with your journey and answer any questions you might have. You can email me or connect through social media.

I also have a recording of this journey on my website to help you go deeper. You can find it at https://www.CarolynMcGee.com/resources

Carolyn McGee is the creator of the Sacred Haven for Empowered & Intuitive Living Community which includes North Carolina retreats, virtual gatherings, powerful workshops, private coaching, and soul-nurturing VIP weekends. She serves women ready to connect with their inner wisdom, trust it to make empowered decisions, then take inspired action and discover the power of nature's cycles to create a life that lights them up.

Carolyn specializes in Amplifying YOUR Intuitive Superpower to listen to, trust, and follow your soul's path to living the most joyful, healthy, connected, abundant, and purposeful life. She has taught thousands of women to trust themselves and their intuition so they can show up in their full power in business and life.

Carolyn is gifted in finding the patterns in relationship to yourself, others, spirit, and money that block ease, flow, and joy and then guiding you to release them.

By showing you the way back to your intuition, she helps you enhance your ability to receive messages and understand your guidance 24/7. This empowers you to take inspired action to release second-guessing for good, and you feel 100% confident in making crystal clear decisions.

With a background of 20+ years in High Tech, Carolyn knows firsthand the importance of living from a blend of her masculine and feminine energies. Carolyn has co-authored 10+ bestselling books, is a popular Radio & TV host, sought-after speaker, and blogger.

To learn more about Carolyn, or to contact her, visit https://www.CarolynMcGee.com

CHAPTER 2

THE ENERGETIC GREEN SMOOTHIE FOR YOUR ANIMALS

SO YOU CAN CONNECT WITH THEM ANYWHERE AND ANYTIME

Maribeth Coye Decker,
Animal Communicator, Medical Intuitive, Healer

MY STORY

If you find that sometimes, you love your animals as much as or more than the people in your life, you're in the right place! I say this with a slight grin, knowing it's an inside joke between devoted animal lovers. Because the truth is, sometimes it *is* easier to find love and acceptance for and from our non-human family than our human one.

To be clear, I deeply love my human family and friends. It's not that I'd prefer life as a hermit. Not at all. But usually, we've had fewer disagreements, and felt less judgment and grudges (or were on the receiving end of fewer grudges) with our animals than our humans.

If that rings true for you, would you like to connect even more deeply with your animal? In other words, would you like to create an intuitive or a telepathic connection with them?

In this chapter, I share my Energetic Green Smoothie™ so you can practice intuitive communication with your animals. But before I do, I want to set you up with the right mindset to be successful. Then I'll teach you the tool and share examples of how you can use it in your daily life.

You don't have to be born an animal communicator to do this.

I'm an example of *you don't have to be born an animal communicator.* I didn't connect intuitively with my animals until later in life, probably because I wasn't aware that I could. Don't make the same mistake.

Before I considered myself an animal communicator, I had an extraordinary experience with my girl dog Eddy. Eddy passed away after a long illness. While Eddy's passing was not unexpected, it was still painful. And the pain increased exponentially as I realized I had to get on a plane to staff our association's annual meeting five hours away. Curling up on the floor and bawling for hours wasn't on the agenda.

As I packed for the meeting, I sniffed, "Why can't there be bereavement leave when we lose someone who's been a part of our family for over ten years? So what if it's a dog?"

I steeled myself for a weekend of outward smiling and inward crying as I made it through the airport and found my seat on the plane.

For some reason, I ended up with an aisle seat even though I usually chose the window seat. "One more thing to remind me I don't want to be here," I grumbled to myself.

After we took off and I was nursing a hot tea, I got the strangest feeling. "Eddy, is that you?" I whispered. Somehow, I just knew she was sitting in the aisle next to me. *Yes, it's me,* I felt her reply. *You need me, and here I am.* Well, okay then. I spent the rest of the trip petting my invisible, recently deceased dog. I can only imagine the flight attendants whispering to each other, "What is going on with that woman?!"

Later, when I checked into my hotel room, I realized I was not needed until the next morning. Eddy jumped on the bed and kept me company that day as I slept.

Because Eddy chose to spend time with me when I most needed her, I was able to pull myself together and perform all my duties during the annual meeting. Too bad my association didn't give awards for "Best and Most Useful Animal Companion." Eddy would have won!

You're connected with your companion animals, too.

You don't have to wait as long as I did to feel the connection. I believe most of us already connect to our animals on an intuitive level. Or, more accurately, our animals are tuned into *us*. A delightful book, *Dogs That Know When Their Owners Are Coming Home,* by Rupert Sheldrake, Ph.D., provides scientific studies in this area. I found these studies of dogs, cats, and even birds who accurately predicted when their people were on their way home fascinating. And entertaining.

All you need to do is pay more attention to this possibility. For instance, have you ever experienced your animal looking at you intently? My sense is they're thinking: *Human, why can't you hear me? I'm making this as clear as I can, but you still aren't getting it!* Many people have had this experience. It's an intuitive connection.

More signs that you and your animals are intuitively tuned in:

- You think about them, and they show up about ten minutes later. My cats are famous for doing this.

- You know that they want to come back into the house, now! When you get to the door, there they are, staring at you, wondering what took so long.

- When you're upset or can't sleep, they snuggle up with you to provide comfort and peace. You sense they enjoy being of service to you.

- Some animals leave the room when you're having an argument with another human or disciplining another animal. Because of past incidents or their particular personality, they may physically feel the energy of the emotions and decide to move away.

- Animals who passed may have visited you in your dreams or let you know some other way that they were visiting you. But you probably thought it was just your imagination because you missed them so much. It wasn't. They wanted you to know they're okay and love you.

- Is there a time when you thought, *If my dog/cat/bunny could talk, I swear she just said, [fill in the blank]?* Your animal communicated intuitively with you.

Take time to recall odd incidents that stick in your mind. Consider other times of synchronicity between you and your animal that you thought were coincidences or your imagination. You may find more examples.

THE TOOL

The Energetic Green Smoothie - Connecting Through Love

Love is the best energy in the universe. And if you've read this far, your love for your animals is genuine and deep. That means you have the key ingredient to help you connect. When you consciously harness this love for your animals, you create a strong intuitive channel to share information. With practice, you may notice subtle changes in their behavior over time. If you're lucky, you may even see a dramatic change in behavior.

Evolution of the Energetic Green Smoothie

When I married for a second time, I had two kids on the brink of becoming teenagers who'd lost their father to a heart attack years before. It was a difficult transition for everyone. I received the download of the Energetic Green Smoothie from Source when I began to learn energy healing techniques. It connects everyone's hearts through love.

At first, I just used it for the humans in my family. Eventually, I mused: *Why aren't I including my animals?* So, I added my dogs, and later my cats, to my Energetic Green Smoothie circle. It's been wonderful to feel everyone's heart connect.

Later, as I shared the Energetic Green Smoothie with my clients, I noticed that adding simple animal communication to the smoothie was the next level of goodness, so to speak. For my family, using animal communication via the Energetic Green Smoothie allowed my cats to shift problematic behaviors more easily.

Learning the Energetic Green Smoothie

First, we're going to learn how to set the Energetic Green Smoothie in motion, so all hearts are connected. Then we're going to practice sharing information with our animals while maintaining the Energetic Green Smoothie.

Key Step – Keep Visualizations Simple and Easy

Some people think visualizing something when their eyes are closed is the same as seeing something with their eyes open. They believe they must see a 3-D picture with vivid colors and incredible details, or they're doing it wrong. That's not what's needed. Instead, picture what you see when you recall a memory. Something as simple as what your front door looks like or your cat's paw. That's all the visualization you need.

Let's do the Energetic Green Smoothie!

Find a place where you can relax without interruption. Don't forget to turn off anything that beeps or rings. Get comfortable, but don't lay down. Close your eyes.

Think about all the beings in your family, all the species, including the humans, and their names. In your imagination, picture gathering them into a circle that includes you.

In case you were wondering, no, you don't have to physically place everyone in a circle, which is good because my cats would never go for that. You don't even have to be in the same room, house, state/province, or country. You're simply creating this circle in your mind's eye.

Now, using your imagination, *look* around and notice where everyone is— remember, your eyes are closed. Being left-handed, I always start to my left and move around the circle clockwise, noticing each being. You can also turn to your right and go counterclockwise. No worries, the direction doesn't matter. All that matters is they're all assembled. It's like looking around the table during dinner and seeing that all your human family has gathered. But in this case, both humans and non-humans are in your circle.

Imagine or pretend or just know that green light the size of a flashlight beam comes out of your heart and travels to whoever's heart is on your left. See that beam move from their heart to the next being's heart and the next being's heart until the green light returns to your heart.

It doesn't matter how many souls you connect with. If it's just you and your animal, great! In your mind's eye, imagine being across from your animal and sending a green light to their heart.

Green Heart Chakra

The color green is associated with the heart chakra, the energy center in the middle of the chest. This center is considered the source of giving and receiving love. From my experience, all sentient beings I've worked with have chakras. If you're not a fan of chakras, just forget that I used the word. Instead, think of your heart as the source of love energy and green being the sign of growth and healing in much of nature.

You now have that green light connecting all the hearts in your family. Good work!

Bring in the Feeling of Love.

Conjure up your love and joy in knowing these beings. Feel the delight of their special selves. As you feel this energy, imagine or pretend that it saturates the green light with your love, moving through the circle of green light. It's as if you've built a small green circular pathway through everyone's heart and filled it with love.

Now imagine you're the engine, moving this loving energy through everyone's heart. You're sending green love-filled energy through this circle that connects every heart.

Run the Energetic Green Smoothie for a while, while it moves through everyone's heart. This should be a slow, relaxed movement. Not fast or frantic. As you feel the peace and joy of being part of your family, imagine they feel it, too. They relax into the knowledge of how loved and connected they are.

Congratulations! You just created your own Energetic Green Smoothie!

By itself, this is a wonderful energy to calm your family members and remind them that you're all connected through love. It's a useful practice for deepening family relationships.

More Ways to Use the Energetic Green Smoothie

In addition to connecting everyone's heart in love, here are additional ways to use the Energetic Green Smoothie. First, get the Energetic Green

Smoothie running. Imagine it running automatically like you've switched on a light as you practice these techniques.

1. When you've got the circle created, tell your family in your mind: *This heart connection is what it means to be a family. We love and respect each other. We take care of each other. This is your forever family. Every day you wake up, we'll be there for you.* Or any other positive statements that express your commitment to your family.

2. Invite family members who've passed on to join the circle. Feel the joy of being connected with all the beings you've loved, how they're still there for you, care for you, and they know they're still in your heart.

3. When you're out of town, create a circle with the animals who didn't get to come with you. In your head, tell them: *Relax, we're coming home soon. We love you and haven't forgotten you. We're having fun, so you should too! Eat, drink and be merry!*

4. If your animal is staying at the animal hospital while they recover from a procedure, tell them: *Don't worry, I'll be coming to pick you up. Let these good people take care of you.*

5. If you have animals who aren't getting along, show them how you wish they'd behave towards each other. By this, I mean create a picture in your mind of them doing the behavior you'd like to see in the real world. As you create this picture, tell them: *I love you guys so much! You'd make me incredibly happy if you treated each other like this.*

6. When their behaviors begin to frustrate or worry you, use the Energetic Green Smoothie to smooth out your own emotions. Then tell them what you love about them; give them specific examples. You will recharge your patience, and they will relax as you do this.

These are a few examples of how to use the Energetic Green Smoothie with your family. Feel free to come up with your own innovations. Know that the loving, peaceful energy you create will affect everyone in a positive way. That's because love is the highest and the strongest vibration in the universe. I urge you to practice the Energetic Green Smoothie often.

Maribeth Coye Decker is the founder of SacredGrove.com—where people and pets heal and connect. Maribeth is an animal communicator and healer, medical intuitive, and bestselling author of the second edition of Peace in Passing: Comfort for Loving Humans During Animal Transitions. A retired Naval Officer, Maribeth found her calling as an animal communicator after becoming a Reiki Master. That's when she heard her Siberian Husky, Mitsubishi, curse her out as she tried energy healing on him. He probably thought his language was okay because of her time in the Navy—think, swear like a sailor! Back then, Maribeth didn't know animal communication was a career option. But when her dog Tibor, who came into her life after Mitsubishi passed, started sharing visions of his life before joining the family, she knew it was time to pursue animal communication. She dived in.

Maribeth works with folks who love their animals as much as or sometimes more than the people in their lives. She addresses physical, emotional, and behavioral issues so that beloved animals can express their best selves and enjoy their best life. She finds delight in watching healing happen for both the animals and their people.

One of Maribeth's specialties is assisting animals and their people before, during, and after the animal's transition process. This includes communicating with animals who have passed on. Finally, Maribeth teaches people to communicate with their own animals through her UConnect animal communication class.

Maribeth and her husband, Charlie, also retired Navy, live with their dogs, Stella and Tibor, and cats, Mac, Bunnie, and Shadow, in Alexandria, Virginia. Her son Patrick also lives in Alexandria. Her daughter Andrea spends time between Grants Pass, Oregon, and Malawi, Africa.

CHAPTER 3

HEALING AFTER THE DEATH OF YOUR PET

A SIMPLE TECHNIQUE TO EASE END-OF-LIFE TRAUMA

Kathy Boyer, Animal Communicator, Energy Healer

MY STORY

I tried to make myself invisible as I entered the L-shaped conference room at Edgar Cayce's A.R.E. Center (Association for Research and Enlightenment) in Virginia Beach, after a long four-hour drive from my home in Staunton, Virginia—it was long because I was in tears all the way down I-64. My beloved horse Jake died earlier that morning, leaving a vacant spot in my heart.

He colicked (suffering severe pain in the abdomen caused by intestinal gas or obstruction in the intestines) the night before at the barn where I boarded him. *Please hang on, Jake. I'll be there as fast as I can.* I drove there immediately, arriving at the same time as the vet who treated him.

Jake responded positively, had multiple bowel movements, and walked around calmly when I left to come home. Someone would stay with him in a confined area and check on him during the night.

I had to be rested enough to make the drive to Virginia Beach in the morning to attend a four-day Animal Communication Conference/ Workshop. I was concerned but confident in his recovery.

I presumed that Jake had made it safely through the night, as nobody from the barn called or texted. My peace was interrupted, though, when the phone rang as I was loading my car—*the dreaded call*—"Jake passed away sometime between 4:00 and 8:00 a.m." He had *not* made it.

It was all too familiar to me to lose an animal, as I said goodbye to 13 cats in 15 years. All their deaths left a huge hole in my heart, along with the familiar feelings of guilt and regret. *If only. . ., Why did I do that? How could I have done that? I'm selfish. . . It's my fault. . . I let them suffer too long. . . I should have let them die at home. . .I should have put them to sleep sooner. . .*

Over the course of 23 years, I lovingly cared for an ongoing population of eight to ten cats at a time, most of them showing up in terrible conditions from neglect or homelessness. This included those with missing eyes, fully blind, deaf, mange, FIV, malnourished, filthy matted coats, severe cases of halitosis, and worms, to name a few.

Helping these cats transform into beautiful, confident animals has been one of the greatest joys of my life. I didn't realize it at the time, but I fulfilled one of my dreams—of opening a cat sanctuary, albeit an informal one.

Jake was my first horse, a 12-year old chestnut quarter horse with a white blaze on his face, grossly overweight, comical yet hard-headed, with a good-natured nicker that said, "Hey, Mom, how's it going?" every time I showed up with pockets full of treats, of course. He was fully aware that I knew nothing about horses and laughed at me during our riding lessons, with antics like intentionally walking backward when I said, "Walk on!" Thus, my riding career began at the ripe old age of 47.

We were together for 12 years, and although I didn't see him every day, the sting of his death felt the same as my cats. And I believed with all my heart that this timing was not by accident. *I'm going to an Animal Communication Conference.*

I walked as inconspicuously as I could through rows of tables at the A.R.E., searching for an empty seat. *Here's one, the front row at the far left corner, out of everyone's view. This is perfect.* I wanted to see and hear the teacher comfortably but not draw attention to myself or my grief.

The instructor, Joan Ranquet, scanned the room of 40 participants and asked us to introduce ourselves by sharing what brought us there. She stared directly at *me*, smiled, and said, "We'll start with you!" *Oh, no!*

I collected myself and muttered, "I'm Kathy Boyer, from Staunton, Virginia, and my horse passed away this morning." *I hate drawing attention to myself, but I'm in the perfect place, surrounded by animal lovers.*

We started by learning telepathy: the transference of pictures, words, and feelings. It's the way animals communicate with each other and how we as humans used to communicate before we developed language. *I love this!* I finally knew what I wanted to be when I grew up: an animal communicator! *Dr. Doolittle, here I come!*

Then we learned the basics of EFT (Emotional Freedom Technique), known as tapping, one of the energy healing modalities Joan teaches at her school, Communication With All Life University (CWALU).

Tapping is a technique that helps release emotional stress from the physical body. You do it by *physically tapping* with your fingers on a series of acupressure points directly on the body or in its energy field.

For those who like more technical explanations, these points are along the meridians (energetic pathways running through the body) associated with specific organs associated with specific emotions. By tapping on the points in a sequential, repeated pattern, emotional energy releases and healing can take place at a deep level. It even works remotely since energy is not bound by time or space.

How does it play out in life? The emotions surrounding a trauma stuck in the body are now lessened or totally gone, and the memory of that event no longer triggers them—the result: emotional freedom.

I had vaguely heard of tapping but was somewhat skeptical, not knowing how powerful it was until I observed it myself.

"Come on, Bandit," coaxed Michelle, a fellow student whose rescue dog's previous groomer slapped him in the face when he was uncooperative. Bandit had a sore on his mouth that she desperately wanted to treat but couldn't get close to his face.

Since almost all the tapping points are on the face and head, this was impossible to do on Bandit. Joan directed the dog, "Come up here on the stage! We're going to tap in the air just a few feet away while directing our hands towards the points on your body." The rest of us followed along, tapping on ourselves.

The results were astonishing, Bandit relaxed, laid down on the floor, nearly fell asleep, yawned, licked, and chewed. Michelle was now able to touch him on his face! *Oh my gosh, I can't believe what I'm seeing. What's all this energy stuff about? I have to learn more.*

After I got home, I couldn't wait to practice tapping on my other horse Nelly, Jake's companion and pasture mate, as a follow-up to Jake's death. *I'm so excited to try this.* Stumbling through the session, I barely remembered all the tapping points, but the emotional release was immediate; she lowered her head, yawned, licked, and chewed. *This is remarkable. She's never done that with me before. It worked!*

I enrolled in the 18-month Animal Mastery Program at CWALU, with classes both online and in-person. I found my soul's purpose, to help animals and their humans!

Tapping has so many applications. I was running on overdrive with emotional stress, particularly after my divorce. I likened myself to the Tin Man in the *Wizard of Oz*. I needed oil to get loosened up, and tapping was that oil!

And then, there was animal-related trauma—another part of my psyche that needed healing. As future animal communicators and energy healers, this was very important.

First of all, the expression 'physician, heal thyself' really comes into play. It's vital to remain emotionally neutral when we work with animals, and the more emotional scars we carry, the more difficult that becomes. Simply put, the more baggage you have, the heavier it is to carry.

Secondly, as we experience tapping first-hand, we learn what it feels like in the body. This helps us when we facilitate a session, better recognizing the subtle energy shifts, helping to make it more effective.

Our assignment with homework partners was to tap through animal-related events from our childhood that continued to bring up strong emotions. This was challenging, as my memories were vague. All I could conjure up were brief flashes of pictures that came into my head. *How could these brief flashes of memories have anything to do with my current life?*

They may have been brief flashes, but the memory and emotional impact went deep within. Here are two examples:

1. **The Fast Horse:** I loved horses, but owning one was impossible since we lived in a small town. When I was 11, my mom found someone in the country willing to let me ride their horse. *At last, this is my big chance! I'm so excited I can hardly wait!*

   There I was, sitting in a saddle on the back of this unfamiliar horse in a large paddock surrounded by a barbed-wire fence—left unattended. I was excited and nervous while my dream was coming true! *I can do this.*

   Well, the horse didn't seem too thrilled. He bolted; I held on for dear life! I miraculously stayed on his back as he ran across the paddock, coming within an inch of scraping my knee against the barbed wire fence! *Whew, what a close call. It feels like my heart flew out of my body.* That was my only flashback—the panic, my knee, and that fence.

   How did this impact me? I wouldn't know until 40 years later when I rode Jake. I quickly realized I was terrified of going fast. Even trotting seemed to scare me. In my mind, I was galloping across beautiful open spaces, my hair bouncing in the wind. My body tensed and gripped with fear instead. *I better change my aspirations of winning the Kentucky Derby!* Jake was the perfect horse for me, as he was the slowest horse at the barn!

   Tapping through the stored emotions from the fast horse experience *completely erased that fear.* The brief flashback triggered enough of the incident to help me feel the emotions still in my body. I can now confidently go on a trail ride, and am comfortable going faster and enjoying myself. *This is emotional freedom!*

2. **The German Shepherd:** A fierce-looking German Shepherd lived up the street from us in a fenced-in yard. *Grrr. . .Woof Woof. . .Grrr* was the sound I dreaded every time I walked by as he came running toward me. I was terrified of that dog before I even left my house,

regardless of the fact that he was in a confined area.

We targeted that fear during the tapping session with more amazing results. I started seeing German Shepherds everywhere, beginning with my Facebook newsfeed the next day. The first post was a heartwarming video of one helping a kitten up the stairs. *I'm not reacting at all.* Then, seeing them at the park, *again no reaction.* I'm no longer afraid of German Shepherds! *I wonder if my cats would mind if I adopted one?*

Soon other animal-related memories came to mind when I opened my heart to look for them. The most difficult ones were related to end-of-life circumstances. As pet parents, it's very painful to talk about the loss of a pet, and we often use words other than 'death' to help ease the pain: crossing the rainbow bridge, put to sleep, transitioning, passing away, gone to the other side, etc.

We store the pain in the silence of our broken hearts, where it can linger for years, blocked from our conscious memory. Sometimes we become incapable of having strong feelings for another animal, believing we're not being loyal to the special one who passed.

I also get so fixated on the stories of the end of my pet's life that I can't remember all the good, wonderful years we had. It's as if all those wonderful years are now encapsulated in a short, unpleasant end-of-life scenario.

I believe many of us still carry huge amounts of guilt and regret pertaining to the circumstances surrounding the death of at least one of our pets. We can be so hard on ourselves that no matter what choices we made, we believe they were wrong.

I'm going to break my silence by sharing my most heart-wrenching end-of-life story (Warning: details not for the faint of heart.)

Big Boy, a large, black and grey striped tabby, and my first cat as an adult, holds the title of B.C.E. (Best Cat Ever). I considered him my true animal soul-mate who slept on my head *every* night, nestled in my hair, and lullabied us both to sleep with his really big purr! He protected me from anyone who rang the doorbell with his equally big, opinionated, "Meow," and his records at the vet clinic included the memo: *Aggressive - needs a muzzle.* I truly loved this cat!

When he was 14, he was diagnosed with cancer, affecting both his vision and hearing. I virtually ignored the gravity of his illness and believed as long as he had the will to live, I would honor that. I live by that belief, but in reality, I couldn't bear letting him go, even as he deteriorated.

The day before he died, I let him outside in the yard to enjoy a nice nap in the hot sun. He looked so content. The next day, I noticed he stopped purring and was no longer responsive to me. *He's still breathing, but it feels like he's gone.* I was devastated.

When I looked closer at his head, some flies had laid eggs in there that hatched. He was infested with maggots. I didn't know what they were right away, but when I figured it out, I was mortified. This was my darkest moment ever as a pet parent.

I took him to the emergency vet immediately and had him put to sleep. *How could I have let this happen?* I berated myself for 20 years for being selfish and waiting too long before I let him go. At least that's what I believed. I shut myself off emotionally towards other animals, even though I took in many more cats after that.

Tapping freed me from the guilt, regret, self-hate, selfishness, and sadness I stuffed for those 20 years. It restored my sense of who Big Boy was and our awesome relationship together! *I'm finally free,* and tapping can free you, too!

To help you process your own experience of losing an animal, here's a simple tapping script related to end-of-life issues.

THE TOOL

TAPPING SCRIPT FOR HEALING AFTER THE DEATH OF YOUR PET

Preparation:

1. Choose which animal's death still has the most emotional impact on you.

2. Write the emotions down on paper that you want to be free from.

Examples:

a. Regret

b. Guilt

c. Can't forgive myself

d. Selfish

e. Heartbroken

3. Write down several transition statements to direct you toward your goal.

Examples:

a. "I'm sick and tired of feeling this way."

b. "I'm open to being set free and moving on."

c. "Maybe it's not my fault."

d. "I'm ready to let go of all this."

e. "I allow myself to move through this."

4. Write down how you would *like* to feel to have this resolved.

Examples:

a. "I'm at peace now."

b. "I know I did the best I could."

c. "I'm okay now."

d. "I've let this go, and I can move on."

The Tapping Portion: Speak Everything Out Loud As You Tap

1. **Setup Statement:** Tap both pinkies together where they attach to the hands, like a karate chop, and say your statement three times.

   Example: "Even though *(animal's name)* passed away, and I feel so much guilt and regret over my choices, I love and accept myself."

2. **Tapping on the Points:** "Use the tips of the fingers on both hands to tap. Focus on the emotions of the story as you move from point

to point. Do at least one complete round **with each emotion** you listed.

Example: One round of tapping, with sample dialogue:

a. *Inside the eyebrows:* "I feel so much regret."

b. *Outside the eyebrows:* "I feel so much regret."

c. *Under the eyes:* "I regret my decision to_____."

d. *Under the nose:* "I wish I had made a different choice, and I regret it."

e. *Under the mouth:* "I made the wrong choice, and I regret it."

f. *Under the collar bone:* "I regret what I did to (name) so much."

g. *Top of the head:* "I feel so much regret over my choices."

As you go, tap through all the rounds, you may feel releases in the form of sighs, yawns, or deep breaths. If so, continue on with step three. If not, go back and do some more rounds.

3. **Transition Statements:** Using the transition statements you listed, do several rounds of tapping using the same sequence of points.

4. **Tapping on your *ideal world of emotions* surrounding this situation:**

Do more rounds of tapping using the statements you listed of how you would *like* to feel. You should have a sense of *'I'm finished'* at the end.

Now take some deep breaths! You have released a huge amount of energy. Notice how you feel over the next few days. When you think of this scenario with your animal, does it still bring up any of these emotions? If not, you have set yourself free! If so, repeat the process, or move to step five.

5. **Follow Along with the Video:** I've posted a free video on my website using this script that you can tap along with. Go to www.thepetconnector.com, under the EFT Tapping tab.

If you'd like to learn more about tapping for yourself or one of your animals, please contact me and book a session—and keep on tapping!

Kathy Boyer, Animal Communicator and Energy Healer is a cat mom and lifelong animal lover. She is a graduate of and now a teacher for Communication With All Life University, bringing her dream of helping animals to life.

Using Telepathic Communication, EFT Tapping, and Scalar Wave Energy Healing, she is truly able to make a difference in the lives of both animals and their human caregivers, improving their relationships with each other in the process.

Kathy is a professional musician who lived in Japan for five years while serving in the Air Force, where she inadvertently started her own cat sanctuary, albeit an informal one. For the next 23 years, she nurtured a consistent population of eight-to-ten felines, primarily coming from environments of abuse or neglect.

Drawing from her experiences, she particularly loves to help animals who have had a rough start in life to heal from their early trauma. In addition, helping pet parents heal from the difficult emotions after their animal passes is near and dear to her heart, as she has said goodbye to over 20 animals in 17 years.

Her love for animals extends beyond cats. She's been a horse mom for 14 years, and if she had the space, she would bring home every dog, duck, and squirrel she sees daily at the local park.

Her mission is to help the animal kingdom feel more connected to humanity while also helping build better interpersonal relationships between animals and their humans.

Connect with Kathy:
https://www.thepetconnector.com
email: kathyh@drnetwork.com

To subscribe to her newsletter, send your request to:
kathyh@drnetwork.com

CHAPTER 4

MY JOURNEY INTO MEDICAL INTUITION

CLOSING THE GAP BETWEEN WHO YOU ARE AND WHO YOU DESIRE TO BECOME

Sharon Joseph PhD., Channeler,
Medical Intuitive, Animal Communicator, Healer

MY STORY

The darkest time in my life was when my dad passed away. I was only 22 years old, and needed to take care of my mom and my maternal grandma, who lived with us. The couple of years prior to my dad's passing were extremely hard on my family. The invention my dad had was constantly being stolen from him and my family was on the verge of being homeless a couple of times. All I cared about was keeping my dad safe and happy. At least, that's what I strived to do. In front of me was a clear (it's clear now; it wasn't then) scenario of giving his power away, or at least fighting for it, and then giving up on himself and life itself. He was diagnosed with cancer, and it took about a year for him to pass.

I was very connected to my dad. He was such a kind and giving person. At 22 years old, my life stopped! I didn't know how I'd get over the pain.

And before even looking at that, I needed to take care of the family. My mom was in the hospital with my brother, giving him a kidney. He lost his kidneys due to a virus. I graduated that same week with a degree in computer science and a minor in business. My soul and spirit woke up. My higher self was calling me to get on board and get into my mission. *There must be much more to this physical existence I was feeling. The body is a vessel for our spirit, our life must have a direct effect on our body and vice versa. I need to investigate this further. I want to help those that hurt as much as I do when their loved ones or themselves go through illnesses or lose a loved one.*

I came into this life remembering how to channel and connect to Spirit and my guides. I was helping and advising everyone since childhood, but I did not know I was doing it until later in life. I only first realized I was doing it when my dad passed away. I knew about energy, that it doesn't disappear but changes form or transforms. Thus, the energy of his soul would be somewhere or something else other than his personality.

I went out looking for answers and came to a metaphysical book store. In the basement, there was a lady who channeled. I immediately made an appointment with her. Among the many things she said (that took the course of 20 plus years to unfold), one comment was, "Dear one, you are a channel just like this vessel we speak through. You will be helping many people this way." At the time, I didn't think much of it. It just seemed natural to me. I kept reading books and expanding my knowledge and tools until I was ready to step into the person she said I was.

At school, my teachers and mentors always said I should go into medicine however, I could not stomach seeing people suffer physically or mentally, so I didn't pursue a medical career. In retrospect, I understand that these people were picking up something in my vibration that indicated I am a healer. But I simply was not ready and did not want to involve myself with other people's ailments, accidents, or troubles.

My first known trauma was during my birth. My mother's placenta was inverted, so as I was trying to emerge, my mother suffered a devastating loss of blood. As a child, I often heard the story of my birth as follows: "The doctor came out and told my dad, 'You have a daughter, but we are not sure yet if you will still have a wife.'" Even though I heard this story repeatedly, I never thought it affected me. Some part of me thought I was protecting myself by not allowing myself to feel anything about this experience. But the trauma still had an impact on me even without my conscious understanding of it. It caused me to be concerned about hurting others. Only by consciously investigating my past and acknowledging this trauma could I understand why I had this fear of hurting others.

For the longest time, I didn't feel qualified to do this work. I didn't think I had experienced any trauma and, therefore, wouldn't be able to relate to people's ailments or suffering. However, that was just a story I told myself. In reality, everyone experiences trauma. I, too, survived traumas from my birth and throughout my life. My coping mechanism was to *be strong* and not allow myself to feel these traumas, and therefore I did not understand how these experiences impacted me.

I was born to Romanian Jewish parents. During WWII, my family's home, which was previously the house of the king of Romania, was taken over by the Germans and made into a military headquarters. I imagine it was a big house, with many rooms, that stood out in the capital of Romania. My grandparents were permitted to stay in the house as servants to the Germans. My mom was very young at the time and understandably terrified. When the war ended, the Russians took over. Under Communist rule, my family lost their wineries, my dad's paper mills, and their most prized belongings. Among the belongings were beautiful hand-made gold necklaces and gorgeous diamonds with sapphire and ruby rings. Those in power also killed my grandfather. For that reason, my mom never wanted to go back or ever visit Romania. It was simply too painful.

On my father's side, during WWII, the roads to my grandparent's farm were blocked, and my dad could not get home to care for his parents. Being isolated, they died of starvation. Even though their death wasn't his fault, my father never forgave himself for not being able to care for them.

My parents risked everything to defect and were some of the lucky ones to make it out of Romania alive. They never had to say these words to me. Their energy said it loud and clear: *Be careful; don't shine too brightly; you don't want to attract any attention; don't take up space.* It's no surprise I struggled to own my gifts. On an energetic level, my inherited traumas informed me that to survive, I should be invisible.

In my journey of self-discovery, I learned that being highly empathic means more than taking on the inherent ancestral resistances and blocks. It also means feeling these experiences in my body and mind. Hence, all of the collective traumas of generations of my ancestors made me resist trusting people and made me fearful of standing out or being different.

One time, when I was about six years old, my friend fell; his knee was bleeding, and his arm was also hurting. I cleaned his knee injury and told him he had fractured his wrist and needed to put his arm in a cast. I had no idea at the time that I was getting this information from his body and from my guides. I didn't realize the information I was sharing required an x-ray or medical evaluation.

I moved from Toronto to Los Angeles about two years after my dad passed. I went about my life working as a personnel manager for an electronic chain while still looking deeper. I discovered another channel and went to see him. Once more, I was told I am a channel. He said, "You love to give. Your propensity and capacity for giving are endless. Clean your vessel. You are a channel. You keep giving of yourself, but you take responsibility for the people you channel for. You need to learn to let these people have their own journey. Your help is only by channeling for them, not by taking responsibility for the outcome!" By vessel, he meant my body, mind, spirit—the channel that I am.

That was my hardest lesson. Detached compassion was not my strong suit. I wanted to personally help everyone I came in contact with. I went in spirals getting the same lesson over and over under different circumstances so many times. It was hard for me not to fix someone or something. I'm sure the healers reading this know exactly what I mean. I can finally say I own this belief: each person has their own journey. I'm not to interfere, and I do not. It's wrong of me to give unsolicited advice. It's almost like assuming the person needs fixing like they are not whole already. And who am I to think that I know better? My guides told me I needed to ask myself where is the need to fix coming from? Why do I want to do a certain thing for someone? For example: even giving a gift. Why do I want to do it? Do I want anything in return? Do I want them to think highly of me? Do I advise because I think I know better? I know now that I'm not to interfere, and I do not. I am only the messenger when asked for a message or help.

My other spiral was (and every so often, I still need to make sure I'm not doing this) is giving my power away. In addition to the inherited behaviors I mentioned above, as a woman in today's society, I felt a collective expectation of giving away my power/authority (especially to males). One of my missions is to balance the divine feminine and masculine energies.

Before I got married, I said to my husband, "Please know that we are in an equal partnership. Yes, there must be give-and-take, it will not be 50/50 down the middle, but we are equal partners." We started out great but being a *loving and fix-it person,* I ruined it. I put his needs first before mine. Why? Because I figured if he was happy and the family was happy, I would be good. This is a common misconception, but it took me many years to get out of that bad habit and put my needs first. I see many women doing this, even my nieces, but each person has their own journey. We all have our ways and our paths to walk on in divine timing.

Not only did I give my power to my husband, I also gave it to other people in my life, like work partners and close friends. I started business partnerships with friends a couple of times. Each time I let them do what they thought was best, even when that conflicted with my beliefs. I shared what I thought but ultimately let others get their way. I ended up spending time and money on these endeavors, and they failed. About 12 years ago, I started a psychic hotline that predated the Zoom era. This hotline would enable people from all around the world to connect to psychics, healers, astrologers, and even therapists on a screen. It was ahead of its time, yet it failed. I didn't listen to my voice, and I let my friend and her husband do what they thought was best. I gave away my power when I should've stood firm. In the end, I lost time and money (which is really just energy), but I gained a deeper appreciation for my voice and my power. And that lesson is priceless.

Thankfully, my mission and light were stronger than my fears—I kept working on myself. I keep asking questions, digging deeper, taking different classes, and reading many inspirational books. I feel that as long as we're physical, especially because of my gifts, I owe it to myself and each person who crosses my path to keep working on myself. Thus, I keep checking for patterns I can let go of and behaviors that no longer serve me. When I become aware of any of the above, I use the following ways to help me release them.

THE TOOL

The energetic matrix that we are is composed of: all of our other life experiences, usually called past life, our in-utero experience, our ancestral energetic and physical DNA we receive, our childhood experiences, and life itself. We acquire many beliefs and patterns and conduct ourselves in the subconscious. We act on these influences and patterns even though we're not aware of them. A good way to start exploring is by answering the following:

1. Do you have needs that are not being met? Examples: Safety, security, worthiness, confidence, significance, etc. You can check out Maslow's Hierarchy of Needs.

2. What kind of spirals or life experiences do you find yourself in over and over again? For example, do you find that you're abandoned over and over in a relationship? Or maybe you need to be in control, so you pick someone that is not capable of providing? Do you feel unseen by your partner, by your boss, or by your friends?

Whatever your answer is if you would like to change it, create a new story. All you're seeking on the outside needs to be felt inside first because your outer reality is the mirror of your inner reality. Since we act 95-96% from our subconscious, we want to create a new neural pathway in our subconscious that will facilitate the way we conduct ourselves from that place.

For example:

Let's say you have a strong need to be in control over a particular area in your life. What you might consider doing is a three-step process:

1. Clear away any experiences you had of no control—more than likely, it's in your childhood. Write a letter to the parent, teacher, or whoever made you feel out of control. Express how their behavior made you feel.

2. Burn or bury the letter (unless you choose to let them read it, providing they are still around). Resolve to start a new way of being.

3. Say some affirmations like: "I trust that this universe is here to serve my highest good," or "I am safe," or another affirmation that resonates with you with the same message.

4. You can visualize your new story, the one you want to create. Use all of your senses, please. Also, pretend you're living this new story. The moment you create something, even if it's only in your mind at this point, it exists in some dimension. To ground it into this dimension, live in it. Imagine you're already living the new story.

Know that the universe usually tests you when you make a big decision or when you're about to open up your awareness. The spiral or whatever you're trying to change will show up right after your decision to resolve it. The trick is not to get tangled in the new situation of the old story. Remember what you decided and stick with it.

Have a powerful journey!

Sharon Joseph has professionally coached people in their personal growth for close to 20 years. She is a Channel, a Healer, an Author, a Medium, an Animal Communicator, a DNA architect, and a Clairvoyant.

Sharon is a mirror for others to explore and embrace who they are, supporting them as they step into the fullness of their being. Using her astute medical intuition x-ray vision, she can interpret the language of the body when it comes to ailments and or energetic blocks. She gives down-to-earth tools on how to release these blocks and uses her fast and powerful healing ability to assist in healing. She also uses her clairvoyance, energy interpretation, and her gift as a medium to help one upgrade their awareness and their life. Sharon helps people uncover and focus on what they can accomplish in any area of life, including personal growth, health, love, relationships, success, and career.

Sharon achieved a Bachelor's degree in computer science with a minor in business and a Ph.D. in Metaphysical Science. She is an ordained minister. As a citizen of the world, Sharon respects all paths to the One. Her passions include animals, laughing, dancing, travel, meditation, and connecting with like-minded people.

She is currently guiding people to release their old stories on all levels and step into their joy. She does it through one-on-one sessions and classes (online and in-person), and she also conducts retreats around the world.

Contact Sharon:

On her website: www.sharonjosef.com

Her Email: sharonjosef8@gmail.com

On Facebook: https://www.facebook.com/SharonNitka/

On Instagram: https://www.instagram.com/sharonjo/

On Twitter: https://twitter.com/sharonJ84151501

On LinkedIn: https://www.linkedin.com/in/sharon-josef-04896a7a/

CHAPTER 5

JOY BEYOND GRIEF

HEAL YOUR HEART AFTER LOSS

Judy Giovangelo, Founder of Ben Speaks,
Advanced Grief Recovery Specialist

MY STORY

Oh my God, my greatest fear had been realized.

That horrifying call from my daughter Jenna will be etched in my mind forever. "Mom, I just found a suicide note on the counter from Ben," she said. "His car is unlocked, and I know there is something terribly wrong."

Minutes later, when I arrived home, my 16-year-old daughter Jenna and I found my 18-year-old son Benjamin dead in our garage. Ben suffered his entire life, as did our whole family, because of his severe obsessive-compulsive disorder and anxiety. He wore his mental health labels like a Scarlet Letter on his chest as his strongest identification of who he was throughout his life until his stage left exit from this planet on that fateful day in 2009.

I often say, "Loving Ben was easy." He was a sensitive, empathic soul with many gifts. Raising Ben was extraordinarily hard. He was tortured with his mental and emotional challenges, his reactivity to his environment, especially school, and extreme bullying from his peers. He did not fit the mainstream box, and we, along with all his educators, continuously tried to stuff him into that box. Losing him was devastating.

Minutes later, we were shuffled to the police station and then to the hospital, where my son's body had already arrived. "I want to see my son," I said.

A nurse charged with the duty of supporting my traumatized family and me led me compassionately to the room where my son's body lay. "Take as long as you need, Mama," she said.

Upon entering the room, I was struck by the beautiful smile on Ben's face, which gave me a knowing that he was finally free from 18 years of extreme emotional and mental pain and anguish. Seeing him in a state of peace and seemingly joy gave me a feeling of deep relief and peace myself, at least at that moment.

I remember saying inside my head: *Ben, I could punch you right now.* To which he responded, "Go ahead, Mom, it won't hurt!" I then exclaimed out loud, "That's not funny, Benjamin."

Next, I saw an energy of light next to his body. I was a developed medium and healer at the time of his death and grateful for the communication that came next. I'm not sure I would have survived his parting had I not received such a powerful message.

The Spirit I knew at that moment to be Benjamin's soul said: *All kidding aside, you and your son have both played your roles perfectly. You and he had a contract before you came into this Earth plane. You have learned well, Grasshopper, and now you will become a voice for change through me and create a mission that will be called Ben Speaks Louder Than Words on behalf of kids just like him.*

My why was born that day to create the non-profit organization

www.benspeaks.org

I was called to healing work over the years of raising my sweet, sensitive, intuitive, creative, and highly empathic son. Through that journey, I developed many gifts and tools as a spirit communicator and healer.

My son benefitted greatly from healing work: yoga, meditation, Reiki, pushing on his back to release the emotional pain he absorbed daily from the world around him. We used a more holistic approach to wellness, and yet, here I was, needing to bury my sweet boy with a mission to be the change for others whose children are still here.

Back then, I was labeled 'weird,' and the holistic movement was still in its very early birth. As much as Ben benefitted from the tools I implemented in his life, he was bullied by the kids in his community because of them. His older brother Mike called me the OG (the original gangster) of the law of attraction and holistic healing. Back then, I didn't feel that way.

My family and I were ostracized, made fun of, and left out of the social fiber of our community with little to no resources to support us. I'm truly grateful for the mission of *Ben Speaks,* as I believe it saved me from my own self-destructive tendencies. It gave me purpose and a reason to get out of bed every day and be the change in my own life while impacting the lives of others in his name.

For the next two years, I immersed myself in the mission of *Ben Speaks,* communicating with my guides and Ben daily. I would go on my God walk every day and ask for guidance. There were many times that I had a sense that Ben was connected to something so much bigger than my limited mind could fathom. The messages were profound and magical.

You can learn more about the full story in my book on Amazon, *The Phoenix Rising, A Mother's Journey Through Life and Loss.* But today, I would like to share with you the incredible gift I received from first Ben and then Archangel Metatron who channeled through me on this crisp day in New England.

I was coming down the stairs from my healing studio when I heard a voice in my head. It was Ben. I went to my computer and the following message poured through me.

Do not fear
For I am here, I am here
Listen for my voice through the stillness of your heart
Come away from the noise of your surroundings
I am always with you
You are always with me
I remember now
I finally remember now
You can remember too

You don't have to leave your body to remember
I got frustrated
I forgot who I was
We all did
You all do

You can remember through me
You can remember through Christ
You can remember by going inside of yourself

I didn't want to go inside
I was mesmerized by the outside voices
I saw no future for myself
I was torn from the outside in
You can be pieced together from the inside out

Go inside and get calm
Your world will change
You can change it
Change your mind
You will change your life

I see that now
I am still with you
I will always be with you
I love you

After receiving this beautiful message from my son's spirit, I went into my kitchen to find my boy Michael and his best friend Chris working on a school project at our kitchen table. I placed the message down for Michael to read it. Just as he was reading the line "You don't have to leave your body to remember," a single droplet of water fell from the tiffany lamp on the ceiling onto the page right next to that line.

I will never forget his buddy Chris searching for the source of the water frantically. "WTF," he said! "Where did that come from?"

Mike exclaimed, "Mom, it's a teardrop from Heaven." We were truly blessed that day with a clear message from Ben.

The next day I was coming down my stairs again and I heard a voice say, *Scribe for me.* I said, "Is that you, Ben?" The voice came back and said, *No, this is Archangel Metatron!*

Whoa! He had my attention! And like a stenographer in a courtroom, I received a profound message and meditation that I was instructed to share with the masses. Thanks to this incredible book for healing and tools, here it is:

It is time to follow your heart from the center outward. You have been looking outside yourselves for your answers. The answers are not out there. The outside is a mere reflection of that which you have projected and thereby created. This is not news to many of you. However, from our vantage point, and I speak for all the Archangels, guides, and angels above, we are still seeing a huge energetic of backwardness to your process of projection from the inside out.

It is my role to see the big picture and hold the space for a greater vision to manifest. So much of what you are creating in your world, even from those who are doing the work as you call it on your planet, are still looking from the outside in. We are calling to you in every moment to seek the peace of God within yourselves. It is time to look inside in every moment before you speak, think, project, create, act, or move forward in any way.

Many of the channels in your world have brought through tremendous tools and awareness for you to continue to grow toward the light. The energies of the crystal, rainbow, and indigo children are being felt at the ground level now. These children are here to be the change that you all seek to see. You must hand the torch over to them and trust in what they know. They have yet to be tainted by the bigger worldview.

There is a new color showing up in many of your meditations. The color is magenta. This color is a mix of Heaven (crown-purple) and Earth (root-red). This is the bridge and the creation of Heaven and Earth coming together to allow for peace, love, and forgiveness to reign on your planet. The more you can focus your energies, visualizations, and meditations on this color, from the inside of your mind, heart, body, and soul, projected up and down through your chakra system, the more you will bridge the gap between your world and mine. Direct, instruct, and allow this beautiful color of magenta to permeate, first your heart center and then your entire being. Fill every cell of your body with this brilliance, and you will be filled with the grace you seek.

We are coming together to create major ascension and, for us, descension. We are to meet in the middle, so to speak. You see, Spirit is wanting to have the experience of being in body and yet having all the benefits of not. This is an experiment that has been working itself to fruition for millennia. We are all in this together, for let us not forget this simple truth, we are one.

There are many, many benefits to your world. Spirit loves the experience of creation in physical form. This project has gone array for many, many, many lifetimes due to the need to control the physical world by ego. It is time to trust in the bigger picture and lift yourselves up beyond that of the ego-mind and see all that you are meant to be. There is so much for you here. There is so much for all of us to experience in the presence of love as our central focus.

As you bridge the Christ-light (violet) of Heaven and the Earth-light of the mother (red), you will be the bridge for great change on your planet. This is the connection of mother and father igniting the heart of their children to live in peace and harmony as has and will always be our greatest wish for you. This transmission is essential for the survival of your planet and this ascension.

With all my love and abiding faith in the highest vision and manifestation for all, I leave you with the blessings of Spirit. - Archangel Metatron!

I was blown away by this message and have been completely on purpose since this transmission to continue to be a voice, role model, and facilitator to provide an inside-out approach to wellness through our programs for youth and families with *Ben Speaks.*

As a grieving mother, it has taken years to heal from the devastation of the loss of my boy. This meditation has been one of my greatest tools in my toolkit to heal my broken heart and the hearts of many other mamas who are losing their children in record numbers as we continue to deal with a pandemic of low self-esteem and self-worth in our culture today.

After Covid shut down my healing studio, I remember sitting on my computer engaged in a Tony Robbins seminar. He said, "Remember, life is not happening to you, it is happening for you!" I took some time to digest his message.

My heart had been broken open not only by the loss of my Ben but also my two sisters, Lynn and Candace, my mom, a friend to a fire, my marriage, and the fresh loss of my brother-in-law to suicide right as the pandemic was rearing its ugly head. How could I survive such heartache?

It was at that moment I signed myself up to become an advanced grief recovery specialist and began my own deeper work to heal myself from the years of resentment, guilt, shame, hurt, and loss. Through this work, I have healed and found my joy again. It's my prayer that you can find yours too. May this meditation lead you down that path.

THE TOOL

Magenta Heart Meditation

Begin by finding a comfortable, quiet place to sit or lay down.
Start to take long, deep breaths into your belly.
Feel your belly rise and fall with each breath.

With every in-breath, breath in peace.
With every out-breath, let go of all stress, tension, or pain in your body and mind!
Release all fear, depression, and anxiety!

Now bring your awareness to the base of your spine!
This is the home of your root chakra.
The color is bright red.
See, feel, sense, or know this energy as a bright ball of red light.
As you plug your awareness into this red energy,
imagine you can breathe it from the base of your spine to your heart center.

Now shift your awareness to the top of your head.
This is the home of your crown chakra.
The color is bright violet.
See, feel, sense, or know this energy as a bright flame of violet light.
As you plug your awareness into this violet energy,
imagine you can breathe it from the top of your head to your heart center.

See it begin to mix with the root red from the base of your spine. Slowly, as the two colors mix, they create the color magenta. Visualize a bright magenta heart in the center of your chest. Now imagine your entire body begins to receive this loving, healing magenta light.

Invite it to spill into the bones of your body starting with your feet, ankles, lower legs, knees, thighs, and hips, deep into your pelvic bowl, up through your spine, ribs, chest, upper back, shoulders, arms, hands, neck, jaw, face, and head. Deep into the marrow.

Continue to draw this light from your heart center into all the organs of your body, your reproductive organs, your intestines, pancreas, liver, kidneys, spleen, gallbladder, and stomach.

Invite it to move into your physical heart and lungs and through your bloodstream, bringing divine grace and love to your body.

Draw the magenta light through your breath up to your brain and down through your nerves to bring your entire being into a state of deep peace.

Send it to all your muscles, ligaments, and tendons as they melt like butter in a warm sun and receive this magenta healing light of love.

Now that you're filled from bone to skin, allow the magenta light to pour into your energy field.

See a giant bubble of magenta light that now surrounds you. You are safe, healed, and whole!

Sit here in silence for some time and feel the love within you and around you!

Judy Giovangelo has been a teacher and healer of energy medicine and the law of attraction for 30 years. She is a certified advanced grief recovery specialist, yoga instructor, Reiki, sound, intuitive healer, hypnotherapist, and spiritual counselor. She offers private healing via Zoom and at her home studio in West Roxbury, Massachusetts.

Her personal mission is to help sensitive and intuitive people permanently remove the blocks that stand in the way of their dreams by providing an inside-out approach to wellness and to support moms who have lost their children to heal and find joy again after tragedy.

She is the founder and director of Curriculum for Ben Speaks Louder Than Words. Ben Speaks is a non-profit organization born through the loss of her 18-year-old son Ben to suicide in 2009.

Ben Speaks mission is to provide positive channels of expression and empowerment for a whole-person approach to wellness through clinical and holistic resources and education.

Judy has delivered a powerful message for change to 100s of youth audiences through Ben Speaks's signature Power of Choice presentation and developed the Power of Choice curriculum for middle school students, parents, and teachers. The mission of the Ben Speaks curriculum is to teach young people to harness their thoughts, words, and feelings to create their destiny through intention in action.

Additionally, through her personal work, she teaches mediumship and intuitive development, Sacred Spirit Circles, past life regression, grief recovery, Reiki trainings, Yoga Nidra, and expressive art workshops in many healing centers throughout New England. All of her programs are rooted in healing and empowerment.

Connect with the author:

Free Magenta Heart Meditation as an opt-in to my website.

www.judygio.com

www.benspeaks.org

https://www.facebook.com/judy.giovangelo

https://www.facebook.com/judygio1

https://www.instagram.com/judygiovangelo/

https://www.linkedin.com/in/judygiovangelo/

www.benspeaks.org

https://www.facebook.com/ben.speaks

https://www.instagram.com/benspeaks/

https://www.linkedin.com/company/ben-speaks/

https://mobile.twitter.com/benspeaks

CHAPTER 6

AT FIRST AWARE,
THEN FULLY ALIVE

ENGAGING YOUR SUPERPOWER
FOR A LIFE WELL-LIVED

Jim Phillips, Certified LIFE Strategist and LIFE Coach

MY STORY

One by one we arrived at the home where the movie was being filmed. Each had a story to tell about a significant, life-changing event that resulted in a new life perspective. The movie's concept was that as the stories were shared, they'd benefit not only the characters portrayed in the movie but also those watching as each considered how their own lives might be impacted by applying these life lessons.

The house in which we filmed was spectacular. It was situated on about two acres in the foothills outside Las Vegas, Nevada. The steep incline at the back of the property was beautifully landscaped with stone pathways, lights, waterfalls, and statuary from around the world. As you made your way to the top of the incline, you found yourself in a large, covered stone patio area from which you had a breathtaking view of Lake Mead and the mountains beyond. The serenity and peace experienced from this vantage point were indescribable.

As the equipment was set up, cast members milled around introducing themselves and talking nervously about the segment they were to film. Never having been on a movie set before, I was intrigued by the process and curious about the story each person would tell.

As I met my fellow cast members and got a feel for their stories, I became concerned. Each experienced a tragic event that impacted them to the extent that their experience was now their life's mission and life philosophy. They wanted others to know that they, too, could overcome whatever challenging situation life might present.

The challenge for me was not having a tragic event like falling from a hang glider from 150 feet in the air to the unwelcome asphalt below. I was not a professional hockey player who crashed into the end boards at over 100 mph, shattering vertebrae and becoming paraplegic. I was not addicted to drugs or alcohol and was not awakened one morning by the presence of a large angel in my bedroom. In fact, I was wondering why I was there about to take part in a movie that featured such extreme life events.

Because my scene was scheduled for the second day of filming, I had the opportunity to listen to some of the incredible stories of tragedy that were turned into triumph. With each unfolding story, my anxiety continued to mount. All I did was author a book which shared various life perspectives that caught the eye of the movie's producer. She felt my message aligned with the movie's, but what was that message, and how could I tell it? A common theme throughout my work, upon which we agreed, was "Life doesn't happen to you, it happens for you."

The day of my scene finally arrived. As I was leaving the hotel where we were staying, I caught up to the woman with whom I'd be sharing the scene. She, in her own right, was an extraordinary person. At the age of three, she lost her sight due to a car accident. Then at age 15, a car hit her as she crossed the street resulting in kidney transplants. And yet, she graduated from college, went on to earn a master's degree, and is living life fully in every imaginable way. In the movie, her character's life paralleled her real life as a young blind woman struggling with day-to-day life.

As we approached the vehicle that would take us to the set, we noticed a flat tire. The producer's assistant, who was driving us, immediately called AAA to get the tire repaired and us on the road to begin the day's filming. As I sat in the back seat with my co-star, I asked her how she felt the previous day's filming had gone. She turned her head towards me, took a long deep breath, and said, "I am so tired of hearing about the terrible lives others have experienced."

I asked what she meant, to which she replied, "As you know, I am blind and have had to overcome my challenges. I've been told I should become an inspirational speaker, share my story, and help others who might be experiencing extreme difficulties in their life. But I don't want to be known for my story. My story is just the life I have experienced. It's not who I am. I don't find it extraordinary in any way."

A little surprised by her answer, I asked, "What or who inspires you?" She immediately looked up, turned her head towards me, and said, "You do." Completely taken aback, I was slow to respond.

"What do you mean I inspire you?" She immediately responded, "You get it without having gone through a tragic event like those in the movie. You didn't have to have something bring you to your knees to get your attention. You see life in a way others don't. You understand that what life presents is what that soul requires for its intended life experiences."

While it's true this is my life perspective, I never had anyone say this to me. I do not believe we have to have a devastating life experience before we awaken to the truth that we can change our lives at any moment with a simple choice. Life always presents what is required to bring about what is needed to fulfill its purpose for each of us. Life doesn't have to be, and for most, is usually not a traumatic, knee-buckling, gut-wrenching, ball-up-on-the-floor-praying-for-help experience.

Some say it requires complete surrender—the white flag, hands in the air, hopeless surrender. I contend that surrender is not giving up, it's giving into. Giving in to the magnificence of what can be, the magnificence of all we are, the magnificence of Self. It's not a throwing of our hands in the air in surrender but the raising of our hands in victory as we realize that life always has and always will offer what we need for the grandest experience and expression of Self.

As we sat waiting, we discussed how we would approach our scene. I still had no specific thought about how I was going to share *the story* that was going to inspire others, and yet the clock was ticking. I looked at her and said, "Why don't we just have a conversation? I will ask questions based on what your character is experiencing in the movie, and we will let it flow naturally."

The producer's assistant heard what I said, quickly turned, and said, "You can't change the script just before filming." I responded with, "Don't worry. We're not going to do anything that would disrupt the flow and message of the movie." So off we went with my wondering how this was going to turn out.

LIGHTS, CAMERA, ACTION

"Okay, you two are up next," said the producer. We made our way to the set, took our positions, and just like in the movies, there was a version of "Lights, camera, action" and the snapping down of the clapperboard. And so, we began.

There was an easy-flowing conversation that ensued. Her answers to my questions allowed me to dig deep into her character's life, and since her real life reflected that of her character, there was a direct correlation between these two lives. As the conversation continued, we shared a deep connection and release of emotions.

We both leaned back and let out deep breaths when the scene was complete. One by one, the members of the production crew approached to tell us how moving the scene was. In their judgment, it was the most authentic scene so far.

What was it about the scene that stirred the emotions in all present? How did she and I connect in such a way that the conversations flowed so easily? The answer is quite simple and a bit profound. We were simply being human. We allowed who and what we are to take the stage and the lead. We got out of our own way and allowed that which had a desire to experience and express through us, and as us, to do just that.

Our *superpower,* the superpower possessed by every person on the planet, is we are human. Being human, we have the ability to think, reflect, feel, be self-aware, create, be compassionate, and experience and express.

We have the gift of free will to choose how we will experience life and how we will *be* within each experience.

And yet, all too often, we squander this power by giving it to others who tell us what they think is best for us. We somehow accept they know more about us and our desires than we do. We give it away by adhering to dogma, misinformation, and limiting beliefs about what we can or cannot, should or should not, do or be. We live in an illusion of who we believe we are while simultaneously living in the illusion of who we believe we are not. We each hold the key to freedom from this self-imposed prison.

Our superpower is being human, not the perfect human, but perfectly human, and embracing what that means. And yet, when an experience doesn't turn out as we hoped, usually due to poor judgment or questionable action, our humanness becomes the excuse for why it didn't turn out. How often do we say or hear, "I'm only human; what do you expect?" Instead of embracing the superpower of being human, we use it as an excuse for our shortcomings.

As a human, there is nothing you cannot overcome, not because you're only given what you can handle, but because there is nothing you cannot handle. Your life is evidence of this superpower. Look at your life experiences, especially those that most challenged you. You overcame them and can now look back at them with the benefit gained from having had the experience.

Of course, while reading this, you might be in the midst of a challenging situation and thinking, *I haven't overcome this; why am I struggling so? Why was I presented this?* It's in realizing there is nothing we have not, and cannot overcome, that we summon the courage and the power within that allows us to do so.

> *We are presented challenging opportunities in life,*
> *not to have the experience of the challenge,*
> *but to have the joyful experience of rising above it,*
> *and the realization of how truly powerful we are.*

Those in the movie who shared their stories of immense challenge could have easily allowed the experience to determine how their life would unfold by becoming victims of those circumstances. They chose instead to acknowledge and understand their reality at that time. Despite the challenging opportunity life presented, they made choices and took action that moved them towards the life they had a strong desire to create and live. Humans, above and beyond all other life forms, have the capacity to live intentionally.

As humans, we are blessed with many gifts (powers) that allow us to live intentionally, the most compelling of which is awareness.

THE TOOL

A Simple Practice of Awareness

What does it mean to be aware? It's to be present, and in that presence, cognizant and attentive towards all that is being perceived, and all one desires. It's through awareness we discern what to do or not do. It's through awareness we appreciate that every moment presents the opportunity to create and experience the life we desire without first being kicked in the head, knocked sideways, or falling into an abyss. It's through awareness we realize life merely responds to us. Life is what we make of it and what it makes of us.

We have an awareness of our Self and our place in the world. Whether exercised or not, we have the ability to be aware of what is happening around us and within us and in seeing the correlation between the two. It's through awareness we can understand what has been misunderstood. We can correct what needs correcting.

It is from awareness that choice emerges.
It is from choice that life unfolds.

The practice of awareness requires no effort. It's the allowing of life to unfold in each moment while consciously observing all that is unfolding without judging any of it. Awareness is the quiet observation and experience of our connection with all things. It's being present to all that is happening within our awareness without attaching to any of it.

Our gift of awareness within our humanness is not something we turn on and off. It's always on and available. It's a matter of being consciously aware, which is simply being aware of when we are aware. Being fully and consciously aware is absorbing the moment while allowing the moment to absorb us.

To understand the power of awareness and our power to manage it, I use a method I learned years ago. The idea is to sit quietly while slowly becoming consciously aware of all that is happening around and within you at the moment. It's not about focusing on the subject or object of your awareness, only your awareness of being aware of it.

You can experience this anywhere at any time, although most often, it's best when sitting quietly and comfortably. As I became better at this practice, I found it more powerful when walking through the woods, in the mountains, along the beach, or, quite frankly, anywhere you can connect with and be in nature. My initial experience was outdoors alongside a lake, guided by a spiritual, intuitive friend.

She had me sit quietly with my eyes closed and said to focus initially on my breathing so I could relax and become more focused. As I relaxed, my breathing slowed and fell into a rhythm of measured breaths.

She then said, "Now place your awareness on the thoughts moving through your mind. Allow them to enter and exit without attachment. If you find your mind has grabbed hold of a specific thought, consciously let it go by bringing your awareness back to your awareness without admonishing yourself for having become distracted or attached."

"As you allow the thoughts to pass effortlessly, be aware of your beingness, your very existence. Be mindful that you do not allow this to become a thought that takes you out of your awareness. Just be aware you exist."

"Now place your awareness on your physical body—this magnificent vehicle through which and as which you experience and express in this lifetime. Experience your presence within this physical body. As you experience your presence, feel it beyond the confines of your physical body. Allow the experience of boundarylessness."

"As you bring your awareness back to the physical body, feel it wrapped in clothing. Feel the texture of the material where it's tight against your skin and where your shirt sleeve ends."

"Feel your feet in your sandals, the pressure of the ball of your foot against the leather of your sandal as it's in contact with the floor, and the pressure of the strap of your sandals against the top of your foot."

"Feel the sensation of the breeze gently caressing your face and your feet and ankles. Hear the breeze as it dances and whispers through the trees. Feel the warmth of the sun embracing your face and your soul."

"Listen as the waves on the lake gently lap the shore. Open to the sounds of nature in all her expressions at this moment."

She concluded with, "Return now to the physical body. Bring your awareness back to sitting quietly. Allow the awareness of your breath once again as it slowly moves in and out. Take a deep breath and slowly exhale as you open your eyes while taking in all you see before you. Be aware of the power of your awareness."

The experience of this exercise isn't to place your awareness on a particular subject for long, only long enough to gain awareness of it. The intention is to gain awareness of our ability to manage and direct our awareness toward anything or nothing. It's only when we are aware of something that we can do anything to change it.

In your daily practice of awareness, pay particular attention to the following:

1. Your thoughts. Not what they are, just the awareness you have them.

2. Your feelings, without questioning them, just that you have them.

3. All that is happening within you and around you.

4. The correlation of your thoughts, beliefs, feelings, and the experiences life presents.

5. Your inspirations. What are you compelled to do?

6. Any resistance towards life. What are you not allowing, accepting, or embracing?

7. Be aware of when you're not aware and quietly return to awareness.

8. Be aware of judgment, especially towards oneself.

9. Be aware of being aware. Who or what is it within me that is aware of my awareness?

10. Be aware of when you're most open, receptive, and present. Set aside time every day that is most conducive to your being quiet and still for your practice of conscious awareness.

As you practice *conscious awareness,* you will soon find it expands into all areas of life, resulting in greater clarity, better choices, a higher level of personal empowerment, a deeper, more compassionate relationship with yourself, a more fulfilling experience, and appreciation of life, and unbridled freedom. It's through awareness you realize that who and what you are is the superpower within all things.

Awareness is our awakening. Once aware, all else falls into place.

Jim Phillips, LIFE Strategist/Coach, speaker, and America's Leading Authority on Living in Full Expression. He authored the book on it—*The Key to LIFE; living in full expression.* He has been engaged in the business world for over 40 years, 30 of which he spent inspiring others to higher levels of achievement and understanding through his strategy sessions, coaching, writing, and more than 20 international business conference presentations.

Jim is a bestselling author with three books to his credit. The aforementioned, *The Key to LIFE; living in full expression, From Inspiration to Intention,* and a collaborative book entitled *The Wellness Universe Guide to Complete Self-Care, 25 tools for Stress Relief* published by Brave Healer Productions.

Jim's work has been featured on CBS, NBC, ABC, FOX, and hundreds of nationally-syndicated television, newspaper, and magazine outlets, including Thrive Global, Bodhi Tree Magazine, Whole Living Magazine, 11:11 Magazine, and Inspire Me Today. He is a regular guest on podcasts focusing on spirituality, wellness, life purpose, and overall wellbeing.

Jim currently lives in Northern Virginia, where he continues writing, speaking, and coaching. www.livinginfullexpression.com

CHAPTER 7

SHINE YOUR AUTHENTIC LIGHT

CULTIVATING YOUR SUPERPOWER USING JOYFUL SELF-CARE

Janette Stuart, Angelic Practitioner

MY STORY

I'd been following the angels' guidance since 2012 when my precious brother was gravely ill. We were close, only a year apart in school. I was always devoted to my faith but watching my brother's rapid decline and bearing the circumstances of his sudden illness made me seek solace elsewhere. In my search for assurance and guidance, I found Illuminating Souls on Facebook, who shared loving words of encouragement from the angels, a healing balm to my aching heart.

At first, I thought only saints or holy people like Mother Teresa or Gandhi could work with the angels, and I didn't know it was possible for regular people like me.

The angels guided me along the way, even when I doubted myself, wanted to shrink, hide, or forgot to trust. I feel like my brother is also helping me from the other side to live more authentically.

Your angels are there for you too, dear heart. We all have at least two guardian angels who love us forever, and they're just a breath away.

The angels guided me through daily interaction, mainly through oracle cards, prayer, and occasional direct guidance of messages such as hearing the guidance, *Name your business Angel Angles. People often interchange the words angels and angles, and with that name, you'd help put a heavenly slant in people's lives with angelic guidance.* As I began contemplating my post-employment career, I was reading everything I could find about the angels and taking lots of uplifting classes, and I knew I'd do something in retirement involving the angels.

I became a Certified Angel Card Reader™ and worked with a mentor and coach to help plan and implement my Angel Angles business. It was both a joy and scary; it felt like my purpose or life mission, and stretched my limits daily.

When my web designer unveiled the business website I'd dreamed about for months, it was exciting and exhilarating. I loved everything about it, from the pink and purple colors I chose to her gorgeous images and even the pretty fonts. I loved the look and feel of it. It was beautiful. Then I saw my logo, including my full name, and was horrified. I had that sinking feeling in my stomach that I'd be sick. *Oh my gosh! What will my friends and family think when I profess to talk to and about angels? Just who do I think I am?*

Have you had that same icky feeling too? Maybe you've asked yourself some of these same questions. It could be imposter syndrome or the sense of not being enough. Sometimes we think we need just one more credential, certification, or training, and then we'll be ready or good enough, which is just our ego's stall tactic.

The angels remind us that we're already enough, just as we are. They urge us to shine our authentic light, our superpower, to bless ourselves and the world. That is our mission; that's what we came here to do. They love and support us unconditionally.

I shared my angst about my name being on the logo, and bless my web designer's heart, she created a new version of my logo without my name and assured me I'd be ready to reveal myself to the world before too long. I had my doubts that I'd ever feel comfortable in the limelight and broadcasting my messages of love to the world using my full name. *After all, what would people think?* Yet, I was so grateful for her talents and guidance, and we launched my website just a few weeks following my retirement in 2015.

At that time, I thought: *Who cares about who writes the loving social media posts, blogs, and articles the angels guided me to create?* I felt safer by omitting my name on the work I produced. However, I was not shining my authentic light when hiding behind anonymity; I was playing small and safe. Can you relate? I dimmed my own light by omission as I let doubt and fear creep in even as I felt inspired and directed by divine forces.

We always have a choice, and I could've chosen to let my fear win. I could've listened to my dear ego, who always wants to keep me safe, or I could be brave and push beyond my fears, stepping into my most authentic light while being held and supported by the wings of my angels.

I decided that where I wanted to be was beyond my comfort zone, yet I felt terrified to cross that line. The angels helped every step of the way as my mission unfolded.

The good news was that I began claiming my work in a very public way only a few months after launching my website. I released my first book, *On a Path of Joy,* Volume One, in October 2016. I didn't know it at the time, but when selecting blue for the color of the cover, I was honoring the fifth chakra. The fifth, or throat chakra energy center, is all about speaking our truth and being visible in the world, which I embraced by boldly publishing my name, photo, and angelic guidance.

I knew I would be an author at age eight as I always loved to write. I just didn't know how or when it would happen. I self-published my first book at age 56, so please believe me when I say you're never too old to follow your dreams.

Following your dreams is a great way to cultivate your superpower. I followed my heart's wild dreams and desires as the angels left me breadcrumbs of inspiration assurance that, *Now is the time to write your book, and we will show you how all along the way.*

I'd always had a strong affinity with the song *This Little Light of Mine* by Harry Dixon Loes, from the first time I heard it in Sunday School over 55 years ago. Do you know it too? Bruce Springsteen sings a great, joyous version live on YouTube from Dublin, Ireland if you'd like to have a listen. Here's an excerpt of the lyrics:

"This little light of mine,
I'm gonna let it shine.
This little light of mine,
I'm gonna let it shine.
This little light of mine,
I'm gonna let it shine,
let it shine, let it shine, oh let it shine.

Ev'rywhere I go,
I'm gonna let it shine.
Ev'rywhere I go,
I'm gonna let it shine.
Ev'rywhere I go,
I'm gonna let it shine,
let it shine, let it shine, oh let it shine.

Jesus gave it to me,
I'm gonna let it shine.
Jesus gave it to me,
I'm gonna let it shine.
Jesus gave it to me,
I'm gonna let it shine,
let it shine, let it shine, oh let it shine."

Even at a tender age, I felt this song connected me to my purpose of shining my radiance, unique light, and superpower. It made me feel joyous, and I especially loved the part about not hiding my light under a bushel or letting it get blown out.

In my case, I was hiding my radiance, my superpower, under a bushel when I wasn't living authentically.

Our light, this authentic, radiant light, is our inner spark. It's our superpower. It's our mission; it's what lights us up and fills our hearts with joy. It's the Divine connection flowing to and through us. We are here to live a life of joy, to be the unique being of love and light that we came here to be.

So, dear heart, what lights you up? What would you do if money were no object? When you can choose fun and creativity, what would you stay up late doing or get up early to do? What has always been fun and easy for you? Chances are, those are the things you need to do to cultivate your superpower.

If you don't know or aren't sure about the answers to these questions, don't despair. We will call on the Angel of Joy, Archangel Haniel, who will help us attune to her divine energy and assist us in cultivating our superpower using joyous self-care in the tool section below.

Archangel Haniel helps with happiness, joy, and soul fulfillment. She, like all of the angels, is pure, unconditional love. Her essence is often portrayed by turquoise and shimmery silver color. Think water sparkling in the moonlight on a still and beautiful night. She is also the Archangel associated with the moon. Picture clear full moon energy where you await her arrival with reverent expectancy.

Here's her definition of reverent expectancy: "A quality of deep respect while believing or desiring this divine connection through attunement. It's basking in loving, gentle, and jubilant energy, which helps magnify your joy."

Don't worry about asking the angels for assistance. They, like the Divine, are omnipotent and can be with everyone at once. Your asking for their help doesn't take them away from more important matters, and they are always here for you.

Since we have dominion over our lives and can choose, we need to ask for the angels' assistance. It needn't be anything fancy. A simple "Angels, I need your help," will do.

My favorite quote about joy:

"You are joy, looking for a way to express. It's not just that your purpose is joy; it is that you are joy. You are love and joy and freedom and clarity expressing—energy-frolicking and eager. That's who you are.

And so, if you're always reaching for alignment with that, you're always on your path, and your path will take you into all kinds of places." - Abraham Hicks

THE TOOL

Archangel Haniel: Angel of Joy Attunement

We will enjoy an attunement into Archangel Haniel's positive energy to enliven and uplift us. We'll be basking in the power of her loving, gentle, and jubilant essence to help magnify our joy.

You can ask any question of her during this attunement. Allow the answer to come easily and effortlessly. Feel the answers come through from your heart. Here are some sample questions you might want to ask as examples:

What lights me up?

What brings me joy?

How can I best shine my authentic light or superpower?

What do I need to do to enhance my self-care practice?

What do I need to know to experience joyful self-care?

Do I have any blocks to joyful self-care? If so, show me.

What five things can I do right away to increase my joyful self-care?

What else do I need to know?

Don't worry; I'll walk you through every step of the way. Allow yourself 10-15 minutes of uninterrupted quiet time to enjoy this joyful self-care attunement.

Here are some things you'll need:

Candle and lighter

Journal

Pen

Water to drink

Turn your cell phone and computer off. Get comfortable in a spot where you'll have 10-15 minutes of uninterrupted quiet time. You're worthy and deserving of this quiet time of gentle self-care.

Light your candle.

Take a few slow, deep breaths.

Have your journal and pen handy beside you.

Place your hand on your heart and gaze gently at the candle's flame.

Continue breathing in and out, slow and easy.

Feel yourself becoming still, open, and receptive.

Envision the color turquoise; hold that vision in your mind for a few breaths.

Next, visualize sitting under the full moon's light near a beautiful calm body of water. You're safe and comfortable, and the temperature is just right for you.

You're now ready to bask in Archangel Haniel's attuned energy. Receive her now with "reverent expectancy."

She comes to you now wearing a gown of turquoise, her wings shimmer with silver iridescence.

You welcome her with an open heart.

You bask in her energy of love, light, and joy. Ah, breathe it in. Allow it to flow to you. Exhale any worry or doubt.

You allow time to melt away.

Nothing matters but this now moment.

There is no rush, dear heart. There is only peace.

Her energy is loving and joyous.

Envision the way the moonlight plays upon the softly rippling water.

You feel Archangel Haniel's essence, and you drink it in.

You're one with her loving and joyous energy.

Now is the time to ask her any questions you may wish to gather her insight and perspective.

It's safe for you to receive.

Allow the answer to come easily and effortlessly. You may receive an answer different than anticipated; please write it down in your journal. Don't overthink or question the response. Know that you can repeat this attunement at any time, and Archangel Haniel will be there for you.

Sit in this loving and joyous space for a few minutes longer. Allow Archangel Haniel's energy to magnify your joy and cultivate your superpower.

Your Archangel Haniel attunement is now complete. Thank her for this precious gift.

She reminds you that you can repeat this attunement as needed, and she will gladly meet you.

Sit a few minutes in quiet gratitude and drink your water to replenish yourself, noting that water is an excellent conductor of energy.

Blow out your candle.

You may feel tired or energized following your Archangel Haniel's attunement, and either response is normal. Remember to hydrate for the next several hours.

You may need some joyful self-care following your attunement. You may want to nap or spend some time in nature to ground and center yourself following this high-vibration healing session.

Did you get your questions answered? If so, fabulous. You can embrace her advice and move forward to help shine your authentic light. If not, or if you have additional questions, Archangel Haniel invites you to connect with her again with a heart full of reverent expectancy. She will be there for you.

In closing, Archangel Haniel congratulates you on your desire to make the world a better place by shining your authentic light, your superpower. You're a unique and wonderful creation, and you're one of a kind in all of the universe. She loves and adores you.

I made an audio recording of the Archangel Haniel attunement as a gift for you, and you may listen to it again and again anytime you'd like to bask in her loving and joyous energy.

Visit https://www.angel-angles.com/resources for this and other goodies to help cultivate your superpower.

Janette Stuart: Emissary of Joy at Angel Angles and Well-Being and Wonder is a beacon of love, joy, peace, and gentleness. She is a #1 Best Selling author, speaker, military mom, and pancreatic cancer survivor who uses the gift of her words and positivity to assist others in embracing their divinity and living a life of joy. She uses tools such as her five devotionals, Drenched in Love and the On a Path of Joy series, 1:1 Angel Readings, and live events.

As an angelic practitioner, she shares goodness and grace and the healing beauty of nature frequently in her work to inspire others. She has developed three inspirational card decks, Drenched in Love and Love Notes from The Divine. She is the co-creator of Words of Wisdom Guidance Cards and shares daily messages of love and encouragement on social media.

She facilities an online monthly gathering celebrating cozy, inspiring conversations at her Sanctuary of Joy on Zoom. Each month the focus changes, all while indulging in joy.

Janette lives in the San Francisco Bay Area with her husband Mark of 39 years and their boxer dog, Spike, who rescued them eight years ago. She has a grown son who proudly serves in the United States Coast Guard and is one of her biggest joys. Retired in 2015 from a career in finance and human resources with 36 years of service, she now joyfully does her soul's work daily.

Janette loves cooking, being out in nature, writing, and has an impressive collection of stationery, pens, and journals. She seeks wonder and delight in her daily walks in nature. Check out her free resources

https://www.angel-angles.com/resources

CHAPTER 8

CONQUERING FEAR TO LIVE YOUR LIFE ON PURPOSE

HOW TO MAKE A GIGANTIC LEAP TOWARD YOUR DREAM!

Kye Sun Rose, Energy Healer, Spiritual Coach

MY STORY

"You won't believe what just happened. I feel like a different person. I had no fear just now." I called my teacher as I drove away from the barn.

There are moments that define you, and change the trajectory of your life. I'd like to share some moments with you. They involve fear. I didn't understand why it was present in my life nor how fear could be one of the most powerful allies to move me toward my dreams and desires.

I grew up next to a horse farm that raised Arabian horses for show and breeding. I loved living next to them. They were beautiful and serene. On occasion, I was allowed to see the newborn horses the day they were born. I always knew I was destined to have a horse, even though it seemed like a big faraway dream.

When I was 30, I completed my post-graduate training as a physician assistant. I spent time with my neighbor to experience taking care of a horse and realized it was a very time-consuming and expensive venture and knew it wasn't the right time.

At 38 years old, when I was planning to have a baby with my partner of five years, I saw myself slowly getting more and more depressed. I realized I was in the wrong place! *How did I get here?* I realized I wasn't committed to the relationship or the baby and extricated myself from the situation. I was shocked that I got so off track even though I didn't know what the right track was. It didn't feel right. I prayed for help to guide me where I was supposed to be. At that moment, my intuition was awakening, and my spiritual life was born.

I found a prayer group that led to a sweat lodge family. We visited the Lakota reservation in South Dakota yearly for their highest ceremony, Sundance. I was ecstatic that I found a community and a place for healing the core wounds that left me living emotionally as a teenager at almost 40 years old. It became paramount for me to heal issues making my world very regimented and small. We call this the rule keeper, and I was living it nearly 100%. It's a way of controlling everything in your life by following certain rules and being unwilling to see any way to live except through these rules. Ultimately, fear of being out of control in any situation ruled my life.

I found a wonderful dude ranch in Arizona in the Cochise Mountains and visited it multiple times. As we rode on horseback amongst the backdrop of desert and mountains, I sensed the Apache ancestors watching us. I felt approval and connection to them. One evening as I walked from the dining hall to my small cabin, it dawned on me how much at peace I felt among the horses, out in nature surrounded by stars with very little hustle and bustle and no TV! It was an important moment. I hadn't realized I wasn't happy where I was in my life. Yet, I wasn't miserable enough to do anything about it.

It was a few years later, during a ceremony, that Spirit told me to get a horse. I felt scared moving forward and adopting a horse as they usually live 25 to 40 years. It's a huge commitment, never mind expensive, as I've mentioned. At this point in my life, time and money were not a problem. Previously it was a dream. Now, it was more of a necessity.

I've learned to allow the Divine to make things happen in my training. I started taking riding lessons, let the process unfold around me, and let the horse find me. One day at the horse rescue where I took lessons, a horse strolled up to me and placed his nose on my chest. He found and picked me. He was to be my partner on a journey I did not understand at that moment.

This gentle soul was only two, and I devoted myself to lessons since I knew very little about training or owning a horse. I named him Dine'— the word for the Navajo people. Some people thought this was a disaster waiting to happen, combining a green owner and a green horse—which means inexperienced. I was aware of this possibility but had trust in the Divine that all would be okay, and financially I could have constant training for the horse and myself.

I remember so vividly the day he came to the barn I found close to home with a wonderful barn manager and trainer, all supplied effortlessly by the Divine. I remember I was scared out of my mind. I felt like I was bringing a newborn baby home, except the baby was 900 pounds.

There was a lot of fear right from the beginning, and it came from a lack of knowledge. This is a good kind of fear. As you gain knowledge and experience, you move out of fear and into confidence—this is a protective kind of fear. Over time I learned more and gained knowledge and confidence. Yet a deeper fear lived inside me. The feeling of inadequacy lingered under the surface.

With a horse, you need to be a leader and show confidence because he is a herd animal who looks to the leader of the pack to make him feel safe. I'm supposed to be the leader; I provide him with confidence and safety. I was lacking this. I borrowed it from my trainer but never owned it in my body, and Dine' knew it. We moved forward and advanced in our skills together, but things never ran smoothly. There were no big incidents that fed this fear of inadequacy. It came from deep within.

I knew early on that horses reflect our emotions and inadequacies. They will quickly show us what we're doing wrong. If you're flighty and not grounded, they are jumpy and possibly explosive. If you're calm and centered, that's the kind of horse you have in front of you.

I was deep down flighty and not grounded. My new trainer addressed this first. She brought my energy down to a place of stillness and calm, and the horse changed in front of my eyes. Instead of him looking away with his head high (a sign of tension and unease, he would drop his head, snort, and lick his lips (a sign of relaxation and integration). He responded to me. He was relaxed, happier, and looking at me finally in partnership. In retrospect, I lived my whole life this way, with adrenaline driving my day, thinking of the next thing I must do on my never-ending to-do list, striving for all the things I thought were going to make me happy.

This is why Spirit wanted me to get this horse. It was my way of working through and attaining confidence, courage, and leadership, expressed not necessarily through words but through my body language. The softer you can express these attributes with horses, the better and the more impact and power they have. I needed to learn this. I'm convinced I'd never have learned it any other way. Someone else can give you confidence through knowledge, but the fear of inadequacy will still lay deep within. It's not an outside job to fix that feeling, it's an inside job.

I advanced quickly in my ability to work with Dine'. I was able to ride him in the safety of the fenced-in arena, but fear arose if I wanted to venture outside the arena and ride him alone in the woods. *I'm not going out there, nope, no way.* With time and more stillness, I could easily feel the fear arise. I could then work with the fear as I learned in my coaching and meditation practices. I worked with harnessing stillness on command, and I could easily move emotion out of the body and see a significant difference in my life in unexpected ways. These emotions are stored deep within our bodies from all the moments of our life. When they're released, a lightness is felt where there was heaviness, tightness, or contraction.

During one session with my meditation teacher, I had to focus on this heavy energy of fear running throughout me. We spent the entire hour moving emotion out of the body. I felt this heavy ball of blackness deep in my left chest. I concentrated on it, honored it, and felt it disappear into thin air. Then, repeatedly a new heaviness flowed up from beneath, looking like a new shape, a new color but always with a tightness or heaviness. I reveled when it moved up and out, but again another heaviness quickly took its place. We did not need to know where it came from or when it appeared, we just had to witness its desire to move, and it did. As I felt lighter, more tightness took its place. It was a bit exhausting. I thought I wasn't doing it right. I was becoming weary. But it was very liberating and exciting in a way. My wonderful teacher just sat and witnessed it and helped me stay in stillness to allow the energy to flow and leave my body. Finally, it felt complete, and we stopped the session. I had no idea what to expect from this one hour of my life.

Two days later, I was at the barn; the weather was windy, and the skies looked dark and ominous like it was ready to rain, but I needed to go move my horse. He needed exercise. I don't know why but I opted to work him outside in the field close by the other horses but not fenced in. As I lunged him, moving him on a lead rope around me, he started getting goofy and even reared up on his hind legs. I felt nothing inside me stir, not a drop of fear, anxiety, or worry. As Dine' felt me stay calm, he responded with the same and surprisingly moved around the lunge line with ease. *What was happening? This usually would freak me out.* I was calm inside. I took notice of it but just moved through the exercise and put him away. It was a moment that changed my life.

I drove away from the barn and called my teacher. "You won't believe what just happened. I feel like a different person. I had no fear just now." I proceeded to share with him the magnitude of difference I felt inside of no feeling of nervousness, worry—nothing. I then realized how paramount it was for me to continue to release stored emotion built up from my life so I can do my energy work healing others from a place of stillness. Dine' showed me how important it's to find this place of stillness, presence, calm, and peace in a very concrete way.

As I reflect on that moment that shifted everything in my own healing and in my desire to help others heal, I understand more deeply that it's the uncertainty in life, the unknowing, that brings fear up, and it's a protective mechanism designed to keep us safe.

When we don't know what lies ahead, we can either be excited or be paralyzed by not knowing. I was paralyzed by not knowing. This fear keeps us small, in our safe place, and sabotages any attempts to move beyond our comfort zone and play bigger in life.

I have been trying to do this for a decade—to leave my medical practice of 31 years and work for myself, providing divinely guided coaching and energy healing. I have strong skills and capabilities for healing and life coaching, but fear was holding me back from starting my business.

I continued to have fears come up as I moved from riding in the arena to the surrounding fields and eventually into the woods, farther away from my original zone of safety. One day when we finally rode in the woods alone, a thought crossed my mind. *This is how all the other riders must feel, nothing—no concerns nor worries, just enjoying a ride on their horse.* How freeing this was. Shortly thereafter, I realized this was to carry over into other parts of my life.

I saw how fear worked. To push forward to live my life on purpose, I had to learn to notice fear and move through it. I realized it's the part of myself trying to keep me safe. As I move the fear out of my body, I feel nothing holding me back like the fearless individuals you see playing extreme sports or scaling Mount Everest.

More recently, fear popped up. My horse was adjusting to us living down south for the winter, in new surroundings all alone. Again, I had to work my way through fear to venture out on the 900 acres by myself. One day after trail riding successfully, he bolted home out of the blue as we left the other two horses who accompanied us. It was too much for him to leave the two horses behind, and in a flash, he was in fright/flight mode. I successfully stayed on his back at full gallop on the pavement faster than I had ever ridden. He wouldn't stop. I jumped off once we hit the sand. It took a week or so to feel the fear. I found myself back in the confines of my fenced-in round pen. The unexpectedness of this event reinforced that it's not safe out there! Anything could happen at any moment, out of the blue.

The unexpected trumped the uncertain. It was paralyzing. Yet, I approached this event differently. I used my methodologies, my stillness, moving the fear, and after three weeks, I moved back out into the woods, and finally I realized I could do anything. I can be fearless despite uncertain times, and even if something very unexpected happens out of the blue, I'd be okay. I would stand tall, be strong, and move through it—even when a family member gets cancer, or a country invades another country without provocation, or worse—I can show up, lead, be strong, and be an example for others to do the same. I saw what the deeper meaning of this scary event was trying to teach me. This is what fear is about, it shapes us and controls us, but you can use fear to move forward and push continuously out of one comfort zone into the next as you strive for your dreams.

How cool is that?

THE TOOL

1. First, have an intention of moving through something that brings fear up. Next, we want to talk to the fear. Be still, take a few deep breaths, and see if you can feel the fear. Connect to it. It will usually feel like a tightness or contraction. Grab a journal and write with your dominant hand. Ask fear: Why are you coming up? What do you need? Move the pen to your non-dominant hand and write. This is automatic writing. The unconscious mind is now free to speak. Once you get an answer, ask fear to tell you more or ask more why questions. Keep speaking to fear until you get an answer to why it's showing up in your life. Have a conversation with fear. Don't stop until you have an aha moment. It will come if you keep writing. Once you have a sense of why fear is showing up, write with your dominant hand that you honor the job fear has done. Thank fear, and let it know you're going to release the stored emotions. Let fear know it can be gentle and easy to release these emotions.

2. Now close your eyes and breathe in from your heart space, and with intention, send the out-breath down from the heart deep into the core of the Earth. Repeat the exhale, continuing to go deeper to the core until you feel it reach the core and come back to your heart. Everything works with intention. Now, breathe in and with intention from the heart, send the out-breath to the heavens above. Continue to send the breath up to the heavens until you feel it come back to your heart. Now feel the connection move up and down through you as you breathe. Fill this area with a colored light of your choosing. You're now connected to the Divine Feminine below and the Divine Masculine above. These energies will help you move the emotion.

3. Concentrate on the tightness within your body, where it is and how it looks or feels. Take note of the energy filled with light moving through you from above and below. Tell the tightness that the light will help it move out of you. It's attracted to the light, and it can pull the tightness out or make it dissolve into nothingness. Continue to do this until the tightness is gone. Do not be surprised if more tightness takes its place. This is a wonderful sign that your

unconscious feels free to give you more stored emotion to move out. This can take time or can go swiftly; do not judge. Let it move. Reflect on how you feel once there is only openness within. Keep a journal daily and watch what unfolds when fear transforms into fearlessness in your life. What can you accomplish? Who can you be? Let me know.

As a spiritual coach, **Kye** is passionate about sharing her gift of ceremony and Native American teachings to help transform and heal your life. She uses the power of prayer and connection with your Divine Source/Self to facilitate healing, allowing faster, easier and deeper transformation.

In 1998, Kye became a student of Native American Ceremony following the Lakota traditions. She is a Pipe carrier and participates in Sweat Lodge, Vision Quest, and Sundance. She has *Sundanced* 15 years at the Rosebud Reservation in South Dakota.

Kye offers a weekly Spirit Horse Healing Pipe Ceremony to guide others in healing their life through prayer, sacred song, and drumming.

In 2014 she became an Ignite your Power Coach using tapping to heal the chakras and she realized she was was guided by the energy of love to shift others to heal and transform, thus creating the Love Warrior Project.

In 2016, Kye became an advanced facilitator in Evolutionary Mystic Meditation (EMM), which guides you to experience your fully embodied, fully enlightened Self thru tapping. This process taught her how to move energy easily out of the body and become connected to and live your life on purpose through the heart.

Kye believes healing at your core can be accomplished with gentleness and ease through the power of Divine Love. Kye invites you to become a Love Warrior.

https://www.lovewarriorproject.com
https://www.facebook.com/kyesunrose

To take part in Kye's Pipe ceremony visit:

https://lovewarriorproject.coachesconsole.com/spirit-horse-healing-pipe-ceremony.html

CHAPTER 9

GOLDEN EARTH ENERGY MEDITATION

MAKING SURE GRIEF DOESN'T MAKE YOU SICK

Renee Moritz, Shaman, Medical Intuitive,
Energy Medicine Practitioner, Animal Communicator

MY STORY

I am not worth the air I am breathing.

These words became my anthem for the first three decades of my life. This belief would show in every thought and decision I made for many years. My childhood was filled with isolation, loneliness, depression, anger, and thoughts of suicide. Things didn't start this way; I remember having a profound connection to nature and animals at an early age. I was perfectly content walking through a field of tall grass, waving my hands over the tops of the wheat-colored blades, singing as I walked. Climbing my favorite tree in the front yard of my house gave me a feeling of being connected to something. I felt held and supported by the large branches. They held me in a way my mother never could. Feeling isolated and misunderstood by everyone around me caused me to internalize my feelings.

Thankfully, we had a dog most of this time because pets were usually my closest friends. I told them my secrets and cried into the scruff of their neck when life felt unfair. When they left me, I took their passing extremely hard, but this somehow prepared me for the loss of my mother at age eight after she was hit by a car. Her death was more like losing the idea of a mother because she physically left when I was four years old. My family dynamics changed after her passing. My father remarried. My stepmother and I only got along for the first few years. Any discussion about my real mother was out of the question by both. My military father's idea of discipline was banishment to my room for weeks, if not months at a time. I had little interaction with school friends or my own family. My father often reminded me of what a disappointment I was and how I would amount to very little in a world that demanded the best. *I don't know where his coldness had come from. Maybe he felt unloved as a child also. Fathers are supposed to love and protect little girls, not tell them how stupid and worthless they are. This only taught me that sometimes love can be unkind.*

We tell ourselves that the bad things that happen to us in our lives are some of the first things we would change if we had a choice. What some don't understand—and took me decades—is that these challenges are what our souls love about this life; these challenges made this life even more delicious.

I never properly grieved the death of my mother. I buried all my feelings deep inside of me for so long I wasn't even aware they were still there. Each time someone left me or broke my heart during my teenage years and early adulthood, it reinforced my long-held belief of being unworthy.

As the years went on, I settled down and created a more peaceful life for myself. I met a wonderful man, and we got married. Things were not perfect, but he understood me and loved me unconditionally. One day while daydreaming out of my kitchen window, a flash of insight downloaded into my being. In a few seconds, a movie played in my mind, lining up all my life events. Some were big, and some small, but each needed to lead me to the next. I was suddenly aware of higher consciousness, some grand plan put in place by a masterful puppet master. This single experience changed the course of my life. I understood each event, from my mother's passing to my parents' role, and how every simple choice was divinely connected to the next.

I started to work on myself from the inside out. My healing slowly began with my wounded heart. I had developed negative personality traits to help keep me safe. These no longer served me, so one by one, I began to release them. I learned about the magic of our body's complex energy fields. I learned our beliefs, thoughts, and emotions could change our bodies on a cellular level. When I began to have clients, I saw the correlation between their beliefs and their personal energy fields. I could see that a wounded heart might have led to their heart issues, and someone that was never able to speak their truth had an energetic disruption on their throat chakra or energy center. One client was never able to discuss or unload a lifetime of grief and sorrow. She eventually battled colon cancer and is in the early stages of her healing process. Grief was a major challenge for some clients, even the pending doom of a gravely ill person can cause a major disruption.

With all my knowledge and abilities, my achilles heel was still grief and loss. I still had my deep passionate love for animals, and losing one of them opened an old wound. During this time, I had six dogs at home, and one by one, almost every year, one of them passed away for different health reasons. Looking back, I can see this was an initiation or invitation from the universe to go deeper. With each passing, I tried to find ways of understanding the afterlife and what became of their souls after leaving their physical bodies. While in that reality, the devastation blocked any mental notes I took along the way. It didn't matter where they were or how happy their souls were, I knew they were gone—*why do people keep leaving me?*

Why is there such an imbalance when someone dies? Do they travel off to a party or reunion in the sky while we are left here in shambles? What was I supposed to do with regrets I felt and the conversations left unsaid? Friends offered kind words of support, but they can be completely unaware of how their words are dismissive. Not everyone shares an incredible bond with a pet.

We spend so much of our life avoiding conversations when we're unsure how to handle a death. Our families typically teach us how to handle these big life events. We make observations as children and assume that is the best way to handle things. Then when it suddenly happens, off the cliff we go.

Death is simply that part of life we can never truly prepare for. Without warning, its cold dark hands reach up from the depths of the water and pull you beneath the surface. Each attempt at breathing will set your lungs on fire. We feel something has physically reached into our chests and ripped out our hearts. We replay the final moments repeatedly, wondering if we could have said or done more.

We're not always given the gift of a long goodbye. In these circumstances, we can leave nothing unsaid. Hold hands, shed tears, and give final kisses. Unfortunately, this is not always possible. Some losses are sudden and unexpected. We're robbed of all those goodbye ceremonies and given no time to process what happened, and this is even more devastating. This type of grief is cruel and filled with many other emotions like regret and anger.

Medical intuitive and energy workers all over the world will tell you that most diseases show up in the body as energy first. As an Energy Medicine Practitioner, I have seen what I call *whispers* of gray energy scattered in and around the bodies of both people and animals. One of the first signs of something going wrong is an energetic disruption in and around the body, usually detected as a slower-moving or dull area. Eventually, other negative energies are allowed to move into this unused space.

When we hold onto grief and all the other emotions associated with it, like depression and anger, we add that lower vibrational energy into our high vibrational bodies. Over time lower energy will grow and join up with other uninvited energies and attach to a particular part of our bodies. In many of my shamanic healings, I've pulled out long black slimy strings of negative energies I intuitively *see* have wrapped themselves around major organs, and on a few rare occasions, I feel have developed a consciousness.

I can do my part as a healer to assist an individual, but the choice to stay healthy is up to them. It's not easy for some to let go of an emotion they've been identifying with for so long. They have to begin to recognize thought patterns and how easily it is to get dragged down that rabbit hole. Yes, bad things will happen in life, but give yourself time for grief and then set a deadline to deactivate grief. Old grief should not feel as raw as it did when the loss occurred. Permit yourself to live.

One of my mentors, Alberto Villoldo, told a story about how the Native American Lakota had a ritual after the death of a loved one. They understood that holding onto grief would make someone sick. The relative would keep a soul bundle with them for one year filled with personal objects of the departed loved one. During this time, they cried, carried it around, had conversations, and dealt with the loss. At the end of the year, the bundle was opened in a ceremony, and the soul was released to the afterlife. The loved one that was left behind vowed to live a harmonious life. The Lakota believed that holding onto the grief beyond that time would tether the soul here in the physical world and stop it from moving on into the spirit world.

A few short weeks before writing this chapter, I suffered the loss of one of my beloved pets. His name was Lincoln, and he was the kindest, sweetest Chocolate Labrador on the planet. He was suffering from a few medical conditions, so his death was not completely unexpected. He lived to be 15 years old. When he passed away, I allowed myself to cry out loud and grieve my loss. I noticed one of my other dogs, Lincoln's best friend Doc Holiday, was growing more and more depressed.

After about a week, I became even more concerned. I realized he was holding onto his grief in an unhealthy way. Intuitively I knew he needed my help. I decided to do a healing ceremony with him. I called him into a quiet space and had him lay down. I got very close to his face, gave him kisses, and began to say all the things I believed he was feeling inside. Whispering between the tears, "I am sorry you lost your best friend," "I miss him too," and "You are not alone." I spoke until I felt there was nothing left unsaid. When this was complete, I placed my hand on his heart, grabbed my rattle, and slowly began the rhythmic movements. The intentions I set for his healing were to bring back his life force energy, heal his heart and bring in a power animal. When the ceremony was complete, I gently opened my eyes and smiled a bit when I saw a gentle smile on his face also.

I still think of Lincoln every day and celebrate how much I loved him. Our mind can quickly take us from gently feeling our pain and loss to raw active grief if we let it. We have to notice the direction of our thoughts and make a change. There are three states of being: past, present, and future. The present is where all the loss and grief dwell. It's where one thought, followed by another similar thought, can quickly take you back to active grief. These thoughts usually focus on what you're physically missing and the void the absence has created.

The past and the future have very different vibrational energy. I like to find the happiest memory in my mind of this person, replay it for a moment, and then imagine a future time when we're reunited in the afterlife. I get imaginative with this one, down to the smile on my face and theirs, who else might be there, and how my heart would feel at that moment. Keep bouncing back to the past and future each time the present tries to sneak in. When you do this exercise, notice the subtle energy shifts with each. Staying in a constant state of the present time, active grief for long periods is the mistake most people make. They do not understand that low vibrational energy is doing real damage to their bodies, both energetically and physically.

Poorly managed grief can cause havoc throughout the body and energy field. It can open you up to health problems down the road. The immune system weakens, and the endocrine system can malfunction, causing problems with our bodies' organs. This is true for both humans and the animals we love.

For me, grounding became the key to everything, the most important first step, regardless of what you seek, whether perfect health or expansion of consciousness. Once you achieve this, you will fully understand.

Not only do we have to keep our bodies free and clear from our own damaging effects, but our bodies are also naturally entrained with the energy around us. When we are not fully in our bodies, by unintentionally sending our energy out, what fills that void? This creates a vacuum, moving in any energy around you. Think of some of the toxic energy surrounding you at work, home, during your commute, and in relationships. What energy has moved into that unused space? What emotions are you caring around that don't belong to you or need to be freed?

A simple daily grounding practice can help you stay grounded and protected. Reclaim your sacred space, bring your own energy back home and live a healthier, happier life. I have included a meditation below to get you started on your journey. Please expand on the meditation in any way you choose.

THE TOOL

Before you begin, set an intention for this healing.

- Get in a comfortable seated position with your back straight and your feet planted firmly on the ground.
- Begin to take three to five deep breaths.
- With each exhale, you're releasing anything that doesn't belong to you.
- Imagine the bottom of your feet opening up and tree roots coming out of each of them deep into the earth.
- Go deep into the earth, past all the layers, past the soil, bedrock, all the way to the center.
- Use your imagination here.
- Your feet begin to feel cemented to the earth, and you cannot move them.
- Move your attention to your hip area.
- Your first chakra is located here.
- Begin to see this ball of light begin to glow.
- Now imagine the roots coming out of the bottom of your feet begin to slowly pull golden earth energy up from the center, slowly up each of your legs.
- This golden energy comes up your legs to your hips and joins the first chakra.
- The energies mix and become even more vibrant and beautiful.
- Now a giant tree trunk comes out of your first chakra down into the center of the earth.
- Pull the energy up from your feet once again, up your legs, and cycle back down into the earth.
- Do this revolution three times.
- Now from your first chakra, begin to pull this energy slowly up your entire body.

- Up your torso, shoulders, up and down your arms, up to your neck, and fill up your head.
- When you feel full of this golden earth energy, move the energy out the top of your head like a chocolate fountain as it flows all around you and back down into the earth.
- Do this complete cycle a few more times. Let the energy flow.
- Run this energy down all the roots of your feet and back down the grounding trunk of your first chakra.
- When you feel complete, release this energy back into the earth and send it with gratitude.
- Place your palms together and thank Mother Earth for helping you.

Authentic, compassionate, gentle, and kind, **Renee Moritz** knows that healing happens on many levels. Renee has the power to *see* and share the most profound insights with great relatability, accessibility, empathy, and humor.

Her clients span the United States, Canada, Mexico, Ireland, United Kingdom, Australia, France, and the United Arab Emirates. Her work in Medical Intuition, Energy Healing, and Animal Communication has deeply touched hundreds of people and their pets.

Renée's endeavors include continued studies in many levels of spiritual, energetic, and shamanic healing. She has trained with global spiritual teachers, including Deepak Chopra, Academy of Intuition Medicine®, Francesca McCartney, Ph.D., medium, John Holland, animal communicator Joan Ranquet, Channeling, Marguerite Rogoglioso Ph.D., Psychologist, Alberto Villoldo, Ph.D., and New York Times best-selling author, James Van Praagh.

Her vision is to help others access the clarity, peace, and direction required to move forward free from emotional blocks. What began as a love for communicating with the animal kingdom has expanded into a love for easing communication, clarity, and forward empowerment for humankind.

Whether you've lost a loved one, need to reclaim your energy, or believe you're experiencing soul loss, Renée is the helping hand and healing heart to help you move forward feeling empowered.

With her ultimate outcome of always being the clarity for others, Renée takes a *listen-first* integrative approach to her work. Attentive to the needs of each individual client, Renée is empathetic with how and what she communicates, taking the time to be fully present prior to sharing her healing insight. Tuning into her human and animal clients at the deepest level, she channels her perceptiveness in relatable, personalized terms.

A true liberator, Renée values self-empowerment and harnessing our ability to each move forward with greater joy and peace. We will all face stumbling blocks and seek answers at various points in time, and Renée carefully delivers the clarity of self and direction we long for. Her purposeful work stems from a personal mission to contribute the clarity she wishes someone could have shown her during the most challenging times in her life.

To find additional information, please contact:

Website: www.shamanicpawprints.com

Facebook: Renee Moritz Animal Communicator & Medical Intuitive

Email: renee.moritz88@gmail.com

CHAPTER 10

ACTIVE INNER STILLNESS

REDIRECTING STRESS FOR NEXT-LEVEL FOCUS AND ENERGY

Sonia Luckey, DNP, MA, FNP-BC, PMHNP-BC

MY STORY

The doors to the ICU swung open, and a full code blue instantly engulfed me. A red light flashed over a room entrance as the code blue alarm blared, summoning all hands on deck. Hospital staff ran down the hall from all directions, surrounding one patient's bed.

Wow, how many people are in that room?

The head and foot of the bed were flat, the entire bed tilted toward the head to help blood move toward the patient's heart and head. The patient was a small older man, and he seemed almost lost in the bed. His blue gown was open, exposing his chest. One nurse was kneeling on the bed doing CPR, the others leaning over, reaching in, and working around him.

The nurses moved in a blur, hanging IVs and giving medications; it was amazing they didn't run into each other. A doctor called out orders, and nurses called them back as they carried them out.

"Prepare for shock. Everyone, stand clear—Now!" Everyone stepped back as the patient's upper body lifted off the bed from the force of the defibrillator shock; then, the nurses and staff stepped forward again and resumed their efforts. Monitors were beeping, alarming, and lights were flashing. The EKG monitor tracing was jagged, erratic, and struggling to find a rhythm. They all worked together like a well-oiled machine. It was loud. It was chaotic.

This is stimulation overload.

As respiratory therapists, lab techs, x-ray techs, and more staff continued to pour into the unit, I pressed my back against the wall and did my best to melt into it.

What the heck was I doing here?

It was my first day at a new job, a pilot program, no less. I was one of three second-year nursing students hired as critical care assistants in the ICU. I felt pretty confident when I applied, but that confidence evaporated as soon as I stepped through those doors. It was a swing shift, so the unit lights were dimmed in the unit as the sun began to set. I knew no one. And right now, I was the only person on the unit just standing there because I had no idea what I was supposed to do.

I am so clueless. I must look like an idiot.

"Hi there, are you Sonia?" A nurse with short red hair and peach-colored scrubs disengaged from the group working on the patient and approached me. I fought down a wave of rising panic and nodded.

"Welcome to the ICU. I'm the PM shift Nurse Supervisor. Let's go over here for a minute." She moved me out of the way and quickly explained what was happening while the jangling of insistent and incessant alarm bells continued.

I wish they would just make the damn alarms stop so I can focus!

As if on cue, the beeping of the code alarm silenced. They had called the code, but the patient had not survived. The noise and energy level in the ICU dropped as the nurses and staff at the bedside slowly began emptying the room and clearing equipment.

Okay, this is not much better. Someone just died. This is not how I want to start my nursing career. I can't handle this. Maybe I'm not cut out for this after all. I felt sick.

"It's time to huddle for the shift change. Let's go." The supervisor jolted me out of my thoughts. We joined the nurses, and secretary crowded around a tiny desk, their voices humming while reporting on each patient's progress in the ICU. Everyone kept their eyes on a large bank of monitors, watching for any changes in patient EKGs and breathing patterns. I tried to take in every word while watching countless heartbeat variations and irregularities lighting up the console.

Only one monitor was dark. The patient that had just passed away had no family present, and none were coming in. The heavy sliding door to the room was closed, lights down, the shade pulled. The supervisor looked at me and said, "Sonia, you can start there. You can get the patient in bed six cleaned up and ready for the morgue."

What the hell? I was supposed to go in there? And do what? That guy was dead!

I thought I was keeping a neutral expression, but the supervisor paused and looked at me. "You've never been around a dead person before, have you?"

I sat still, frozen. *Of course not! What am I doing here? This is crazy. This place is crazy. What made me think that nursing was my dream job?* Dealing with dead people was not what I had in mind.

Apparently, my face said it all because she sighed. "Okay," she said. "Let's go in, and I'll show you what to do."

The room was dim. Only the bedside lamp was on. The silence in the room was eerie—no EKG beeping to reassure me of a heartbeat, no sound of a ventilator's steady whooshing. No machines, no talking. No breathing. I found myself holding my breath too. *He was so still.*

His skin looked different, drained of blood. I was half expecting him to move, and I was ready to bolt out the door if he did. *I've watched way too many horror movies. Am I really able to handle this? It would be so embarrassing to fail.* I tried to calm myself.

The supervisor flipped on the lights and moved briskly. "First, we need to take out these tubes like this." I tried not to gag as she removed the breathing tube and the IVs. I stood as far back as I dared. My mouth was dry; I couldn't swallow. She filled a basin with water and got out some soap.

"I want you to bathe him, change his gown and finish getting him cleaned up. I'll check back with you in a bit." And with that, she was gone.

I'm alone with a dead person. And they want me to bathe him.

The bright lights seemed to glare. It was unbearably stuffy in the windowless room. My heart was racing; my breathing was ragged. *I don't know if I can do this.* I leaned against the wall, feeling the blood draining from my head, starting to see stars.

Good grief, Sonia! All I need is to pass out after being on the job for less than an hour. I've got to pull it together.

Though it was the last thing I wanted to do, I took a deep breath. And then another, making myself slow down.

How did I get here? What made me want to be a nurse? Why would I take on an insane challenge like a critical care assistant pilot project? There were plenty of normal jobs out there. I wanted to help people and make a difference in the world. I did not see how bathing someone who had just died would help me achieve that goal.

I leaned against the wall, willing myself not to panic. *Pull it together. You got the job for a reason. At least one person in the world thinks that I can do this. Maybe I can.* My breathing started to even out. I felt my body shift and start to calm.

I looked over at the small still form in the bed. *Breathe.* This was a human being who deserved the dignity of the last cleansing after his final battle with life. *Breathe. There's no one else here for him. I can be that person.* I breathed in dignity and calm. I looked at his face and quickly glanced up and around. Was he floating above me, watching me? Just in case, I better do a good job. *Breathe, be calm. I can do this.* I picked up the washcloth and gently cleaned his face and hands. *Keep breathing.* I settled into a rhythm.

You know, it could be cool if he was watching. It would be like working with an angel—a spiritual connection. I felt a new stillness, a change. I didn't feel alone anymore. I paused and breathed into my heart, and everything stood still. In that sacred moment, something shifted.

And I fell in love.

The patient looked so peaceful—*what an honor to participate in someone's transition like this. Angels are indeed present.* I could feel the air around me change and lighten as I carried out my task with calm and reverence—my panic was transformed by remembering the privilege of loving humanity in this way. I was embarking on a transformative career that would span over 25 years. By changing my thoughts and breathing into my heart, I discovered an inner stillness. I just needed to slow down, connect within, and change my mind.

THE TOOL

In a world greatly in need of peace, it is more important than ever to first focus on inner peace. Mindfulness practices help us find that calmness. The way we think helps us keep it.

Before you do an inner eye roll because you don't have time to stop and meditate, just hang on a sec. This is written exactly for people like you, who think inner stillness and peace is a luxury they can't afford.

The stressors and challenges we face on a daily basis take a toll on our mental, emotional, spiritual, and physical health. Think of how tired you are after a stressful event or situation. Stress is a huge energy drain. It also interferes with the brain's ability to focus and think straight. There's a reason you run around looking for your keys when you're rushing out the door and then find them in your hand. It's called cortical inhibition. Your brain literally shuts down higher executive functions when it detects that you're stressed. Not because some inner jokester wants to have a laugh, but because the brain thinks it's protecting you by redirecting and conserving your energy so you can react and run.

Uncontrolled stress is hard on the body. If it continues unchecked, it can cause anxiety, depression, and disease over time. It interferes with our enjoyment of life. The worst part is that people feel like their stress is running the show and that they can't do much about it. They certainly can't sit in a corner and close their eyes to meditate. As stressed as they are, it's possible they couldn't calm themselves enough to do it if they tried.

So here's the game-changer: you can train your brain to help you when you're stressed instead of just shutting down. You can literally stay calm, be focused, and change the situation. When you learn to look at a stressful situation differently, you can calm yourself and activate that still point where you can be calm, cool, and collected, all by changing the way you think.

It's a given that everyone has to deal with a certain amount of stress in their life. Many people feel like they have no control over it, so when the going gets rough, they start to panic, get upset, and yes, stress out. And then everything starts to spin out of control. Things fall apart, your day is ruined, and things go from bad to worse. What if you could stop it right there and change the trajectory? It's possible with a technique based on Cognitive Behavior Therapy (CBT).

A psychiatrist named Aaron Beck first developed CBT in the 1960s. He noticed that the inner dialog that many of his patients carried on had a huge impact on their feelings. These "automatic thoughts" were usually negative. So he developed a therapy (originally called cognitive therapy) to help people improve their coping skills by changing the way they think. This type of therapy actually alters brain activity! It has been very effective in treating many health conditions like sleep disorders, anxiety, and mood disorders. It's equally effective in dealing with everyday situations and helping you be the kind of human you want to be.

The way you think affects the way you feel. The way you feel affects the way you behave. Thinking, feeling, and behaving are all closely related. If you want to see and download a graphic of how this cycle looks, check out the resources page at the end of this chapter.

Often, a trigger event starts the negative thinking. It can be as simple as someone saying that something you did was wrong or strange, or telling you "no" when you ask for something, or asking you to do something you don't want to do or don't know how to do.

Say, for example your boss asks you to complete a project. She tells you that it has to be done a certain way. You may start having an inner conversation that goes something like, *"This is too hard, I'll never get it right,"* or *"This is stupid; I can't believe I have to do this."* These are negative thought patterns. What happens next is that the inner conversation continues, and you start in with negative self-talk: *"I'm such an idiot. What made me think I could even do this? I can't do anything right. I'm totally going to embarrass myself."*

First, you have to be aware of your negative thoughts. Your thoughts about certain situations can become automatic and happen without you even realizing it. The good news is that by analyzing the situation differently and practicing some positive self-talk, the outcome can be totally different. Using positive self-talk is a good way to change negative thinking. Some people are so used to negative self-talk that they might find positive self-talk difficult. It takes practice, but it's a critical step in helping you change your thinking.

The next step is to look at your beliefs about the event or the situation. What do you automatically think about it? Do you think your boss is really looking for an excuse to fire you so she can hire her friend? Do you think you are being set up to fail? Do you think that people just don't like you? What objective information do you have to support those thoughts?

How do you want to feel? It's also important to notice those situations where you find yourself wanting to stay angry—but that's a whole other conversation and skillset to learn. Let's stay on track with the basics.

Next in the cycle comes the consequences of your beliefs or thinking. If you're convinced that nothing good is going to come out of your boss's request, you might push back and get into an argument or react and say that it's a bad idea. Or you might avoid the whole thing and hope she forgets or doesn't notice if the job doesn't get done. The whole situation puts you in a bad mood, and now you remember how much you hate your job anyway.

But consider this: What if your boss asks you to do this project because you're an excellent employee and she is thinking about a promotion for you? What if she asks you to do this project because you are knowledgeable and mature, and she knows she can trust you with it? What if she sees your potential and wants to help you grow? And finally, my favorite consideration (one that I use all the time) is this: What if this situation is being presented to you to help you evolve spiritually? How can you react to this situation in a way that helps you live in service to your personal beliefs, mission, and values?

So, again, how you think affects how you feel and behave. A good way to remember this is ABC:

A = the Antecedent event that triggers your thinking.

B = the Beliefs or thoughts about the event or situation

C = The Consequences of your beliefs or thinking, i.e., how you feel (your emotions) and how you behave.

Once you learn the techniques, they are super helpful when you get into stressful situations and need to calm yourself down; and find that inner still point so you can make good decisions. You can redirect your stress and actually focus on what you need to do. You'll have much more energy to carry out that next-level plan because you won't be exhausted by your body pumping adrenaline to feed that stress reaction and all the strong emotions that come with it.

So here's how you put all this to work. There's a downloadable worksheet you can use by following the resources link at the end of the chapter. You can also remember the following steps as the three C's: Catch it, check it, and change it!

THE STEPS

1. Catch it. What is the situation that is irritating or upsetting you? Describe the situation and the trigger that started you thinking negatively.

   a. What are you thinking?

   b. How do you feel?

   c. How do you want to (or how did you) act or behave?

2. Check it. What are your beliefs about the situation? What are your beliefs about yourself in this situation? What objective evidence do you have to support those beliefs? Do you want to stay mad?

3. Change it. Use positive self-talk and examine what other possibilities exist in the situation.

   a. What are alternative explanations for why this scenario is happening?

b. How else could you feel in this situation? How do you want to feel?

c. How could you react to change the situation positively?

d. If this situation is here for your personal and spiritual growth, what can you say or do to honor that?

Finally, acknowledge yourself for having the courage to be honest, and doing the extra work to be honest with yourself, change your thinking, and make the right choices.

Remember, anything the mind can conceive and believe, it can achieve. You create your life situation. The scenario may not change, but the way you react to it can be changed. You can get away from the mindset where you are a victim and instead change your mindset to one where you are calm, cool, collected, and successful. Life is for you, not against you. It's all about the way you think. Change your thoughts, and you can change your life.

Resources:

To learn more about how to work with Dr. Luckey, and to access more information and resources about how to change your thoughts—and your life—visit her website:

https://sonialuckey.coachesconsole.com/resource-request--the-ultimate-guide-to-spiritual-living.html

Dr. Sonia Luckey is a nurse practitioner with over 25 years of experience, board-certified in Psychiatric Mental Health and Family Practice. She is the president of The Nightingale Way, a nurse-owned education and consulting company.

Sonia has been following a breadcrumb trail of holistic healing modalities her entire career, including Reiki, shamanic training, bio-field, energy medicine, functional medicine, and HeartMath. She took everything up a notch by earning a Master's in Spiritual Psychology and a doctorate in nursing, applying scientific principles and evidence-based research into these healing modalities. This created an amazing toolkit that she uses to help her patients and clients be more in control of their well-being and health care. Through her writing, workshops, and coaching, she teaches them how to shift their thinking and connect with their inner guidance; then apply spiritual principles and universal laws to their personal lives, business, and relationships to live authentic, heart-centered, soul-aligned lives.

Sonia loves to write, read, and meditate. She loves connecting with water and nature spirits, listening to music while taking it all in with a tall glass of water garnished with mint and cucumber. She works by pools and fountains whenever possible, and her ideal getaway always involves beaches and the ocean. She enjoys a little bit of heaven with dark chocolate and a nice glass of wine.

One of Sonia's greatest pleasures is facilitating and witnessing the transformation in people as they evolve into their complete authentic selves. Her goal is to help them cultivate the best in themselves and live in ways that create positive influence, lasting change, and true peace.

Connect with Sonia:

Website: www.sonialuckey.com
Facebook: DrSoniaLuckey
Instagram: @sonialuckey
LinkedIn: www.linkedin.com/in/sonia-luckey-dnp-285b019

CHAPTER 11

THE BREAKDOWN BEFORE THE BREAKTHROUGH

ACHIEVING UNTOUCHED LEVELS

Chris Stoner, The Fascia Performance Coach

MY STORY

I'll never be that fucking vulnerable again!

I asked, "Mom, can I go to Laurie's house?"

"Yes, just be home in time for supper," she said.

I was nine years old and wanted to play with my best friend as much as possible. I walked to Laurie's house many times, but I had no clue this time would change the course of my life.

I saw two teenage boys looking, talking, and pointing at me. Every hair on my neck stood up, and I had a massive knot in my stomach.

Run! Run now and run fast!

But I kept walking toward them. "Please help us. Our grandpa is sick, and our mom is working. We would call her, but our phone doesn't work. Will you sit with him so we can run and get her? We don't want to leave him alone."

No! Run!

"How far away does your mom work?" I asked. "Just down the street. It won't take us very long," they said.

"Umm, yeah, okay."

Chris, why are you following them? Stop! You have no clue who they are! You're in danger.

But I kept ignoring the voice. *How can I say no when someone needs my help?*

The smallest boy led the way onto the long narrow porch, and the biggest one was walking behind me. As we walked into the house, I looked over my shoulder and noticed he had stopped following. Instead, he stood like a guard, looking out onto the street.

Once inside, I asked, "Where is your grandpa?"

In a flash, he grabbed me. His eyes were as cold as ice as he thrust a knife's blade onto my throat and said, "There is no grandpa!" The other guy came in, locked, and dead-bolted the door as he told the other guy he had such-and-such amount of time before he went into another room and sat down.

On the inside, I was frozen, scared shitless, and I could barely breathe. *Stay calm, Chris. Just do what they say.*

He told me, "Take your clothes off, and if you try to fight, I will kill you!" I did as he told me, and then he threw me on the ugly maroon couch, pressed the knife on my throat, and raped me repeatedly for several hours.

It's as if time stopped but in a very calm way. The details of that moment, and that house of horror, were being imprinted in my mind. The living room had so much red—a red couch, red curtains, and even the velvet-textured wallpaper had red. My eyes repeatedly traced the patterns in that wallpaper to escape what was happening.

I couldn't stand the way he was breathing in my face, and the smell of cigarette smoke hung in the air.

God, I want to go home.

Either he was finally done, or his time was up, I do not know which, but he instructed me to get dressed.

"What do we do with her now? Do we kill her, or do we let her live? She will probably tell her family, and then we will go to jail."

I stood there staring at this floor-to-ceiling window while they were discussing my fate. I heard every word they were saying, but I kept staring at that window, trying to decide whether I was big enough or fast enough to break through it and run home.

I don't want to die. I wonder if I can bust through the window? I am fast but am I fast enough? I've seen people run and smash through windows on TV. Wait! The glass could cut me. I'll have to use my arms to protect my face. If I have scars, people will stare at me. I better not. I don't want people staring at me.

"We will let you go if you promise not to tell anyone," they said.

"I promise I won't tell anyone," I said.

They both said, "We know where you live, and if you tell anyone, we will kill you and your family,"

"I swear I won't tell anyone," I said. I repeated it several times, hoping they would believe me and release me before they changed their minds.

I find myself short on the words to describe the feelings I felt hearing and watching them unlock that door. Holding my breath, scared to death they'd still change their mind and kill me. I walked slowly past them, keeping an eye on the hand with the knife, but as soon as I crossed the threshold of that door onto the porch, I ran faster than I had ever run before.

"Chrissy, what happened to your throat," Mom asked.

"Laurie and I were chasing each other, and I had a branch snap back and hit me," I said.

"You need to be more careful," she said. I ran upstairs to my bedroom, knowing I had to act normal to keep my family safe. Lying on my bed, at that moment, I made a vow to myself: *I will never be that fucking vulnerable again!*

I was 42 years old, and had another discussion with my doctor about the right course of action for my health. Fifteen years of chronic pain, digestive problems, test after test, and desperation to find answers. Also, 15 years of refusing medication because I knew the drugs were only a quick fix that would cause other health problems.

Finally, he said, "Chris, I'm concerned that if you don't take medication, there is a good chance you will end up with stomach or esophagus cancer or another kind of disease. Your body can only handle so much."

"If I take medication, I won't feel what is going on in my body, and I want to get to the root cause. I want to heal, not mask the symptoms by slapping a band-aid on them."

He shook his head and said, "Okay."

I had a lovely home, a good husband (number four) and kids, a fit body, loved dancing, hiking, and exploring new activities. On the outside, I looked great. On the inside, I was in pain—a lot of it. The pain was debilitating and caused havoc in my family and marriage. I constantly felt angry. I constantly felt like my entire being was under pressure. I constantly felt stressed, like my soul had no room to breathe.

Shortly after that discussion with my doctor, my fourth marriage was ending.

What the hell is wrong with me? Something has got to give because I'm done living this way! Four failed marriages, my health is shit, and there's only one common denominator—me. At that moment, I decided to be my own healer and take ownership of my life. The time had come for me to heal a 33-year-old wound—the rape.

The next day, I made an appointment with a counselor, Deb. That was the beginning of a lifelong quest of curiosity and understanding that continues to this day.

As I sat in the waiting room at Cornerstone Counseling and wondered: *Am I failing again, or am I weak by not being able to figure this out on my own? Dad always said anyone who needed therapy was weak, and here I sit.*

"Chris, I'm Deb. I'm ready for you," she said. *There's no turning back now.*

We sat across from one another in these beautiful, super comfy blue chairs as if I was sitting across from a friend and having a normal conversation.

"So, Chris, what brings you here today?" asked Deb.

"I think I'm broken and not capable of truly loving someone," I said.

With a smile, she said, "I promise you you're not broken, and you're capable of truly loving someone, but tell me why you think that."

I told her about the rape, my failed marriages, and relationships. Deb listened, took notes, nodded her head, and offered an occasional smile, which gave me comfort.

"Thank you for sharing all this with me. Will you repeat the vow you made to yourself when you were nine?" she asked.

"I will never be that fucking vulnerable again!" I said.

Deb asked, "And have you honored that vow? Have you ever allowed anyone fully in, or do you keep them at arm's length?" It's as if she'd opened a window of hope.

She gave me a book to read. I remember opening that book, and a sentence jumped off the page, "Your thoughts create your reality." At that moment, I completely lost it and had the biggest breakdown of my life because nobody in my life had ever told me anything like this, that I had the power to change my life by changing my thoughts.

As I began to release all this pent-up anger, frustration, sadness, and hurt, I felt something very strange: spaciousness. For the first time since I was nine, I felt like I could take a full, deep breath without feeling like there was body armor squeezing my chest.

I craved more. I was like a sponge. So, I began searching for holistic solutions from some of the top leaders in our industry. First, I learned that eating real food is vital for life. Who knew Aunt Jemima syrup wasn't real syrup? Not this girl. So I completely changed my diet and began training in the emerging fields of integrative and diagnostic nutrition, and became utterly obsessed with our body's master connector—the fascia. It's truly magical!

"We start every single class in the belly position because, most importantly, we want to engage and strengthen this powerful muscle, the diaphragm," my mentor Deanna said.

Holy shit, talk about pain! Releasing fascia is no joke. Wait, my what? No one has ever told me to strengthen a diaphragm.

"Deanna, what the heck is the diaphragm muscle?" I asked.

"It's pretty awesome. The diaphragm is designed to pull air into the lungs, feed and cleans the entire body, and is like turning on the furnace in the body. But when we breathe, using the muscles of the chest, it's like having a space heater in your body. Only that room will be heated, not the whole building," she said.

I never even considered using my body as a starting point for healing.

I am a reliable resource, ally, and guide to release hidden pain deep within myself.

So, layer by layer, breath by breath, my body released and shared past events and the emotions attached to them. I was hooked.

How can we feel alive, beautiful, and sexy when living in a house full of clutter, dirt, and waste?

The body is our home, but my body was a house, not a home. Light, air, and energy flow through the house in a lively home instead of being trapped and stagnant. Remodeling is a slow process and takes time. It isn't always elegant or pretty. But it needs to be done to make it truly livable. There are several rooms in a house, and all those rooms turn the house into a home. So I began working through my body, clearing, healing, and restoring— room by room.

Reconnecting the relationship between my mind and body is a whole-body rebirth—a coming home.

I realized that the overwhelming majority of people I knew didn't know any of this stuff. I knew I was going to spend the rest of my life mastering myself and teaching others what I was learning. I now had a responsibility and mission to share this with the world.

I invite you to listen to your own body's inherent wisdom and apply these principles in your journey to recovery, health, and vitality. I inspire you to say "yes" to life.

THE TOOL

Achieving Untouched Levels

When dealing with the fascia system, the adhesions are what cause pain, aging, and disease due to a lack of blood and oxygen flow to the cells. This sampler begins to create body awareness and address adhesions that have you bound and stuck. Fascia is the communication highway between every cell. If the roadways are open and clear, there is an immediate response to the call, and the body knows what to do. But the challenge arises when the fascia becomes sticky and glued together, blocking those 911 calls. It's a whole system approach to training and plays an essential role in our bodies' health, strength, and movement.

What you will need:

A hardback or paperback book or a rolled-up laundry towel.

- Try to roll it as tight as you can, and if you have a thick elastic band or something, you can put it on to hold it together. If you don't, that's okay.

A phone or something with a timer set to three minutes.

Today is the belly position, which will teach you to connect to your diaphragmatic breath. This can be done at any time and helps if you feel stressed or anxious. It activates your parasympathetic nervous system to bring you into a state of peace and calm and will benefit issues with the gut to improve digestion and elimination.

We always start with the belly position. Place the prop (book or towel) on the belly button and lay belly down on the floor. You can start up on the elbows or take your rib cage to the floor. For the first minute, focus on the inhalation phase of the breath. Inhale for a count of six. Exhale for a count of four. The goal is to strengthen proper diaphragmatic breathing and use the abdominal muscles to gain access to the diaphragm muscle. So initially, let's focus on inhaling into the towel. You want to feel your belly moving into the prop, even getting a sense that your body is lifting toward the ceiling with each full inhalation.

The very first thing I want to mention is that your breath is your guide. As long as you're breathing in a relaxed way, you'll be feeding and healing yourself. If anything hurts so much that it takes that relaxed breath away, that's your body saying, "This is too intense." You also want to always breathe in and out through the nose.

The nostrils and the base of the nose are designed specifically to send oxygen to all of the body's cells, keep everything hydrated, and keep the body clean. When we breathe through the mouth, it's a very different physiology that occurs inside. So in and out through the nose at all times, unless you have a stuffy nose.

For some people, it's better to do this just simply lying on the floor. You can also try it on a bed where you've got a little extra cushion—it will be a little less intense.

You may feel some interesting sensations. Pain and pressure are normal, and you may even feel a pulse. That's the aorta. As long as you're breathing in a relaxed way, all is good. If it takes your breath away, your body is letting you know to back off.

Shift your attention to the exhalation phase of the breath. Inhale for a count of four. Exhale for a count of six. Also, allow your body weight and gravity to do the work as the towel sinks deeply into the core. And if it feels good to bring the ribcage to the floor, that will get you deeper access. But of course, you can always stay up on the elbows if that makes more sense for you, with your breath being your guide. So we want the breath to be full and complete in its range but not forced. If you can hear yourself breathing, see if you can back off the intensity slightly. And I'm going to add one more element here, after you exhale fully, see if you can hold for a moment or two before engaging that inhalation. And with each exhalation, see if you can let that towel sink a little more deeply into the core.

When you breathe with the diaphragm, you're doing so many things. It changes the entire physiology of the body. First, it gives the abdominal organs and the heart and lungs a continual massage. It's also changing the brain frequency to a more relaxed state. Also, because we literally collapsed into the core of the body over time from unconscious posture, and from not keeping the diaphragm muscle strong, we create adhesions, which cause us to become ballooned in the belly, we inflame, we also don't eliminate effectively, so that attracts parasites, bacteria, they create waste, and we become toxic.

So as you're going through this process, you're breaking down and releasing adhesions, moving the waste out of the body through proper exhalation and detoxifying. And that creates the most aligned, clean, healthy body that you can have.

As you're focusing more on the exhalation, as you're spending more time here, you may be feeling more pain or sensation, which is all completely normal. By understanding pain equals restriction to blood oxygen flow, we need to use a combination of body weight and gravity, with the proper breath to fascia decompress, break down those adhesions, and create space to improve blood and oxygen flow. So as long as you're breathing through the pain, you're safe, and it will benefit you faster.

And when you're ready, you're going to place your hands under your shoulders, and you're going to very slowly exhale up and off.

I hope you enjoy your newfound space and achieve untouched levels.

If you would love more resources, please head over to https://www.chrisstoner.life/resources/

 **Chris Stoner,** a.k.a., The Fascia Performance Coach, speaker, and author, truly cares about people, our planet, and that all things are possible. Chris is on a mission to inspire people to create permanent change by breaking down the adhesions that keep them stuck so that they can say yes to life. Her passion extends to empowering people to achieve untouched levels as they dive into their body-mind healing. She is committed to helping people live a healthy, active life, with the body being the starting point for true lasting transformation.

Chris helps highly active individuals create sustainable enjoyment and performance on a daily basis. Chris works with entrepreneurs, executives, career professionals, and competitive athletes who pursue a wide range of athletic passions: gymnastics, golf, martial arts, dance, tennis, cycling, water skiing, and even competitive limbo. She teaches these active humans to recover more quickly and take their performance to new highs, or in the case of limbo, to new lows.

Chris recharges by living an active full life through reading, walking, hiking in nature, and dancing to the beat of her own drum.

She currently resides in Texas and enjoys spending time with her family and friends.

Chris has trained and holds certifications in the fields of fascia mastery, block therapy, integrative and diagnostic nutrition, and health coaching.

Institute of Integrative Nutrition - health coach certification

Block Therapist and Instructor Block Therapy Certification

Fascial Fitness Trainer Certification

XPT Breathing Performance Coach

Wim Hof's Fundamental Breathing Course

Connect with Chris:
On her website: https://www.chrisstoner.life
Email: chris@chrisstoner.life

CHAPTER 12

SPILLING THE TEA

AN EXTRAORDINARY ACT
OF REBELLION

Deborah Hodiak-Knox, Transformational Coach, Designer

MY STORY

It was an ordinary afternoon, about a week and a half after my physical separation from my soon-to-be-ex-husband. I was alone for the first time in I don't know how long. I stood in the kitchen of my brand new-to-me apartment. It was a gorgeous studio that once housed the likes of countless budding musicians as a former orchestral practice hall. The hardwood floors glistened in the afternoon sunlight, and the high, rounded ceilings cradled me in their promise of possibility.

I was putting away a box of chamomile tea. As I opened up the door to the cupboard, I had an overwhelming feeling of awareness wash over me. I experienced almost instantaneous flashes of all of the times I remained quiet, agreed when I didn't agree and did whatever it took to seemingly keep the peace. But right here, in this very moment, it felt like I was free! I was free to place my favorite type of tea into my cabinet, wherever I so chose. It was a concrete representation of my pending divorce. It was so deliciously satisfying.

I remember the grueling process to get to this very moment, reenacting the countless nights of lying awake in bed, all too aware that I was growing increasingly unhappy. *Is this really how it's supposed to be? We have no connection—no conversation, we don't even hug or kiss anymore!* Dinner after dinner with my dad filled with the same topics of conversation: "I don't think I can do this anymore," I said over and over and over again.

It's tough to know exactly what it was that brought me to that realization. *Where did this habit of sacrificing myself and pleasing people come from?* We were married for just over a decade. He always wanted children. I, on the other hand, was not as convinced. And then it hit me.

I was probably right around five years old when I asked my mother, "Mom, where did Dad go?" My then binge-drinking father had been gone for the previous week. This happened often, and most of the time, I knew better than even to broach the subject. For some reason, though, on that day, I finally got up enough gumption to ask the question. "I don't know what you're talking about—your father didn't go anywhere," was her cold, stoic reply. It took me aback. I mean, I may have only been five years old, but I still knew what I saw or, in this case, didn't see—my father.

It was very confusing to never really know what was real.

I mean, I knew my truth but clearly, that wasn't the acceptable version of reality. And so it began years of discounting and questioning myself and always looking to others to find validity.

Growing up, I took all of these early lessons to heart. I learned that good grades were desirable, so I became a straight-A student. Upon graduation, I wasn't ready for college but quickly found that waiting was unacceptable, so I dove right in. I studied what everyone thought I'd be good at and immediately began working a nine-to-five job in the said field upon graduating. I met a guy who got along with my mother better than I ever did and shortly thereafter found myself quitting the pursuit of my Master's degree. Before I could even begin to process that decision, I moved out of my home state, away from family, friends, and the only support system I ever knew. I was going to get married. I mean, I was, after all, nearly 30, and it was certainly about time.

I was never truly happy and found myself moving from job to job and dodging the incessant pressure to have children. Marriage was certainly not at all what it was cracked up to be, and I often dreamt about what my life would be like had I made different choices. Little did I know that that was all about to change.

Driving through a small New Hampshire town one afternoon for work, I had an extreme feeling of gratitude overcome me. I suddenly noticed everything—every single detail—the way the sun was shining, the intensive blueness of the sky, the sheer beauty in all of my surroundings. I felt an enormous sense of peace wash over and engulf me. Seconds later, I received a phone call from my father. "Your mother just had a heart attack," his voice shaking. "I'm on my way to the hospital now." I honestly don't remember much of anything during the 45-minute drive south along Route three back into Massachusetts. There were only vague pictures of blurred-out trees passing by with the increased speed of travel.

What I do remember and still cannot shake from my mind was the image of my father sitting in the waiting room, alone, holding on tightly to my mother's handbag. She died before I could make it back.

After my mother's death, I decided to make some changes. I wanted to see what it would be like to actually do something for me for a change. It was an unspoken desire to own a flower shop and become some type of designer. I had dreams about it since I was a young girl. So I quit my job of three years, enrolled in a well-known floral design school out of Boston, and studied under one of the top designers in New Hampshire. Six short months later, I opened up my first shop, *Somedays Floral Design*. This was it! Total freedom, doing something I loved.

Or so I thought.

The monotony of the business slowly began creeping in, while my relationship with my father began creeping out of my life. I found myself lying awake at night with the all too familiar hole in my stomach that was with me for what seemed like forever. *If this isn't it, then what is?* I had no answers.

Fast forward a year or two. After selling that first initial flower shop and opening and closing a second, I decided to fall back into my old ways of looking to others for approval and direction on the next right thing. I would often hear from my aunt, grandmother, or anyone else who looked in from the outside, "When are you going to have kids? You're not getting any younger."

I gave in and finally became pregnant. In the beginning, it seemed to help out with our dying marriage, as we partnered up on caring for a newborn and were both awestruck with the newness of it all. However, it didn't take long before a subtle subconscious resentment slowly began to settle in. Once again, I found myself back under the dark cloud of my own fragmentation.

They say every cloud has a silver lining, and this was no exception. This baby was born five days past his due date. He did not want to come out! When he finally did, he had no problem letting everyone know of his dissatisfaction. And my colicky, what-the-hell-was-I-thinking-becoming-a-mother newborn son changed my life forever.

Nothing, and I mean nothing, would console this child. He cried nearly 24 hours a day, seven days a week, and was only soothed by one thing: love. I realize that may sound corny, but I loved this sweet boy with all of my being, and I intuitively knew what he needed. Sure, I asked everyone else what I should do, but not one of those answers ever endured. This feisty little creature created a spark in me as I'd never felt before, and for the first time ever, I found validation within myself.

Feeling validated as a mother (or simply as a person) was not something to be taken lightly, especially given my track record. I sought out other like-minded women and soon found myself at a presentation one evening entitled, *Tapping Into The Power of Your Women's Intuition*. This intuition thing seemed to have something to it. The more I learned about it, the more I realized it was my truth—the one I felt at five years old and that I'd always known. The one that had always been unspoken.

From that moment on, I began my journey home. I made decisions based on my likes and dislikes, curiosities, and experiences. I started to use my voice. I followed the speaker from that evening's first class on manifesting abundance and went on to go through each and every one of her courses as they were birthed, giving more and more life to *Deborah* along the way.

I grew enough courage to revisit my interests in design, gave birth to a daughter, and became immersed in alternative/peaceful parenting styles, allowing nothing to come between me and my newfound path of expansion. I ended up leaving my marriage as a result.

Despite the fact that the decade to follow would be filled with personal attacks, threats to take my children away, and an overarching attempt to invalidate, discredit and essentially take me down a notch, I never once regretted my decision, even despite it being an impossible act to carry out.

You see, my tendencies to be that good girl, people-pleaser, were never far behind me. I swore I would never not work, and yet here I was, a stay-at-home mother who dropped everything aside from the role. I was dedicated, determined, and desperate. It was an extraordinary act of rebellion for my personal betterment.

I went on to become an oracle card reader, certified life coach, and master intuitive teacher. For years, I worked magic through the power of touch as a holistic massage therapist and energy worker. I'm an ordained minister and most recently revisited my childhood passion for design.

It's an unbelievable feeling to be able to live authentically as who it is that you truly are.

Today I have a clear understanding of the next right thing for me.

Whenever I falter, I remember that box of chamomile tea and the feeling it gave me of being free to choose. I'm proud to say that today, as I write this, I have changed the lives of many through concrete, hands-on ways of living and more enlightened and empowered spiritual ways of being.

The journey **HOME** (**H**onoring **O**ur **M**emories and **E**xperiences) has developed itself into a beautiful union of my intuitive coaching and teaching, spirituality, and design work. It's something I have coined Extraordinary Living. There are five core values/beliefs, all stemming from this journey of mine, that I often jokingly liken to The Boston Tea Party Rebellion.

THE TOOL

A bit more on Extraordinary Living:

The play on words here is delicious. It's a state of being that allows our everyday, ordinary lives to be experienced as remarkable. Living in an almost childlike state of wonderment and awe allows us to believe in magic and bear witness to everyday miracles. It's the true manifestation of abundance, and should be celebrated!

Core Value/Belief #1
Divine Abundance

The ability to tap into your deepest inner self—that part of you connected to something greater—while allowing that power to provide for your needs, wants, and desires.

The steps to achieving divine abundance are, first and foremost, the belief in and knowingness of something greater and your connection to it. Once this connection has been acknowledged, there is no longer an experience of lack. Instead, one becomes aware of the plentifulness of magic and miracles in their everyday life, allowing for a new state of being in the world to emerge.

Core Value/Belief #2
Your Intuitive Nature

Intuition is the innate knowingness of your truth. It's your inner guidance system that is directly connected to your higher self, which connects to the Divine. It's the communication hub, your own personal Google if you will. Harnessing this power involves about 95% remembering and 5% strategy.

Once you claim this power and learn to cultivate it, there will never again be a lack of clarity for you.

Core Value/Belief #3
An Attitude of Gratitude

A quick internet search will yield a definition of gratitude as "The quality of being thankful; readiness to show appreciation and to return kindness." Having an 'attitude of gratitude' is an acknowledgment of Spirit. It comes from feeling into our connectedness to something greater and witnessing its ability to provide for us on a multitude of levels.

This leads to a deep sense of peace, serenity, and being held/supported. In short, it feels like **home**. As a result, the spark becomes ignited within to return the favor by taking action and being of service to others and the world at large.

Core Value/Belief #4
Always an Adventure

This is a saying that came from many years of adventures as a single mom with my two kiddos. It was something I used to say whenever there was a snafu, plot twist, or change of plans, for these were the times where adventures were sure to be had!

Although a cute way to teach kids to stay positive, it's also a great philosophy to apply to the ups and downs of everyday life in general. Make a habit of seeing challenges through the lens of an adventurer, and always search for the golden nuggets along the way—I guarantee you they are out there!

Core Value/Belief #5
The Art of Creation

Creative expression is at the heart of extraordinary living. It's the true art of devotion. By physically expressing ourselves via whatever medium is suited to us, we are breathing life into our divinity. It's through the art of creation that we find and fulfill our purpose—giving birth to our own individual Divine essence.

This work has been such a gift. It has allowed me to help others step more fully into who it is that they truly are. It has also impacted me personally. It has transformed me into a better mother, a more present partner, and a mindful contributor to the planet through my up-cycling and redesign work.

It's all about creating space for you to come home—to you!

To find out more, please visit www.deborahhodiakknox.com and see how you, too, can live a life of Extraordinary proportions!

Deborah Hodiak-Knox

Transformational Coach, Designer, and Believer in Magic

I had always been someone who just 'knew' things. The problem was that I couldn't figure out how to trust that knowingness as most of the time, it went against the norm and wasn't exactly met with great approval. Being an only child in an alcoholic home only served to reinforce this dichotomy.

In my formative years, I searched for ways to make sense of it all and found myself writing, creating, and designing anything I could get my hands on as a way to stay sane. As I grew older, I began studying psychology and sociology, attended various 12 step meetings, and stumbled into metaphysical and spiritual ways of being.

I was never a big fan of labels or being pigeon-holed; I slowly found my own unique way of being in this world. Today, I see the beauty in every day and the extraordinary in life's most basic moments with grateful eyes.

Healing happens on so many different levels in so many different ways. At the end of the day, it all comes down to faith, trust, and knowing yourself inside and out. ~ xoxox

Deborah is an Interior Designer, certified Life Coach, Master Teacher, Licensed Massage Therapist, and Ordained Minister. She has dabbled in hypnotherapy, guided meditation, EFT, various energy therapies, fashion, floral and interior design; is an Angel Communication Master Intuitive and most recently celebrated her attendance at the final School of Womanly Art's Mastery Program in New York City.

She was the proprietor of Co-Creations Cottage Artisan Community and currently owns AbracaDeborah - ExtraOrdinary Living, which includes elements of interior design, professional organization, transformational coaching, and community education.

CHAPTER 13

FEAR TO FREEDOM

THROUGH COURAGE AND DIVINE TRUST

Sunshine Beeson, Iridologist, Hypnotherapist, Retreat Facilitator

MY STORY

Getting off the plane and stepping into Hollywood, California, feeling the heat, my body instantly had a new relationship with the sun! I was ten years old.

In November of 1964, my family moved from my hometown of Vancouver, British Columbia, Canada, to the infamous Hollywood, California. Even though the 60s were a radical time in history, I wasn't star-struck, even though we lived amongst the famous actors and musicians alike! The natural world was more enticing to me, seeking nature wherever I could.

My sense of spirituality formed at age 12. I had this uncanny protectiveness when I heard people cursing at God. I believed in a higher power and angels. I also had an invisible companion from the natural world: I had a vision of a statuesque, white horse, rearing up with mane flying, and he would whinny in my ear! This went on for many years, and it felt like a Spirit Guide. At this time, I prayed, *Dear God, Higher Power, please allow me to assist in helping the world be free of pain and illness.*

At the age of 18, my interest was deeply invested in meditation and the healing arts. Coming from Canada, my family was set up with permanent resident alien cards. *What an odd thing to be considered an alien because of bordering countries.* Every ten years, this card needed to be renewed. I had such fear whenever having to deal with immigration—my body would seize up in a panic with my heart racing. I couldn't explain or find logic to this fear, however, it seemed to appear uncontrollably anytime I had to deal with the government.

I loved connecting with people. I preferred to connect with someone's heart and soul rather than chit-chat. Intuitively, I'd connect with people's eyes, and felt that was the entry point into the soul. During my path into the natural healing world, I studied plants and herbs and was able to see the auras of plants. I loved the world of energy!

After my studies in psychology, counseling, nutrition, herbology, and hypnotherapy, at age 38, I came across a healer in California who taught a healing modality through the *eyes! What?!* I couldn't believe this; I was super excited and amazed!

During the process of learning this dynamic, profound, and insightful modality, hundreds of irises are photographed, then the class views the iris structure on a screen. The eyes were blown up to the size of a globe. Within the iris, the colored part of the eye, there exists a whole world of information unique to each person.

I was amazed and blown wide open to witness the deepest parts of a person's history, being able to see into their soul. It allowed me to drop any judgements about people, seeing the innocence deeply embedded into each person. I felt a renewed compassion for humanity. To this day, it's an absolute honor and privilege to do Iridology sessions with my clients, being able to see into the depths of who they are!

The Iridology system became the foundation of my healing work. The iris of the eye displays links to one's physical and emotional health and behaviors, beliefs, and imprinted patterns.

While living in Hollywood, I had a lot of trust during the sex, drugs, and rock and roll days. I didn't *fear* people. My mother, however, even though she was very outgoing, had some innate fears that were energetically passed down to me. Mom was always worried about me. There is a newer science called Epigenetics; this my friends, is when our cells hold onto memories and traumas from our ancestors which are not even our own experiences!

Fast forward to a marriage, then the birth of my daughter Fawn. Fawn was eight years of age. We moved to Colorado, where I then knew I had arrived in Heaven! One year later, my son Ethan came into the world. When flying over Durango, Colorado, *I had an inner knowing from the air this was going to be home.* I was into Native American culture for some time, and during the flight over Durango, I had a vision of a Native American elder. I was at his home, he was teaching me about sweat lodges, and he made flutes. I'm *seeing* all this in a vision in my head. He said to me, "The sweat lodge is a sacred place of purification for the mind and the body. We pray for all living things and the earth. It is an honorable place to come and give your pain and sorrows to Great Spirit. The eagle bone whistle is used to carry the prayers up to the Creator."

Well, within a month of living in Colorado, I was introduced to the chief of the Southern Ute Tribe by a friend of mine who had adopted a Ute baby. "Sunshine, I would like to take you to a special ceremony that will absolutely transform your life. You will feel a huge spiritual renewal. I will introduce you to Red Ute." He was a flute player, and he taught and led sweat lodges! This was the vision I had flying over the land. He lived 20 minutes from our home. The tribal leader and his family became my new family, and they taught me the sacred ways of prayer and purification of body, mind, and soul. During my first sweat lodge experience, I felt a shedding of old energy. I was renewed and reborn into a new me, a new identity. After a while, the tribal leaders initiated me to facilitate sweat lodges—OMG, what an honor. I ended up having my own lodge for 25 years! This experience highlighted my committed awakening into the sacred.

The time came when I left the father of my children. Thankfully, we are friends now; the form of the relationship just needed to change. When I left the marriage of 18 years, it was time to get into some serious internal emotional healing work. I knew the only way out of suffering was going deep into the core. My inner healing journey took me into transformational inner child work and getting in touch with the emotions I was too afraid to feel. For most of my early years, I felt invisible, not seen or heard. I would never raise my hand in school. I had a great fear of anger.

Growing up in a household where my mother's emotion's erupted often, my nervous system would be in fight or flight mode. I didn't feel safe expressing myself or showing anger. When I finally embraced the anger that was hiding inside of me, it became a pivotal point in my life. Allowing that emotion to surge through me was like a damn that opened, and incredible vitality ensued! I found my voice underneath the rage.

My mother was in her 80s when she visited me in Colorado. I now had the opportunity to express my truth to her, even though my body would freeze at the thought of it. I sat her down and said, "Mom, I know you don't understand the work I do helping people share their deepest darkest emotions with me about their families. However, I have a request, and you can help me very much with this. Are you willing?" Of course, she said yes. "Okay, there are some rules, you must let me outflow, express anything and everything, and you can't interrupt or try to defend."

This surprised and shocked her, as I never expressed my deepest emotions. Often, she would tell me not to cry, it was too painful for her, and she couldn't hold space for my feelings.

Down from the inner depths of my soul, buried memories came flooding like a river. Tears came, and I felt like the insides of me were being washed clean to be able to express my truth from my heart. Having her witness and not react was a miracle in itself! Mom was able to listen and hold space for me. I felt forgiveness underneath all the blocked emotions— true forgiveness, not just from the logical mind. I could feel another layer of healing present itself. My heart expanded, which created more ease in giving and receiving love with more depth. Then a couple of months later, my mother passed. I felt so grateful I was able to have that experience with her before she transitioned.

I believe there are two kinds of forgiveness. One is conscious logic forgiveness when the mind knows or thinks it's the right thing to do. This type doesn't really convince the internal younger self, so there can still be lingering resentment or other emotions that hide out in the body organs.

The second forgiveness is cellular or embodiment, in which the forgiveness comes about through the subconscious, through hypnotherapy work, or deep work accessing the younger parts of self, where imprinted patterns get stuck. This allows responses to life's situations and relationships rather than reactions or triggers.

I'd like you to imagine a pond. You are a rock, diving down into the dark, murky pond, not knowing what's underneath. This pond symbolizes the emotional body. Imagine this pond is being flushed clean and effervescent bubbles are coming to the top and start to ripple out, going far and wide. The rock represents you and stays in the center of the pond, being cleansed and cleared of numbness and stuck emotions. Now, the ripple effect happens from within you, going out to family, friends, and business.

I received guidance from many different healing modalities. One teacher said, "Go vertical before going horizontal." That phrase has molded part of my life. Going vertical became an anchor point for my spiritual connection, then my heart was able to connect to the world without losing my identity.

Ever since my early years of being clairaudient, hearing that white spirit horse in my ear, I have a strong belief in the etheric plane. I love anything to do with angels, fairies, and the world of magic! Divine trust is the place where my heart feels embraced and held. I invite guidance from the spirit world, and I hear downloads of messages or information.

I was doing my healing work part-time while raising two kids and didn't have the finances to support myself. I started a cleaning business I named Shine to Shine Cleaning. For a few years, I did the cleaning myself and enjoyed it. I love altering the energy of spaces to bring in positivity, and with the way I did the cleaning, people tangibly felt the difference! This business continued to the point where I hired 15 independent contractors, had contracts, and made sure all the legalities were in place.

The women that came to work for me generally were single moms. Many of them had low self-esteem and worthiness issues. I began to mentor those with an interest. I was like a mother hen to these gals. One of them became so confident she started her own cleaning company. Even though she could've been my competition, I admired her courage to initiate herself. Another became like a daughter as her mother passed when she was quite young. To this day, she calls me Mom, and we have a close relationship.

After a while, the Department of Employment wanted to do an audit on my company. My records were all clean, and they found nothing. However, the person—I'll call her Mrs. Jones—wanted to call a hearing and take me to court. My fear of legalities from the government brought on that unshakable fear. My body was unable to move, I couldn't think, and I felt shut down. I had my CPA work with me on the appeal. He said, "Business owners who go through this process usually don't win. The agency is trying to prove you have employees and not independent contractors." I told him I would be consulting with my team, my personal counsel, the one's from the Angelic realm! He didn't get it right then.

Round two—Mrs. Jones called a second appeal. The judge cleared my business again, saying all was legitimate. Mrs. Jones was determined to take me down with the system. She called for a third appeal! The fear was trying to have me acquiesce, and it took all my inner tools to keep grounded and centered. Every day, twice a day, I prayed, meditated, and did my manifestation magic techniques. *I received a download that there was some karma and past life issues at play.* I used the information revealed and did some atonement. Courage started to rise, and deep trust in the Divine spread through me like a woven sacred cloth embedded into my bones.

All the while, my CPA was in shock at the consistent unwavering pushing from Mrs. Jones to take me down. I told my CPA, "We are going to win this!" He didn't quite have the belief I did. Here it is, the third appeal.

The judge was still steadfast in his decision. "Sunshine Beeson and her business Shine to Shine Cleaning do not have employees; they are Independent Contractors!"

The final decision was made! I went from fear to freedom, cultivating courage and divine trust. This was a huge victory for me! I'm grateful to my angelic team!

THE TOOL

It's called The Chakra Clearing Tune-Up. It is important to clear our Electro Magnetic Field, the aura, and the chakras due to the accumulation of outside influences and stresses that build up day to day. We brush our teeth and shower; well, it's just as important to clear our field of energy too!

If time permits, this is good to do at the start of your day, perhaps before getting out of bed in the morning.

Place your left hand on the heart—it remains there as you go through each chakra. The right hand will be touching each chakra from the first through the seventh.

First chakra: right-hand on pubic area, breathing in and imagining red spiraling light filling up, bringing in the qualities of being rooted, grounded, supported. Breath this in deeply.

Second chakra: right-hand moves up above pubic bone below the belly button, breath in orange light, bringing in the qualities of activating your sacred sexuality and divine feminine essence, breathing in inspiration and creativity.

Third chakra: right-hand moves to the center of the body. Bring in brilliant yellow light, filling up with knowing you're enough, amplifying your self-esteem and self-worth, feeling into your purpose and identity.

Fourth chakra: place right hand on top of left, over the heart. Breath in green healing light, soothing the heart of pain or wounds, then imagine an overlay of pink light like a soothing salve feeling into self-love and self-acceptance. Open yourself up to give and receive love unconditionally.

Fifth chakra: Keep the left hand over the heart and move the right hand gently over the throat. Imagine bright blue light filling up the throat, activating your communication center. Strengthening your voice and the ability to fully express your truth from your heart, being heard and respected.

Sixth chakra: right-hand moves up to the forehead, third eye area. Bring in either indigo or violet light. Connect with your intuition and your higher self. Letting go of the part of the mind that wants to judge or be critical of yourself or others. Also, imagine flushing the pineal gland to open the psychic center.

Seventh chakra: right-hand on top of the head. Imagine your crown chakra opening like a column of light, connecting with your personal team of angels and guides.

Keep your focus on the crown chakra, imagining a clear crystalline waterfall of light flowing down from above, coming through the top of your head, flushing through each of your body centers, rejuvenating, cleansing, and clearing all the cells of your body, bringing in fresh new vitality, up-leveling your frequency and vibration. Keep the breath flowing deeply.

My journey of healing and self-transformation has enabled me to come from feeling invisible, not having a voice, being in fear to doing live presentations, talking on the radio, doing podcasts, and facilitating retreats. I now rejoice in coming from fear to freedom!

My business of 39 years is InSpiral Iridology and Alchemy Hypnotherapy. Iridology is an innovative assessment tool analyzing the iris of the eye for physical and emotional health. I specialize in helping women, men and teens uncover and unlock the challenges of relationships, pain in the body, and stuck emotions. I assist in getting to the deep-rooted causes of anxiety, stress, and unresolved issues and help to instill identity, purpose, confidence, peace, and exuberant health. I create a space where clients can relax into feeling trust, so they may experience a profound sense of their true selves. Their deepest, buried, hidden emotions can be expressed freely.

I facilitate retreats for women: Divine Feminine Rising-Awakening Sacred Sexuality, Ceremonial Manifestation Wand workshop, Masculine/Feminine – The integration – The Shadow and The Sacred.

When **Sunshine** is not working with clients, she spends time with her husband Eric, daughter Fawn, son-in-law Sean and amazing twin grandchildren Brooklyn and Xander.

Sunshine enjoys time with her sisters Eli and Amie when they can visit from Colorado and Canada.

She loves horses, hiking, hot springs, meditation, and all things spiritual!

Her contact information is:

www.whatisiridology.com

Facebook: Wholistic Wellness Coaching-InSpiral Iridology

Instagram: inspiral_iridology

CHAPTER 14

ACCESSING YOUR INNER TRUTH

HOW TO EXPERIENCE LIFE-CHANGING SPIRITUAL GROWTH THROUGH MEDITATION

Donna O'Toole, RN, B.Ed., Massage Therapist, Druid Priestess

MY STORY

I am feeling safe tonight. Then unexpectedly, I'm startled in the dark as I felt him reach out and touch me inappropriately again.

I looked directly into his eyes. And then. . .

Power Over No More

I remember saying, "I'll tell her."
When rapidly, his hands found my neck and tightened.
And I looked back at him defiantly,
sending him the message,
you will never touch me again.
I remember.

I remember experiencing no fear;
a knowing I needed to remain calm and not fight back
so the message could reach him within;
Risking all, I was determined and brave.
I remember.

I remember the freedom and joy as my spirit left my body.
Floating near the ceiling,
my spirit was looking down at my body and him,
knowing the void of pain and fear,
as if I were the observer.
I remember.

I remember the moment he realized
What he was doing,
for the fury in his eyes had changed.
He let go of his death grip about my throat,
and I felt my spirit re-enter my body
as I began gasping for air.

I remember.

But I knew at that very moment
between the thin veil of life and death,
he had no more power over me.
I remember.

It was a life-altering defining moment. One juncture in time profoundly changes everything. It was the day I took my power back. I was no longer the victim.

I was sexually abused from the age of five to the age of 17. Every night before I fell asleep, I knew the utter terror of *'is he sneaking into my bedroom tonight.'*

Things were different in the 1950s and 1960s. You didn't talk about these things to anyone. You didn't tell your parents, siblings, family, friends, teacher, minister, or any other human. It was taboo to talk about your family secrets—to anyone.

You just endured such atrocities. You held everything inside. These raw emotions of fear, anger, bewilderment, abandonment, guilt—would leave their marks with emotional scars and physical diseases.

He would whisper eerily in my ear every time he came in the middle of the night to my bed: "If you tell anyone about this, who will feed you, your brother, and your mother? Where would you live? Your mother can't take care of you. How would she support you? If you tell anyone, I will go to prison? Is that what you want? All of this would be your fault!"

I would always sit trembling in silence as I shouldered this huge responsibility and family secret. Which was worse? The constant psychological threats or the physical abuse I experienced day after day, night after night, year after year.

But somewhere deep within my mind, I always heard: *It's not your fault. He is your father. You're the child. He is the adult.*

I would often pray: *Dear Heavenly Father, please make him stop. Please. I'm begging you to help him know this is just wrong. I don't understand why you have not answered my prayers. I don't understand why this is happening to me. I don't know what I did to deserve this, but can you just make him stop doing this to me—now? I feel so alone. I feel so abandoned. Oh, and—please forgive him too. In Jesus' name, I pray. Amen.*

I was confused because my biological father was also the respected minister in town. *Who would believe me? I have no one to turn to, no one to talk to. I am all alone battling this monster. I came to the sad conclusion no one would believe me.*

The deadly silence of victimhood.

Saturday nights were always the hardest. His study was across the hall from my bedroom. He would be there late at night preparing for his Sunday sermon. I knew what would happen on those nights. Then I'd have to listen to him about eight hours later, standing in the pulpit preaching his sermon while extolling his love for God and how everyone who sinned was going to go to Hell. *I guess he thought he was exempt from going to Hell.*

I believed that my mother did not know, but she might have held it within her subconscious mind. I firmly believed that Mom was not emotionally strong enough to withstand the ugly truth. How could she believe this man she loved and married could be this amoral person who would stoop so low to take repeated advantage of a small defenseless child? Consequently, I became her protectress. My mother was one of the sweetest women you could ever imagine. She had a huge, loving heart, and she showered me daily with so much love. *Mom was my saving grace.*

My brother was 14 months older than me. I knew in my heart if he found out, he would kill our father. I had to protect my brother by hiding this family secret from him. *I had to protect him for myself because I could not live with the pain if he went to prison for killing Dad.* I'm surprised I don't feel any remorse or sadness if Dad was killed or died. *Whoa! That's an aha moment because it would finally be over if that happened.*

So, with no other path to choose, I learned to hold the anger and fear inside at a very early age—not letting anyone in, not letting anyone figure out what was going on. I became an excellent little actress. Fear had a seat in every room of my house. I was the obedient smiling child on the outside as fear and anger dwelled silently in me. I became the protector of everyone except myself.

You might be wondering why it took me so long to stand up against him. I was tiny and short growing up. My father towered over me. It's akin to a dog that, as a puppy, learned it could not jump over the fence. Hence, as it grows up, it believes it never can jump that fence.

How did I survive the 12 years of sexual abuse? The body is smart and resilient. Interestingly, somehow my body would cause my menstruation to last 7-to-14 days, and I would have a period every two or three weeks. At least during those times, I could sleep peacefully. I welcomed those nights. *It's interesting what the body will do.*

And then, one day, I reached an important pivotal point. What shifted? Were the planets and stars aligned just so? Is it divine timing? What made this day so special? *All I knew was it felt like something snapped inside me.*

It was 11 p.m. on a dark, cold wintry night when I became very thirsty. I could hear the branches of the trees scratching at my bedroom window from the blowing wind. I opened my bedroom door ever so quietly as I attuned to the sounds of the house. It was commonly quiet in my home at this time of night as everyone was ordinarily in bed. *I feel safe tonight.*

I decided to tiptoe down the stairs to the kitchen to get a drink of water. Reaching the bottom of the staircase, I walked noiselessly through the dark unlit living room, when unexpectedly, I was startled as I felt him reach out and touch me inappropriately again.

He immediately pushed me, pinning me against the living room wall as he pressed his body into mine.

It was at this precise moment when I thought: *This had got to end now.*

I defiantly looked directly into his eyes. And then, as I took my power back and lived through the thin veil between life and death, I knew he had no more power over me. I was no longer the victim.

This was when my journey of forgiveness, healing, setting boundaries, and finding my unique spiritual path began to truly unfold.

My journey is akin to the path of the labyrinth, weaving through the spirals, stopping, turning to reach the center.

Years of psychological stress, holding the anger and fear trapped inside me, led to the diagnosis of autoimmune Crohn's Disease. I had multiple hospitalizations and surgeries as I experienced systemic manifestations of this chronic, devastating disease. Through years of forgiveness work—I must say my biggest soul lesson so far—I have been 30 years with no signs or symptoms of Crohn's Disease.

I healed my body through forgiveness. I cleared my emotional auric body, which directly correlates to the first, second, and third chakras. These areas of dis-ease are associated with autoimmune, intestinal tract, and reproductive organ diseases. I had health issues or diseases in all these body areas.

All people have experienced some type of trauma that create wounds and/or gaping holes. Light will always find a way to enter those wounds so healing can occur.

I didn't overcome all these psychological or physical issues overnight. Were there times I dreamed of him dying, that I killed him? Absolutely, but these were scenarios I played in my head as I worked through the many layers of deep emotional scars. Again, the body and mind protect oneself, revealing hidden memories when it knows you're strong enough to process them. I was like a blooming onion, peeling back one layer at a time only to discover another layer underneath that one. At times, it was extremely frightening, like being on a roller coaster ride, knowing what is coming after you reach the top. Over the years, the processing only takes minutes rather than years, weeks, days, or hours. *It was my journey, one day at a time.*

For the first time in my life, I tell this story to more than an extremely small select group of people. My hope in telling this one life story of mine is it may help others who have lived and survived childhood sexual abuse. If it just changes or helps one life, that is enough for me.

The main question is: How did I take my power back?

The one tool I kept on using to regain my focus, search within, find meaning, gain peace, and receive clarity, but most importantly, to access my inner truth, was in the form of prayer and meditation.

There are many different modes of prayers. I firmly believe meditation is a form of prayer, a conversation with the Divine Source, the Supreme Creator of all. Meditation is very contemplative and serves as a connection to one's soul core, a place where peace, love, compassion, well-being, calm, and gratitude live. The Divine speaks to us during meditation in the form of intuition. This is the voice that you will hear. *You know what I am talking about.* This is the place of your inner truth. A knowing that what you hear is what you need to hear at this moment or time in your life.

There is a multitude of different kinds of meditations. There is always at least one kind of meditation that will personally resonate. It may be walking in nature, communing with the beauty of the sounds of the forest, or sitting quietly in a room in the lotus position or some other comfortable position. Have fun exploring to find the types of meditations that make your soul sing! You want your soul to sing! It's a feeling of coming home— my spiritual home.

One kind of meditation that resonates for many is guided meditation. This takes on the form of someone walking you through the meditation as you listen and experience it.

I prefer to use the "I AM" statements or affirmations within guided meditations. "I AM" affirmations connect you directly to your subconscious and *alert the universe that effectively says reflect or manifest my inner reality into my outer reality or physical world.* Examples of affirmations I wrote are: "I AM aligning my thoughts, energies, intentions, and actions with and to the Divine while I AM surrendering my attachment(s) to the outcome." And "I AM living gratitude, and I AM loving wisdom. And it is so."

The beginning portion of this meditation has originated from many years of study as a Druid Priestess and information learned from the book *Mary Magdalene Beckons: Join the River of Love* by Mercedes Kirkel.

THE TOOL

GUIDED MEDITATION ON GRATITUDE

Sit comfortably with your feet firmly planted on the ground. Inhale three deep breaths, breathing slowly in and out. Imagine you have roots extending from the soles of your feet going down into the earth. Deep down into the earth through every rock, even deeper through the earth's inner layers until those roots reach the center core of the earth. You feel firmly grounded in Mother Earth.

Begin by drawing unconditional love, which is the love of the Divine Feminine, which you can visualize as coming from Mother Earth. You draw this divine love up through the soles of your feet, through the lower three chakras, and into your heart space.

Continue drawing love into your heart as you simultaneously draw Creator-light, the light of the Divine Masculine, which you can visualize as coming from Father Sun, Grandfather Sky, the heavens, or the great central sun of the universe. The light enters through the crown chakra of your head, which is the gateway to your higher self and thus to the Supreme Creator of all. From there, bring this divine light down into your sacred mind, third eye, throat chakra, and then into your heart, where it merges with the divine love from Mother Earth.

In that merging, this divine love-light energy becomes activated and so empowered that it can be sent out to the rest of your body, engulfing every cell down to the most minute particles, and then with the exhale, you send this activated, empowered love-light energy through a thousand points of light to the rest of the world for each highest good.

Imagine golden and violet threads with this activated love-light energy, weaving infinity symbols, connecting you to the realm of all possibilities.

Continue to coordinate this process with the breath, drawing love and light into your heart with the inhalation, merging the two, and then, with the exhalation, sending out the activated and empowered divine love-light energy. Know that this will happen automatically without you even thinking about it.

Visualize a violet light that surrounds you and your auras completely. This violet light protects you and only allows divine love, light, and energy to enter or leave freely.

Next, visualize a sacred place or place of power that holds special meaning to you. Feel its unique energy and infuse yourself with it. Breathe this unique energy into your heart space.

As you sit in this sacred place, you continue to breathe in the divine love and light. Ask for your spirit guides, animal guides, angels, ascended masters, or the presence of a higher spirit to come and sit with you here in this sacred place.

Breathe in love.

Breathe in compassion.

Breath in gratitude.

Feel the love, compassion, and gratitude in your heart and heart space.

Send love to your wounds, known and unknown, for healing. See this empowered and activated divine love and light mixture finding and reaching all your wounds. Feel the love, compassion, and healing taking place.

What are you grateful for?

Who are you grateful for?

What one family member are you most grateful for?

Whose friendship do you cherish?

Who is someone who listens to you when you need to talk?

Who or what has made you laugh or smile this week?

What or whose voice do you want to hear?

What three relationships are you most grateful for?

What are you grateful for about yourself?

What are the gifts that you are grateful for?

Have you helped someone recently?

What random acts of kindness have you received recently?

What random acts of kindness have you given recently?

Who has crossed over that you would like to share your gratitude for?

Continue to meditate as you hear these affirmations:

I AM grateful for each breath I take.

I AM grateful for myself.

I AM grateful that my heart always receives more to be grateful for in my life.

I AM grateful that I AM allowing joy and bliss to live in me through gratitude.

I AM grateful that I know love.

I AM grateful for the people in my life.

I AM grateful for my soul tribe.

I AM grateful that I AM connected to and guided by the Divine Source.

I AM living in the vibration of gratitude.

I AM accessing my inner truth.

I AM ushering in life-changing spiritual growth.

I AM experiencing life-changing spiritual growth through meditation.

Listen to the message your spirit guides or the divine source have for you at this moment in time?

Kindly thank them for their special messages you received.

You are now bringing yourself back into your body so that you're fully aware of all your senses. You feel relaxed and calm. You will take this feeling of well-being and gratitude with you throughout the rest of the day.

And it is so!

Namaste!

You can meditate on just one of these questions. Do you take a walk, sit with your back against a tree, repose in a chair, walk a labyrinth, or lose yourself in a painting? It's your choice on how, when, where, and why you meditate. You're the master of your life.

Through this process, you will access your inner truth and thus experience life-changing spiritual growth through meditation.

And it is so!

Donna O'Toole, RN, B.Ed., Massage Therapist, Druid Priestess, Intuitive, Energy Healer, Awen Awakener.

After caring for her husband of 14 years, who died from ALS, Donna knew something was missing from western teachings. This led her to search and study across many fields. As a result, she merges the western and eastern philosophies to enhance and enrich how one lives their life.

Donna bridges this work with many other teachings as a Reiki Master, Karuna Reiki Master, Crystal, Sound and Color Healer, clearing and blessing homes and spaces, intuitive, poet, actress, singer, and guided meditation leader. She is in her third decade of embracing the healing arts, energy work, sound healing, crystal healing, crystal grids, Celtic and Irish study, druidism, and meditation, to name a few of her varied interests.

Donna focuses, as she feels called, on those individuals who need help with alternative healing options; transitioning from this earth plane; and those who have had the trauma of childhood sexual abuse.

Donna started writing poetry 11 years ago and found this method of writing, as well as journal writing, has led her to further healing for herself and her readers.

She also brings healing through guided meditations using focused "I AM" statements. Through Donna's years of stage and theatre work, she has learned how to use her voice and lends those talents to her voice-guided meditations, setting the right tone for delivery.

Donna truly believes it's important to live your authentic spiritual life and to be guided to dwell where it *makes your soul sing*.

For further information and resources, go to
https://www.AwenAwakener.com

CHAPTER 15

DIAMONDS AND SAWDUST

CREATIVE EXPRESSION
FOR JOY AND MANIFESTING

Anna Pereira, CEO and Head Goddess of The Wellness Universe

MY STORY

Okay, I'm a manifestor. I want something; I usually get it. I do put in the action, patience, and allowing needed to bring what I seek to manifest into my life.

I first realized this a few years ago upon revisiting what I did, specifically, to attract the man and life of my dreams. I wrote about how I manifested my husband in *The Wellness Universe Guide to Complete Self-Care, 25 Tools for Happiness* book introduction. It's a great story and proof that we truly can manifest our desires, and if we're careful, we can be blessed with even better results than we can possibly imagine.

For the last several years, I've been building a community of support for the world to find help, healing, and health. In my heart of hearts, I know we need each other to be able to heal through what we suffer from once we're aware and take responsibility and the steps needed to allow healing and transformation.

I'm passionate about wanting the world to be healed because I believe a happy, healthy, healed human leads to world peace. I'm also equally passionate about community—a place where like-minded wellness leaders and folks who make the world a better place find each other. We're a peer network of support and a support network of well-being leaders for the world to tap into, connect with, and find what helps them to heal—that best describes the unique utopia known as The Wellness Universe.

This vision came to me in 2013. As if God spoke directly to me, I heard in my head and my heart: *There needs to be a place where people who change the world come, collaborate, co-create, and can be found, and you are the one to build it.* Not too big of an undertaking, ya think?! Well, I followed the instruction, and in 2014 The Wellness Universe was seeded and launched online in late January 2015.

I DO THE WORK TO MAKE MY DREAMS COME TRUE.

Manifesting doesn't just happen because you dream of something big. You can't be an iconic singer just because you want to. You need to have the talent, get out there and perform, make the right connections, and learn a little about the business.

I know there are some conditions beyond the practical that the quantum, energetic, or spiritual realms help us with—if we're doing the work in those areas—to help us manifest our dreams.

From my observation and experience, my theory is that you have better chances of manifesting your dreams when you engage in self-love and self-care. Feeding your soul feeds your joy which raises your vibration, helps you heal, and allows the Universe to bring you what you desire and are ready for.

DOES SCIENCE SUPPORT CREATIVITY AS A PORTAL?

Recently, I was inspired to change my home office in Portugal—a long overdue redo. It leached my joy and was a daily environmental energy-zapping factor I ignored, procrastinated on doing anything about, and avoided. Finally, I got off my ass and gave it the attention it needed.

For the last several years, I was always too busy to take care of this. My workspace was toxic, invasive, and impacted my self-care. Drowning in the day-to-day work was toxic enough; my space made it more burdensome.

My cats claimed my office, and half of the space was a spare bedroom with leftover clothes to iron and a mishmash of other items all over the place. I classified it as a 'level 1 hoarder room'. The décor was never my own—the energy never claimed by me.

Embarking upon the metamorphosis of this space to be completely mine, it thrust me into what would have made a really good reality show episode of a makeover. I do not have 'before' photos, but the 'before' was too horrendous to revisit and be reminded of.

As I began feeding my soul with the transformation of my space, I realized I was opening the portal to manifesting.

I turned to one of my dear, trusted, and respected friends, Jennifer Whitacre Gardner, who works as a trauma specialist and is described as "one who straddles the line between science and woo-woo."

"Jennifer, I'm trying to connect the dots between being creative and feeling good, which leads to manifesting the life of your dreams. My head is so full of thoughts and feelings around this, and I know that when we're in joy, we can allow dreams to come true, but I wonder if you can help me with a more 'sciency' way to explain this?"

"I know the science between play being the antidote to anger and play and creativity are related, however scientific evidence behind creativity is a little harder to nail down. Creativity is not something you do, it's the result you get when you allow your inner passions to emerge and merge."

I marinaded on that for a moment. Very interesting. And what she added after that, I found fascinating!

"As you know, I work with internal family systems, so many times it's like doing couples therapy as you're working with different parts within that have conflicts. A lot of those conflicts come with adult, mature parts overriding young childlike parts that want to be creative. That creativity gets overridden with protocol-driven, systematic practices that come with work-life. For example, we can experience a lifeless, colorless droning on from day to day because we can't put our passions and creative pursuits into action. When we explore our different parts and the different creative passions within those parts and allow them to emerge and *merge,* emotion is behind that (i.e., passion). If there's no emotion, then it isn't creative. When we're exploring our creativity and being in the action of creativity, our head, heart, and gut are most in alignment. And when we can get to that—that alignment—then yes, we're gonna manifest the life of our dreams."

She nailed it!

As soon as I heard her 'science-splain' what I was feeling, I felt validated.

I share all of this because it's been an ever-evolving eight years of bringing to life my passion project known as The Wellness Universe. Lots of experimentation. Lots of funding. Lots of time. Lots of heart. Lots of putting my self-care and needs in the back seat.

"I'm mentally, emotionally, and spiritually eroded," I recently shared. "I cannot keep going like this." The leadership I embody and show up with every day comes with a cost.

For the past two years, I've been working on rebuilding what I've put my entire life into, feeling accountable for it not becoming all I expected. I've seen where I needed fine-tuning. Finding a sustainable way to have The Wellness Universe make the world a better place took sitting down and reevaluating, redesigning, and reinvesting, all while I've been running on a treadmill I cannot seem to get off of. It all has become overwhelming and seemingly impossible.

So much reflection. So much mustering up the emotional fortitude to say, "I am taking care of me. I'm going to take a hiatus after SoulTreat."

That break after my third huge retreat event never happened.

As a business owner (maybe you are one, too), there is no vacation. There is no space for rest in my schedule. But I knew I'd shatter into a million pieces if I didn't take a break.

On the heels of acceptance, finally saying, "You have to put you and your self-care first, Anna," releasing the guilt, and aligning with my team to express that I'd be taking a break after our last book launch for *25 Tools for Goddesses,* I was ready.

Then my team fell ill.

No rest for the wicked! The break never came.

Then I got Covid.

My team came first, and their health was the most important thing. I was so stressed and pulled in a hundred directions—still struggling with what I was doing with my business.

I happened to be in Rio de Janeiro. One would think to enjoy paradise, yet I was filled with stress and contemplation while sitting at the window (or lying in bed) of a beachfront hotel room, nursing my health, and staring out over the beautiful ocean in Ipanema. As I watched the Majestic Frigatebirds fly in every morning, I would sit with a knot in my stomach, spiraling downward, pressuring myself to have all the answers and everything buttoned-up, but the lack of answers led to darkness; *Where do I go from here? I don't even know where to start. Am I crazy? Who am I to think I can make this happen? Do I have the strength? How do I proceed?*

I needed self-care more than ever.

One of the ways I experience joy and submerge into self-care and self-love is by working with my hands, heart, and head. Being creative is where I heal and feel my purpose. I feel like a child again. I have the power to make and do anything I want. I create, and the process brings me joy, a sense of accomplishment, and knowing I created something that only I could make, the way I made it, exactly how I want it to be, from my imagination.

Typically, I will make jewelry, soaps, or custom dye, paint, and print t-shirts and other garments. But this time, since I was under renovation with my office, I was inspired to grab a hammer and build.

I entered my garage, claimed it as my new workspace to channel my joy, grabbed a hammer and some wood, and went to work.

There was not much more thought. I didn't take off my jewelry, file my nails, or prepare. I just made sure I had sneakers on rather than flip-flops to protect my feet and took action.

Diamonds on—surrounded by sawdust; I was in heaven.

As I was feeding my soul, the Universe was my witness. As I was in motion with my self-care, feeding and nurturing my inner child (everything I advocate for healing oneself), the portal for manifesting opened.

In the end, I combined my talents and designed and built custom-created, and beautifully-adorned storage boxes painted in the colors inspired by the ocean and sun on the coast of Portimao and Madeira Island, Portugal.

For the aesthetic handle, I took leather lacing I had in storage from jewelry making, copper wiring, and an array of crystals, beads, and gemstones to adorn them, giving them a bohemian look. They are as much décor as they are functional. I can seriously have an orgasm over something aesthetically pleasing AND functional!

The process brought me back to life! I was rejuvenated and felt like I reconnected with a part of me I sadly ignored and put in the backseat for far too long.

"Come see my boxes!" I said.

"Wow! Great job, babe. I'm so proud of you." Hugo said with a smile and gave me a big hug.

Hugo's words made me feel so good. I felt like a child, and although approval isn't needed to validate me, it sure feels good to be appreciated and recognized by the love of my life.

I was proud of my masterpieces. You would think I just carved the David.

With childlike excitement, I said, "And wait until you see what I do with the handles! There's the functional handle here on the side, and the front will be just for decoration and beauty. This made me feel so good. I needed this more than I realized."

"I'm glad the wood wasn't a waste of money then," Hugo said with a chuckle, and we had a good laugh. Hugo and I are like those Muppets, Statler, and Waldorf. Remember them, the two old men in the balcony box of the Muppet theatre? We'd poke fun at each other all the time and have a great laugh.

The result? I fed my soul and so many new opportunities were coming in left and right that found ME—manifesting opportunities and dreams (like I said earlier) beyond what I could imagine.

THE TOOL

So many experts have their recipe for manifesting. For example, the one I shared in my *25 Tools for Happiness* book is my personal, detailed description that delivered a life-awaited dream to me.

My tool regarding self-care and opening the channel to manifesting through being creative is another way we open a portal to manifest dreams.

The Universe will plug up a hole. You must allow the space for this. If you keep filling a hole (mine was with work and putting everyone before me and my self-care all the time), it will stop up the superhighway to manifesting.

Manifesting is a balance between doing the work, practicing self-love, setting our intention, and believing the Universe to have our best interest at heart and allowing it to take place.

The Universe could only see me doing what I do—day in and day out. My routine demonstrated to the Universe: "Well she must like what she's doing because she keeps doing it over and over."

Although I asked for and wanted very specific things to manifest in my life, was I making the room or showing the Universe I desired something different?

Also, was I showing the Universe I'd take care of the blessings I received and love my life experience if it were to reward me with what I think I want? I had to ask myself if that was the message I was sending.

After all, behind the person, place, or thing we want is the desire for what we believe will fill us up to experience joy, happiness, fulfillment, pleasure, accomplishment, and live in the highest vibration for ourselves.

Doing something creative allows us to express what is inside of us. We can *all* do something that brings us joy. We don't have to be great at it. We can be terrible at something, but it doesn't matter! Because you're doing it for *you* and your inner child, not for anyone else.

The reward lies in that.

That is when manifesting happens.

Serve yourself from a place of love and joy without expectation. Do what you do for the sheer joy in the doing.

An apple tree blossoms, bears apples, and repeats the cycle again. It does what it does.

Life is about love, creation, and transformation—diversity and experiences. When we play in that energy, get completely lost in it, and enjoy life, we allow a portal and clear channel to open to opportunities and events.

I encourage you to open the portal for allowing blessings to manifest through immersing yourself in something creative, fun, fulfilling, playful, or perhaps relaxing.

Turn to creativity and expression of your inner self and serve your heart, mind, body, and soul with creative expression. Here are some ideas:

- Paint
- Dance
- Sing
- Sculpt
- Build
- Color
- Write
- Play/Write music
- Reupholster/Up-cycle furniture
- Knit or crochet
- Sew
- Make note cards
- Origami
- Make jewelry
- Make holiday ornaments
- Bake and decorate cookies
- Tie-dye old shirts (it's always in fashion!)

*These are just some suggestions, and the bonus is, that many of these can be shared, gifted, or donated.

Do something you really enjoyed as a child! Revisiting a childhood activity is powerfully healing.

My inner child found great joy in building my boxes! I was reliving a happy memory of when I was a child. My grandmother gave me a block of wood, a hammer, and nails. I would hammer and remove them from that piece of wood for hours. It was fun for me, but it was also a skill builder.

GETTING CREATIVE!

1. Deciding what to do may be a challenge if you are a highly creative person or not creative at all. Ask yourself:

    a. What brought me joy as a child?

    b. What do I love to do that I lose myself in?

    c. What can I do that would add to my life in other ways? Think aesthetic and functional, for gifts, or donating to an organization.

2. Do you have a space ready for you to get to play? Where can you dive in uninterrupted?

    a. Claim your space.

    b. Be as initiative-taking in the prep of your space as possible. Once you start, you don't want to have your flow interrupted. Tidy up and allocate space to work in peace with everything at your fingertips.

    c. You may want incense, a candle, or music. Make a ritual out of the set-up and prep.

3. Gather your tools, bobbles, what-it's, and necessities to get creative! Prep, protect, produce.

    a. Make a list. Check it twice.

b. Think about everything needed, not just the components/ingredients needed to produce your product: Are you painting? You'll need drop cloths, a bucket of water, and rags, for example.

4. Enjoying your experience and 'me time.' Schedule it and tell those who may use your shared space to respect that time/space and not interrupt you.

5. Dive in. Get crafting, building, baking, or painting. Feel the feels. Smell the smells. Liberate yourself in the process! Boy, do I love driving a nail accurately on the first go. The physical activity coupled with the skill of driving it straight, without poking through the side, is so rewarding.

6. Well done! Pat yourself on the back, compliment your work, effort, and expression of self-love.

May you find your own way to express yourself and find joy through creativity, self-expression, and self-love. May it lead to manifesting your dreams beyond your expectations.

*I intentionally kept vision-boarding off my list as it keeps your headspace in the future. That may sound counter-intuitive since vision-boarding is a tool for manifesting, however, this creative journey is for you to detach completely and sink into your present and joy.

Anna Pereira is the CEO and Head Goddess of The Wellness Universe, a woman-owned business where her mission is to make the world a better place. She's an inspirational leader, mentor, and connector for business owners who are changing the world. As an author and creator of wellness events, projects, and programs, Anna is an expert at showcasing, promoting, and supporting the world's most talented wellness professionals and empowering organizations with group and corporate wellness programs.

Never too far from a beach, Anna enjoys them regularly as she lives between Portugal and her birthplace, New Jersey, with her husband, Hugo Varela. The couple has rescues, one dog and two cats, and cares for two neighborhood strays. Their most entertaining pet is Big Red, an African Gray. Being creative, artistic, and getting out in nature is part of her self-care regimen. She is dedicated to serving her calling and leaving her legacy as a 'conduit for change' by bringing more health, happiness, and well-being to the world with a collaborative spirit and intentional action. Learn more about Anna and The Wellness Universe at
TheWellnessUniverse.com
https://www.thewellnessuniverse.com/world-changers/annapereira/

CHAPTER 16

HEAL YOUR INNER SABOTEUR

IGNITE YOUR ABILITY TO ATTRACT GREATER ABUNDANCE

Jacqueline M. Kane,

R.T., LMT, EFT, Master Energetic Healer

MY STORY

"Why do I never reach my goals?"

"Why do I get so close to my goals, and then something happens to derail my success?"

"Am I destined to be a failure?"

I've heard these words from clients, fellow healers, coaches, and in my own head. The inner saboteur is so sneaky it took me years to realize she was hijacking my life, relationships, and success.

At first glance, there's always a reason for missed opportunities and goals not being met. There are plenty of reasons to use as excuses about why I didn't achieve my yearly goal, year after year. I was good at blaming it on the economy, that I didn't promote my event in time, or the weather was bad so people didn't want to come out, or my family needed me more.

Looking back, there were plenty of times I planned something big in my business that could've changed everything for me, and then I got the phone call or the text. A demanding text from my sister yelling at me through her words asking "Can't the Dr. give her something to improve her memory? Did you ask him about it?" Instead of clearly asking for what she needed, she would get angry and vent at me for how frustrated she was with her life—leaving me to jump in and fix everything.

This was the family drama pattern I had unconsciously created. It was how we handled situations. It was normal for my parents, siblings, and I not to ask for what we needed at the moment. We were taught to get over things and move on and then explode when we reached our limit of not feeling heard or seen.

Instead of speaking up and clearly stating what we needed, we used manipulation and condescending habits to get our needs met. Because how we do anything is how we do everything, I unknowingly was using this habit in my business relationships. It showed up when I was looking into shifting my massage therapy business into more of an online healing business.

It was an entirely new way of running my business, and I had no idea what I was doing. During this transition, I hired many coaches to help me learn how to create and promote this new business into an online presence.

Every new coach told me if I did what they said, I'd be able to create a very successful business. There was specifically one coach I was introduced to that sounded like she was the one to help me grow my online business. She was very creative and experienced in creating online programs that helped healers and practitioners showcase their programs and attract their ideal clients. I had high hopes she was the coach for me.

She was going to help me create a free video series called Three Myths Keeping Moms in Pain. Even though I was very scared to be seen and heard on camera, I had this big passion and desire to help moms living in pain release their pain to feel better and be able to enjoy their children. That passion was bigger than my fear of being seen.

I was excited to begin working with this coach, Sandy, and was ready to put all of my time, energy, and focus into soaking up everything she'd be teaching me. We scheduled our meetings, and I got to work. In the beginning, our meetings were going well, and she was putting everything she had into creating the content for my videos. She was a master at creating interesting and fun content for videos that would convert into sales.

As time went by and the months were running one into the other, I began to feel some irritation from her. I began to feel like Sandy was feeling resentful for all the time she put in and that she was feeling like she was giving more than she was being paid for. I'm an empath and could feel her annoyance. Back then, I wasn't good at speaking up and would shrug it off as *I'm being too sensitive or analytical. Get over it and keep working.'*

It was turning into one problem after another. The annoyance in her voice was getting more noticeable, and because I wasn't comfortable standing in my power and sharing my concerns with her, I did what I was used to doing, not saying a word, judging her in my head, and making her the problem.

Of course, I was in the energy of being right. *It's not my fault! She's the one who is creating this disappointing circus again for me in my business. She's the one being unprofessional, not me.* My resentment over this business relationship was building, and I did what I normally did, suppress it, suck it up, and keep going. Because I didn't believe I could do it on my own, I felt desperate to complete this with her.

Everything around this project became a huge waste of time. The videos took forever to record. I purposely scheduled time to record my videos in my office when I assumed the building would be quiet and free of other people. Whenever I tried recording outside my door, I'd hear other practitioners laughing over the latest Seinfeld episode. Or the camera would record me in the wrong position. The excuses and technical difficulties went on and on. My excitement was now turning to resentment and frustration for saying yes to this project. Any hope and joy had drained out of me like a deflated balloon, and it was turning into drudgery.

Needless to say, the results were disappointing. Only a handful of people registered for it, and even less showed up for the live event. It would go into my memory as another disappointment.

My normal routine after a disappointing event would be to allow myself to feel the feelings and then get back to work—find the next coach whose marketing resonated with me and try again. There were many coaches I signed up with, and there were moments of wins and of disappointment.

It wasn't until I started working with Alan Davidson, creator of *Evolutionary Mystic Meditation,* who taught me about our inner voices, when I suddenly realized: *My saboteur is driving the bus of my life! And oh, by the way, she's two years old!*

He learned voice dialogue from Hal and Sidra Stone, the founder of this work. They would have someone move across the room into a different chair to acknowledge what voice they were. Some examples of these inner voices are the procrastinator, the perfectionist, the inner judge, and many more.

Alan combined voice dialogue with the Emotional Freedom Technique (EFT) or tapping, which showed me how to get in touch with these inner voices. I learned that we have inner defensive voices and inner enlightened voices. For most of us, we live our lives in our defensive voices. The well-known defense voices are your inner critic, inner saboteur, and inner perfectionist.

I learned these voices developed when I was hurt at a very young age. Also, this part of me created defensive habits and patterns from the mind of a child. It's keeping me safe from the thoughts and beliefs created by an immature, wounded part of me.

As I got to know and tune in to this part of me, I realized that it was here to keep me safe. The patterns it was using to keep me safe were outdated, no longer working for me, and immature.

For example, my saboteur believed that if I was seen, I'd get hurt by people—even those trying to help me. In response to this, I found myself sabotaging my results to hurt me before others hurt me. My way of doing that was to find a problem with the coach I hired.

This is the complicated voice of the childlike saboteur. In my healing journey, I allowed my saboteur to be seen and heard so that we could release this unhealthy cyclical pattern I found myself in. The more I allowed this inner voice to share the fear it held on to, the more this part of me relaxed and felt safe being seen and heard.

It wasn't until years later, talking with my healer friends, when I sat at my desk and looked out the picture window watching the birds at our bird feeder and had a huge realization: I was the problem. Not the coaches I hired.

"OMG, I'm just realizing now that about five years ago, when I worked with that coach, I sabotaged those results! It was me! Oh, man! I'm the common denominator! I created all that drama about her not doing enough for me! My own fear was coming up and creating a situation to blame her for my results."

Wow, that felt like a mic drop ah-ha moment! As I was becoming aware of my saboteur and how I sabotage my results, I began seeing all the ways my clients sabotage their goals and intentions.

It was like a lightbulb went off in my head, and now I couldn't unsee it. And I saw it everywhere. It was fascinating to see these patterns in a new way. Not something to be upset or disappointed about, but in an enlightened way. I was now able to see my patterns. It was like this huge energetic shift in my body and awareness.

Everything changed for me at that moment. Suddenly I had this compassion for myself and for these parts of myself that held on to those hurts and wounds. From that point on, I could see it in my clients and help them heal their saboteur, which created huge shifts in their lives and businesses.

Now we can see it coming and stop it before it derails us.

Here are some of the sabotaging patterns that I saw:

- Getting sick, especially with allergies acting up
- Cold and flu symptoms
- A family member getting sick and the client jumping in to help them
- Shiny red object syndrome (become busy with other projects)
- Get stuck in the downward spiral of world events and negativity
- Get devoted to my to-do list, which is busywork, not productive work
- Become convinced that they are not sabotaging and they are right to stop working on their dreams and move on to something else

- Getting into overwhelm
- Not sleeping
- Feeling depressed
- Confusion
- Family drama

All of these patterns are good reasons to stop moving forward. Except when you find yourself in business for years and still making the same amount of money year after year. Or when you find yourself sick and tired of not being further ahead. Or you feel that your siblings leave you out of major family decisions. Or your children's friends' mothers leave you out of girl's night out. Or you see your peers moving ahead and making huge progress, and you wonder: *When is it my time?*

The exciting thing is when you become aware of these sabotaging patterns and begin the process of healing that part of you, your life can shift in a new exciting way, faster and easier. For example, when I worked with my client Jane her life changed at the exact moment she connected with her inner saboteur. As I was asking her questions, her phone started buzzing and wasn't stopping.

She was trying to sell a couch for which she no longer had any use. She posted it on Facebook to sell three weeks ago and had no takers. She couldn't even give it away; no one wanted it. The first text said, "I can come over right now to purchase and take the couch."

The other text was from an old friend who texted and said, "Things have not worked out for my new boyfriend and me, and I'm leaving him. All of my possessions are packed into a u-haul and will be arriving at your ranch next week." This woman was the only person with who Jane and her husband felt comfortable maintaining the ranch so that they could take time off and go on a vacation.

Basically, at the moment, Jane was healing her saboteur and creating a better partnership with that part of herself. All the right people and situations were working themselves out to accommodate her desires. That's how powerful your inner saboteur is. Once you connect with that part and become friends, life becomes magical.

THE TOOL

First, you have to be aware of your sabotaging patterns. Because this inner voice is so sneaky at first glance, they don't look like patterns. They simply look like life events and circumstances are happening to me and not by me.

Your inner saboteur is actually protecting you in a very old limiting way. This is the part of you that was hurt at an early age and has never grown up. This aspect of you has been stunted at that traumatized age and is still in the background making decisions for you. It's protecting you in very childlike ways.

The first step in creating a partnership with your saboteur is to become aware of your saboteur's pattern to keep you safe. Many times the pattern doesn't even make sense. Remember, this is a very young childlike aspect of you.

Maybe you don't want to fire your saboteur because this part of you has been protecting you for your entire life. It's a very strong part of your personality. What if perhaps you create a new friendship or partnership with this part of you? Then you can work together to create the life you desire.

Take a moment to get comfortable and take a seat.

This is your time to self-reflect and gain awareness so that you can move forward in a new empowered way.

Light a candle to create your sacred space.

Then take three deep breaths and bring that breath of air all the way down your body to your feet. This will help you get out of your head and become grounded in your body.

Now think of the times in your life when you had your mindset on accomplishing something, and it didn't go the way you had hoped it would.

What happened that caused you to not receive that desire?

Did you become sick? Did you go into battle with someone?

Release any judgment on what happened. You are looking for the pattern that continues to play out in your life.

Imagine you're watching this story like it's playing like a movie in your mind. You are the main character.

What is the common energetic thread that plays out for you?

Is it disappointment or frustration, or do you get sick or someone else gets sick, and you have to abandon your dream to take care of them?

One way to clear this pattern is to do EFT or Emotional Freedom Technique.

You can go to my youtube channel, where I explain Tapping at https://youtu.be/w56AakSG-cI

You can also go to my resource page, where there is a video recording of this tapping routine. https://jacquelinemkane.com/resources/

There I am
Really wanting that goal
And wow it didn't happen
It just didn't happen
I wanted it so bad
If it all worked out it would have changed everything for me
It would have changed everything for my family

All this frustration
All this disappointment
It keeps happening
I see it all now

I get so far, and a part of me gets scared
I'm actually scared to achieve this goal
I'm actually afraid to be successful
To feel pain-free and energized
To have all the money I desire
To have that much attention

Who would I be if I actually achieved that?
I'm not sure
Right now I'm ok with that

In this moment I allow myself to honor me in this story
Because I had it tough
No one taught me these things
I had to learn it all on my own
I had to do it all on my own

There was no support
It's all me
And I haven't given myself enough credit for all that I'm doing
And all that I've accomplished
I am doing a lot
I am enough in this moment

I release these old limiting sabotaging patterns
I acknowledge that I do deserve more
I do deserve to go after my dreams and achieve them

Starting right now in this moment I honor this old limiting story
I honor the gift in my saboteur
And I am open to listening to this part of me that is keeping me safe

I'm open to releasing the fear from every cell in my body
So that I can be seen and heard in a much bigger way
Thank you saboteur for keeping me safe

I'm letting you know that I release you from controlling my success
I will be taking it from here

I'm ready to receive more success
I'm ready to allow in more fun, clients, money
And everything else I desire
In a fun new exciting way
And all of this starts right now

Stop tapping and take a deep breath. Focus on your body and the sensations you feel in your body. Does your body feel lighter? Do you feel less tension or more tension? This is all awareness in creating a new relationship with your inner saboteur. Great job!

Jacqueline M. Kane is a Master Energetic Healer who guides women to uncover their hidden energetic and karmic blocks that keep them in physical, emotional, and financial pain. By using her Uncover The Root Cause process, we unravel negative thoughts and clear limitations, including Inner Child and Ancestral Karma, which have held them back for decades.

With over 20-years in private practice as a healer and over 35-years in health care, Jacqueline has merged her innate wisdom with a multitude of healing modalities, including Bowenwork, Emotional Freedom Technique, Evolutionary Meditation, Soul Clearing, and more, to create unique, results-oriented methods for healing. Her clients are able to quickly and easily achieve major shifts to create a new level of health, wealth, and lifestyle they desire now.

Jacqueline's powerful programs, available to individuals, groups, and organizations, liberate clients from physical pain and financial struggle, creating a path to energy, health, the ease with money, and personal fulfillment.

When Jacqueline is not working, she enjoys bike rides with her husband on their electric bikes, golfing with family and friends, and traveling to new exciting destinations.

You can connect with her:

Website: https://jacquelinemkane.com/

Free Soul Activation

Meditation: https://jacquelinemkane.com/qmb-meditation/

Facebook: https://www.facebook.com/jacqueline.kane.313/

Facebook Group:

https://www.facebook.com/groups/healingcirclebyjacquelinekane/

LinkedIn: https://www.linkedin.com/in/jacquelinekane/

If, after reading this chapter, you become aware that you would like to create a new relationship with our saboteur, I invite you to click this link and let's have a chat about what you could do to create a new friendship. https://JacquelineMKane.as.me/RealPainRelief

I would love to hear what you thought of this chapter. Feel free to email me at jacqueline@jacquelinemkane.com

CHAPTER 17

ACTUALIZING YOUR IDEAL LIFE

MANIFESTATION STRATEGIES TO HELP YOU ACHIEVE PERSONAL FULFILLMENT

Leslie Fraser, LMT, JFB MFR Expert

Today I feel healthy, balanced, and fulfilled. Today I feel positive and excited for the future. Today, I'm focused on expanding the thriving business I've created and realizing my vision for my dream home—doing much of the work with my own hands. Today I'm deeply in love with a partner who appreciates and values me and is my equal.

If you think these words sound a bit like a self-actualization dialogue, you're not wrong. I'm mindfully describing my current state of mind, body, and soul using the language of self-actualization because I've personally experienced the tremendous power of visualization and manifestation to heal myself, create that thriving business, and find true love.

And as you may have already guessed, things were not always this way for me. Like so many, I struggled profoundly and for many years with challenges that trace to my own origin story, which left me struggling to feel good about myself.

MY STORY

Today people often tell me I'm fearless. It used to disarm me. But now I find it validating. My long journey to personal and professional fulfillment was bumpy and began under a shadow.

As a young child, an adolescent, and into adulthood, an influential loved one in my direct orbit (we'll call this person Louise) engaged in what felt like a relentless and deeply personal campaign to undercut my sense of worth—using hurtful words to take me down at every opportunity, hobbling my ability to gain strong footing by constantly pulling the rug out from under me.

Often this was done in front of people to elevate the impact of my humiliation. It made the holidays particularly uncomfortable for guests and was horrifying for me. I was the direct target of Louise's venom, everyone in our family knew it, and they mostly stayed silent because no one knew how to stop it.

As a result of that early conditioning—firmly in place from when my young character began to develop and I started to find my voice—I had little self-confidence. I lacked the scaffolding children need to grow up and be successful in love, life, and career. I was seen for decades as type ADHD, not as the visionary, creative, and able person buried beneath the labels.

The general expectation from my family was that I would not amount to much, so I didn't put a whole lot of effort into doing anything special in terms of a career. And I found myself involved in unhealthy relationships with people who did not value me, because I did not value myself.

Years after it occurred, I learned that Louise called me when I was newly engaged. I happened to be out, and so she instead had a chat with my fiancé. "The thing about Leslie is that she gets too full of herself sometimes," my fiancé was informed, "So you have to take her down a notch or two, now and then. Otherwise, she becomes unbearable."

Can you imagine, that someone who was supposed to love you and lift you up could say such a thing, to your future life partner, no less?!

My fiancé and I married in 2001, and I settled into married life. After a few banal administrative jobs that gave me little gratification and no real career path, getting downsized from a corporate job at Polaroid was a blessing. Finally, I could choose a path that suited me. I became a massage therapist in 2007. I chose bodywork because I always felt such power in the human touch, and I felt deeply compelled to put my hands on people. But even enrolling in massage school was a challenge. My husband said, "Leslie, you have a pattern of not following through on stuff you start. This sounds like another one of those situations." I had to convince my husband and the career center that even though my testing stated I should be in the creative arts, I wanted to learn the healing arts. I knew it was the right path from the moment I entered massage school.

That same year I graduated from massage school, I became a mother. I built a small business over the next ten years. At best, I had a scant five clients a week, and my fee was tiny, which was fine during early motherhood. When my son was around six, it became increasingly clear that my home life was not at all authentic. I wasn't being true to myself. I was supposed to be happy, but I wasn't. I was happy being a mother, but playing the role of a 50s housewife was not sustainable for my soul. I knew this was not who I was meant to be.

I was adopted as an infant. I had a lifelong yearning to learn my original story. In 2012, I found the courage to connect with my birth family. When I cracked open that door, the floodgates burst open. I found both of my birth parents, my birth grandmother, siblings and cousins, and aunts and uncles. I connected with many people who looked like me, laughed like me, and shared my blood—my original tribe! It redefined my sense of self-identity; I finally felt whole, and my self-confidence soared.

It was around this time that I was first exposed to a healing technique called myofascial release. For months I had been experiencing debilitating neck pain, and no one in the medical establishment could help. I finally asked a gal with whom I shared a massage space if she could work on my neck. She spent 45 minutes working on my abdomen.

Okay, I will play your silly game. It's my neck that hurts, not my stomach.

I trusted, took off the brakes, and went quiet. My legs and body twitched a bit, startling me. Afterward, I got up and, for the first time in months, my head floated back on my shoulders where it belonged, and the pain vanished!

What is this sorcery? I need to learn more!

That experience was so profound that I knew I needed to go straight to the source to learn more.

The leading authority and most prominent teacher of myofascial release is John F. Barnes, known internationally for developing an innovative and highly effective whole-body approach for the evaluation and treatment of pain and dysfunction. John F. Barnes believes that trauma and pain are often linked through the fascial system. Thus, myofascial release (MFR) is commonly the treatment of choice to resolve past traumas in our bodies.

It took me about a year to get myself to my first MFR class. Finding my birth family gave me the confidence to start getting out of my marriage, which required my focus. Yet, I knew I zeroed in on something profound that would change my life and the lives of others.

During that first MFR course, a random student was called up onstage so John Barnes could demonstrate a technique. What ensued was this stunning emotional and physical unwinding that left *me* flattened. After her unwinding, when the floor was opened to questions, my hand involuntarily shot straight into the air. "She's so vulnerable," I said, more a statement than a question, with tears pouring down my face. I was so moved by her open display of raw vulnerability. A 'yes' nod from John Barnes followed my statement and a collective nod from the silent room of students.

At that moment, an experience I thought was mostly about professional development became something much more—a portal into my personal journey of healing and becoming.

Over the following five-to-six years, I traveled the country to immerse myself in every class that John Barnes offered, sacrificing time with my young son in the process. I repeated many courses to soak in every iota of depth, connection, and underlying nuance. It fed my light and my soul. It taught me to tap into my abilities to help others heal from trauma. I found empathy and compassion and discovered I could hold space for others and help them heal—not just with my hands but with my presence, intuition, and insights.

These experiences also helped me start my own healing journey and learn how to forgive Louise. The power to change the toxic dynamic of that relationship was profound. And a week before she passed to the other side, I felt at peace and could genuinely tell her that I loved her as I bid her farewell. Through tears, the words spilled out, "I am grateful for you and our journey together, in spite of how hard it was. I love you."

With that, I stepped into my power and found my voice. Certain strategies I've continued to learn throughout my MFR journey have helped me visualize and manifest the life I desired.

THE TOOL

You have surely heard about manifestation. It has become quite the buzzword in the healing community. You have the ability to invite wonderful things into your life by focusing on your daily language and employing the gift of your imagination. You will use positivity, visualization, and language to actualize what you want to invite in.

What I'm about to present to you is a collection of nuanced gold nuggets collected along my healing journey for you to weave into the tapestry of your life.

Choose your battles thoughtfully. You don't have to attend every argument to which you are invited. Oh, how I wish I understood that simple truth during some of my conflicts with Louise. Today, I devote my heart and imagination to diffusing conflict rather than stoking the drama. Most of us have experienced some version of this in our lives with a close friend or loved one. Giving yourself permission not to engage in the moment can be empowering.

Talk about your plans and dreams. Surround yourself with people who say, "Why not?" to your ideas, instead of those who say "Why?" and obsess on obstacles instead of opportunities. Think about how many times you've had a wild idea that might make sense to you. You share your idea with a loved one who lacks your imagination, vision, and drive—and they proceed to tear your idea apart. Bam! Your balloon popped. You can do anything you want, especially when you think in terms of solutions instead of problems.

Journal the ideas, feelings, and dreams that excite you. Dedicate a notebook to outlining the finer details and creating manageable action items related to those dreams. Because building your future starts with a foundation: What needs to happen first so the next thing can fall into place? Prioritize. Begin taking action to make new things happen. Rewrite your list as you cross things off.

Truly *believe* in your dreams. See and believe in what you dream about inviting in. Live in gratitude for the things that you already have. How can we ask for more if we don't already appreciate what we have? Make time in your daily routine for daydreaming, gratitude, and taking action to achieve your goals.

Be *specific* and *positive* in your mental imaging. A friend used to tell me, "The universe loves a laundry list, but be very specific." She was right! When we spend time talking or thinking about what we don't want, we feed a negative idea. And the ideas you give the most oxygen to are the ones that live and breathe. I used to talk a lot about the type of partner I didn't want. I thought I was just unlucky in love and would become an eccentric old maid, destined to die alone.

Well, that relationship sucked. I don't want a man who doesn't value me. He never calls. I always have to call him. And when I am with him, he doesn't appreciate me.

When I altered my thoughts to visualize and imagine a loving partner who saw my worth and wanted to be with me, guess what happened? Yes! My current partner appeared in my life, and we fell deeply in love. It was not the next day, but we connected within six months or so.

It works with the little stuff, too—a good place to start. I remember once noticing that several clients who used to be regulars had dropped off the planet. I looked at my calendar from a few months before and read the names.

Huh, this person has not been in for a while; what happened?

The phone rang the next day, and they rebooked. Sometimes setting an intention can put energy into motion. During my myofascial release training, I discovered that the moment I decided to take a class, I began to experience shifts in energy as if I was already at that next class.

Declutter. If there is a lot of *deadwood* surrounding you, and taking up space, declutter and cut the *deadwood*. Think about how trees grow big and strong when you cut the dead branches away. Eliminate the clutter around you to make room for the fantastic stuff you will bring in. This can refer to a messy workspace, a clogged to-do list, and even folks who aren't healthy for us. Decluttering helps you reclaim the time you waste on things that impede your productivity.

Quiet your negative inner voice. We all have an inner monologue. Ideally, that voice is positive and empowering; however, many of us struggle with negative thoughts. When you find this happening, I encourage you to recognize what is occurring, take a beat, and intentionally reframe negative or critical internal self-talk to emphasize more positive, empowering thoughts and feelings.

For example, ever find yourself saying something like: "Wow, that was a stupid thing to do"? What would happen if you dropped the harshness? "Oops, I'll sure know how to handle that better next time," might be a kinder approach.

This also applies to specific word choices. For example, the word "should" can be empowering, but many of us use it in ways that fuel anxiety about where we are in relation to where we'd like to be. The word "should" can be used to challenge ourselves to grow. For example: "I should earn my master's degree to help achieve my next career goal," but we can also use it to shame ourselves, "I should get my act together." Language choices can be impactful, so be mindful about using kinder self-dialogue.

Use visualization techniques to magnetize all the juicy things you want to invite into your world. Here is an MFR gem: Create an imaginary reel of how you see your ideal life. Then periodically play that mental video in your daily routine. When you loop this short clip into your thoughts, it becomes part of your consciousness, and you can begin to take actionable steps to bring it to life.

Imagine yourself feeling healthy and strong in a setting that makes you happy. Perhaps you're picturing a dream home in your favorite location, your golden job, true love, or all of the above. Add in fine details—sights, smells, and sounds. Who are you with? What are you wearing? Do you hear birds singing? Is the wind lightly whispering in the trees? I'll bet it's sunny there.

Feel the sensations of how healthy and happy you are. See yourself as care-free, with plenty of money in your pocket. If there are words in your video clip, make sure they are positive ones. For example, "I feel strong, balanced, and grounded in my body." Make sure your thoughts are in the present tense. If you always use the future tense in your self-talk, what you wish to attain will always be just out of reach.

Believe it. So, you have taken the time to create this amazing vision of how you want your life to be. You're dedicating time each day to visualize it. Now you need to believe in it. Feel it in your core that these things that you want are attainable. And that you deserve them, because you do! We are meant to live happy and fulfilled lives, and you *can* build a beautiful existence with your thoughts and language, imagination, and will.

Take action on these goals to begin building the life you want. Along the way, replay your aspirational mini-movie in your mind's eye. Envisioning your ideal life in your simple, powerful video reel will help you begin to make it real.

Leslie Fraser, LMT, is an expert level John F. Barnes Myofascial Release practitioner and has also done UMA Reiki levels one and two. Leslie is the sole proprietor of Fraser Massage and Myofascial Release, a thriving healing practice in Framingham, Mass.

Ms. Fraser is in the process of transitioning her practice to an expanded healing facility at her childhood home on the coast of southern Maine, Rivermede, a 1750s farmhouse surrounded by seven acres of fields and woodland with spectacular views of the York River.

Here, clients enjoy mini intensive weekend retreats featuring myofascial release sessions while relaxing in a peaceful, antique inn-like setting that includes five fireplaces, a completely remodeled kitchen with modern amenities, two large living rooms (one summer and one winter), and a newly renovated sunroom that overlooks the field and river, plus ample guest quarters for a small group of four-to-eight people to stay on site.

In her downtime from practicing her passion for healing, Leslie enjoys spending time with her teenage son, sitting by the fire with a glass of wine, writing her memoir, creating in her pottery studio, building pallet walls and furniture, homesteading, gardening, splitting wood, fixing up her home in Maine, kayaking and sailing. All this while sharing adventures and life's marvelous journey with her partner John, a former journalist, gifted writer, and creative soul.

Leslie is always dreaming up what she will manifest next.

If you're interested in learning more about having a mini-intensive myofascial release experience at Rivermede, please visit http://www.RivermedeRetreat.com and reach out at LeslieMFraser@gmail.com

Connect with Leslie on:
LeslieMFraser@gmail.com
RivermedeMaine@gmail.com
www.RivermedeRetreat.com
www.FraserMassageMFR.com
https://www.facebook.com/RivermedeMaine
https://www.facebook.com/FraserRustics
https://www.instagram.com/rivermederetreat/
https://twitter.com/LeslieMFraser
https://www.linkedin.com/in/LadyRivermede/

CHAPTER 18

A MOTHER'S HEART

EMBODYING YOUR INNER NURTURER

Dawn Simpson, Intuitive Spiritual Life Coach,
Energy Healing Guide

MY STORY

"If you leave here today, I disown you as a daughter, turn in your key to this house, and you will never be allowed back here again." I still remember him saying these words to me like it was yesterday.

In June of 1984, I graduated high school. In September, while my dad was at work, my boyfriend (now husband) and I, packed up all of my belongings to finally leave behind a life of living in an alcoholic, abusive home. When my dad came home from work, I prepared myself to come downstairs to tell him what I'd done. His response was, "Go and get your stuff and move it back in." I said, "No, I'm leaving." He then said what no child could fathom coming from a parent's mouth, "If you leave here today, I disown you as a daughter, turn in your key to this house, and you will never be allowed back here again." I was not prepared for that reaction. How was I to walk out that door and not be able to visit my mom and three siblings?

My dad was an abusive alcoholic. He also grew up in an abusive alcoholic home with his parents and five siblings. My mom lived in a quiet small town with her parents and brother. It was a loving home blessed with support and resilience. My parents began dating in high school, and my mom became pregnant and had to quit school her senior year. She was 18, and my dad was 20. They married in January, and I was born in August.

In 1976 my sister Jennifer was born, I was 11, and I already had two younger brothers. Being the big sister to three siblings was a job I took seriously. Being the oldest put me in that role, but it also came naturally. I wanted and needed everyone to be taken care of.

Being the big sister meant I was a role model, teacher, and protector. There were many times as a child I stood by helplessly watching one of my brothers being treated terribly at the hands of my dad. My dad's words and hands did irreparable damage. I had no power as a child to help him but have tried multiple times as an adult, to no avail. Alcohol continues to rule his life to this day.

My escape was staying in my room and writing while growing up. I wrote in my diary about the day's drama, trauma, or simply my thoughts.

Why is this happening to me? Why me? How can I make him happy? How can I be more lovable?

I also found comfort in writing poems. I mostly wrote about love and sometimes about pain. These were very cathartic and enabled me to express myself, nurture my pain, work through my challenges, and try to process what was happening in my small, inescapable world. Due to my environment, I did not have a lot of friends with whom to talk and vent to. I did this writing unconsciously as a nurturing practice, and I now believe it was what saved me from deeper emotional challenges.

Having and practicing ways to release emotions and nurture my wounds have set the stage for my emotional and spiritual growth. I nurtured my spiritual growth by attending Catholic school for seven years. While there, I was taught about connecting to and having a relationship with God, how to pray, and how to forgive others who have hurt me. This was a huge challenge for me, feeling deeply hurt on a daily basis. I remember crying every single day for years. I distinctly remember on really bad days saying to myself: *It won't be like this forever. I will get through this day.*

Some day's tears were simply for my sadness, but most day's tears were from fear, being a witness to daily mental abuse for myself and my three siblings, and physical abuse.

The main physical abuse was my dad abusing my mom. My tears were also a release of so much pain, which was also a nurturing in disguise. When you're able to free yourself from even some of your emotional pain, you allow yourself the space for nurturing. We'll never be free of all pain and suffering. I believe it's part of the human experience and process. But we can certainly work through some pain or trauma that may be holding us back.

This behavior and environment went on for many years until the last day, the final straw day. This day was the worst day of them all. My phone rang, answering this call; I heard my mom's voice; she was in tears. I can hear her body shaking through her voice as she utters these words, "Dawn, can you *please* come to the house right now?! My dad was fighting with my brother, and it was bad. Without going into the harsh traumatic details, this was the last day my dad was in that house, and my mom filed for divorce after 25 years of marriage. My dad moved on (not peacefully) continuing with his drinking. On the final day of his week-long, alcohol-binging vacation in 2009, his girlfriend stepped out for ten minutes to get some items from the store. He took a sleeping pill, went to bed, had a heart attack, and died. Saying goodbye to him was not easy, but it came with a level of peace. That chapter in my life was over.

I married Kevin, the love of my life and high school sweetheart, in 1987. This was a very big deal for me. My whole life, I was made to feel I wasn't good enough. If my father couldn't love me for who I was, then who could possibly ever love and accept me? This was all very confusing for me. I was not a problem child and didn't get into trouble. My grades were never that great, but there wasn't a way for me to improve them living in his environment.

I knew Kevin and I would be married forever as soon as we started dating. I wanted him as my partner in life. There is one thing he still professes to this day, that he saved me from my dad and my dysfunctional home. His nurturing of my mind and definitely my soul was the life preserver I truly needed. Along with being Kevin's wife, another thing I most wanted to be was a mother. I wanted children on a deep soul level.

In February 1993, at the age of 46, my mother gave birth to my new baby sister. If that wasn't crazy enough, I was also pregnant. When my mother shared the news of her pregnancy of six months, I said to Kevin, "Wouldn't it be great to be pregnant at the same time as my mom?" First try, it happened!

The day before my mother gave birth, I received the news that the child I was carrying had died in the 8th week; I was 12 weeks along. My mother was distraught. While lying in her hospital bed preparing for delivery, she says to me, "I understand if you can't be here for this, it is truly okay if you need to leave, I am so sorry you are going through this." This was not an option. I needed to be there for my mom. My sister Jen and I were there for the entire experience. I cut the cord and welcomed my new baby sister onto the earth plane. Wow, what a wild emotional experience that was!

The following day was my time to have a surgical procedure to remove the deceased fetus from my womb. It was also my time to start the process of nurturing myself from what started to be one of the most exciting times of my life to being one of the most devastating. I deeply wanted to be a mother!

In March of 1995, that dream came true! Kevin and I had our first child, our daughter. Then in 1996, we had our son. My life filled up with people and pets to nurture.

Connecting to my inner nurturer has always been my main focus. I was always asking the question: *Who is on my radar at the moment, and how can I serve?* When I became a mother, I struggled with nurturing myself. There was always someone needing something. I was on call 24/7, 365. FYI I still am, but I have grown over the years with nurturing myself. Meditation happens daily, in and out of the shower. Reading soul-nurturing books and enrolling in and practicing new and deeper ways of helping others heal their emotional, mental, and spiritual bodies is where it's at. I have used Reiki, crystals, essential oils, color, mediumship, and intuitive spiritual counseling for starters. As a mother nurturer, I am following the calls and whispers from my soul.

Kevin and I were both raised Catholic, and we continued following our upbringing path. To give you a taste of my dedication to nurturing my spirituality, I went to church every day before school started when I was in Catholic elementary school. That was my raw hunger being fed as a child.

When our children came of age to perform their first confession and first communion, I signed on as a teacher in our church, teaching our children's classes. It brought me so much joy knowing I was sharing teachings of love, forgiveness, and overall doing good deeds in this world. After all, this is what we're here for, right?

My entire life up to that point and a few years into teaching CCD, I had this deep feeling and utter hunger for going deeper—much deeper than I was being taught. We're talking soul deep. That inner knowing told me this was my time to raise the roof and step out of the box—like *way* out of the box I was being kept in. My mind was being fed a little of my spirit but none of my soul, and I really needed some soul food.

The searching began! I became a Reiki master/teacher, which opened up my intuition on a level I hadn't experienced before. I knew things at a deeper level, for myself and also for others. I think I possessed a level of this deeper knowing my whole life, it just didn't get much attention. I have visions and knowings happening more and more frequently, so I nurtured and grew this new level of spirituality and these experiences. These experiences have been healing for myself and my clients, as I have now begun to branch out and help others on their journeys.

One spiritual thing led to the next, and I followed this path, allowing the growth of all parts of me. This new level of living and thinking has played an enormous role in the continuing of moving on and up.

Learning and growing through all the experiences, classes, modalities, and connections—both human and angelic—I can honestly say I am where I am because of the trauma and beauty that has come my way. Life has its way of teaching through pleasant and unpleasant experiences, and we—individually and collectively—inevitably grow. I didn't believe this as a child living in my environment, but through resilience, support, and deep nurturing, here I am, writing this for you, for me, and for all of us.

Your truths change as you grow. You are normal, just as you are!

Spend moments of your precious time connecting and reflecting, learning your truths, whatever they are. Grow and shine your light even brighter than you did yesterday.

THE TOOL

Connect with your Inner Nurturer

I now invite you to spend a few moments learning a new process of connecting to and going deeper with your inner nurturer. Feel free to hold a crystal, light a candle, invite your angels and guides to be nearby, or whatever you're comfortable with while connecting and plugging in.

Close your eyes softly and bring your awareness to your heart. Become aware of its beating, knowing this process is how your life began. Place your left hand on your heart and your right hand on your belly. Take three deep cleansing breaths, inhaling through your nose, exhaling out of your mouth. You can even say "ahhhhh" out loud as you exhale. Notice a bright white light shining out from your heart center. As you focus on this light, it grows brighter and brighter, shining out in all directions. Connect with this light, becoming one with it. This light has much wisdom to share with you. Now see this light going up, higher and higher, connecting to your higher self, God, or what you believe in as your Divine Being, your Divine Nurturer. Now see this light going down, deeper down into the center of the earth. Connect to its heart. Feel the rhythm of her heartbeat. Feel yourself being connected above and below. You are a divine being of this connection.

Bring into your consciousness a question or challenge that you would like guidance on. As you remain one with this light, you begin to receive images, sounds, feelings, knowings, perhaps even smells, coming into your awareness. These experiences all have messages for you within them. Sit with this connection as long as you'd like, receiving, relaxing, and allowing all that wants to come through you to do so. When you feel complete in this sitting, bring your awareness back to the present time, wiggle your fingers and toes, and open your eyes. As soon as you are back in your awareness, I invite you to write down all that came through so that you can use it as your guide and follow its wisdom.

Use this practice often to create an automatic response to your inner nurturer, so when you're in need of this connection, you will be able to be in the flow of this wisdom with much more ease. This practice is yours, use it, tweak it, grow from it, and most of all, connect with your inner nurturer in a way that serves your soul.

As a side note, if you use a crystal or candle or sit in the same chair or space, this can be a great tool to use to connect more easily each time you sit with this practice.

I am signing off for now and sending much love and blessings to you on your journey.

I hope our paths cross again. Until then, be well.

Dawn Simpson is an Intuitive Spiritual Life Coach, Energy Healing Guide, and Medium. She uses the many tools she has learned to assist others with connecting to their higher selves and the Angelic realm so they too can create the changes they are seeking. With her angelic healing team, Dawn has also created classes/workshops and a line of Divine sprays that assist with moving forward, meditation, love of self and along with others, chakra cleansing, and much more. Dawn's passion her entire life has been to help others feel better, allow opportunities for healing, connect them to their higher selves and the spirit realm, and create space for living from their souls.

Dawn is also a Reiki/Master/teacher, ordained minister, and works with crystals.

Being on many radio shows, TV shows and writing a children's book have also been some big accomplishments.

One of Dawn's deep passions is connecting to horses and bringing messages through for their people or their foster parents.

It's her belief that as we go through our lives, learning from our experiences and living our truths, we deepen in our soul's growth.

Becoming a wife, mother, and grandmother all play a role in helping me deepen as a Divine being living on this earth plane. To connect with Dawn, and see her current classes/workshops and products, visit https://www.angeldawning.com

CHAPTER 19

THE DEPTH AND BREADTH OF LOVE

AN UNEXPECTED JOURNEY

Rev. Joy Resor, Spiritual Mentor, Joy Bringer

MY STORY

L O V E...
O ne
V oluminous
E nergy

    L O V E...
    O ur
    V aried
    E xperiences

We're loved, loving, and lovable.
Let's repeat that, dear reader—
We're loved, loving, and lovable. . .

. . .though we may not know this, feel this, or act like this is true. . .until we do.

May this chapter offer a view into *The Depth and Breadth of Love* through my experiences, informing your journey of loving.

Love at Any Distance

Let's observe a youthful, alluring couple early in marriage, loving their first-born daughter. When she nears two, they conceive anew; I'm who they await. Weeks before my on-time birth beneath July's Thunder Moon, expectant mom and toddling sister slumber in the liver-scented Brooklyn apartment of her parents, close to Ebbets Field.

Is mom's older brother Harvey present, too? I'm not sure.

To this day, I still have the delightful book he sent for my birthday over 50 years ago - Loudmouse by Richard Wilbur, 1968

Uncle Harvey

You are mom's only sibling,
her big brother who builds radios, loves opera,
the one who lights her night sky with stars.

As a young man, you join ROTC,
find yourself on active duty in a fox hole
where your brain waves crash in tumult.

Institutionalized, medicated, isolated.

Mom's parents tell her to sail far away,
to float a happy life, not to tie a rock
around her ankle and jump overboard.

She sinks anyway.

I think she stows you away, holds you
bone to bone until she indents her soul
with boulder-sized guilt.

As a little girl when I ask about you,
mom's stormy answers keep me quiet.
I stop casting your name out loud
but I continue to drop lines.

On Valentine's Day in my 45th year,
you surface by phone, tell me
you've saved all 18 of my letters.

I float on the waves of your voice,
sit down to pen my 19th letter to you.

Uncle Harvey, across the miles, we share love uncle to niece and back again. While we've barely been in the same state or room, we never stop loving.

Aunt Bobbie loves from her full life in New York. Rarely, she travels to Ohio for a visit, or we travel east. Annually, I skip to the mailbox for this long-distance aunt's card, which thrills me. Inside, she's straightly underlined <u>Happy Birthday</u> *twice* in red pencil, adding matching dollars for the years I'm turning: $7 turning seven, $8 turning eight, $9 turning nine. . .

In every photo, Aunt Bobbie displays finesse, wearing a smart frock and a bright red-lipstick smile beneath a flowing crown of thick, black hair. This maiden aunt teaches students in NYC, traveling across the world when she's free.

On dad's side, meet Aunt Beth, his oopsie-daisy baby sister who enters when he's 18 years old, with brothers 16 and 14. Their Racine, Wisconsin mom is Ruth/Nana, a 7Up-loving, domineering woman who tells Beth she's a mistake, treating her as such while hounding her. Beth eventually joins the Red Cross to serve in Vietnam during the war, traveling where Mom won't follow.

Again, though we're seldom together, Aunt Beth and I share love as we're able. On long car rides in the back seat, she teaches us fun songs as her fists gingerly pummel our backs before a tickle.

Family History

> *. . .Nana pays us*
> *a dollar to write her*
> *a letter.*
> *I hunch over the task*
> *with a gaggle of spinning*
> *thoughts hanging near.*
> *My father hates his own*
> *mother, this Nana who*
> *whines from Wisconsin.*
> *When dad was eight,*
> *she threw his birthday watch*
> *against a wall,*
> *shattering it*
> *along with something*
> *inside my father that*
> *rages the rest of his life.*

We're (usually) conceived in love to be loved, loving, and lovable, followed by days, events, and people that may hamper our journeys to feel loved, loving, and lovable.

Are you riding the waves of blessed days?

Are you lamenting intentions gone awry?

Have you suffered long enough?

Life has fleet feet. We're designed to love what's before our hearts that are open rather than living in our heads that spin with issues from the past or worries of the future.

Love Relayed Heart to Heart

It's bigger than both of us! Blares the card Wally (not his real name) hands me before we drive to Fanny's Restaurant for dinner.

Yes! There's something palpable between us that feels like love or a connection we can't resist. Is it karma?

We're engaged after nine months, married less than a year later, and raise two sons in an arrangement echoing an earlier era. Wally leaves for work before we awaken, often traveling to connect with clients while I manage our sons and home, rehashing or releasing past issues, depending on the day. Returning, he's a joyful and playful dad with the boys; random objects and little ones catapult through the air to a chorus of squeals and laughter.

My sensibilities are routinely challenged by exuberant male antics since I straddled the Rambler's hump on the floor as the quiet, long-legged, middle of three girls. Retreating to calm myself when needed, I fingered piano keys in the basement or sat on a large rock in the sun, penning poems in my own little corner in my own little world.

Early in our parenting days, Wally instructs me.

"Joy, a mom wakes up to feed her children breakfast."

Really?

I literally didn't know that a mom gets up with her kids because our mom loved us differently.

> *Alone in the tiled kitchen on silent feet,*
> *I pack my paper sack the same each morning—*
> *half a jelly sandwich, Twinkie, bag of chips.*
> *After school, I fish the house key from my blouse*
> *as fear nibbles, slip into a silent house, lock the door. . .*

Wally's teachings give me gratitude for guidance to do better, along with sadness that my mom inadvertently left out key utensils in a mother's tool kit.

As our sons mature, something vexing occurs. Rage flies through my lips onto Andrew when he heatedly badgers Kevin, and I'm aware that my dad's intense anger from long ego erupts through me onto my son—unbidden, unwelcome.

I pray on my knees until I'm freed; please release me from passing down to Andrew the irate words dad slung at us. This isn't how I want to speak to him.

Unlike Mom, who was always late, I retrieve our sons on schedule when practices end. Andrew pleads to transfer schools due to bullying and to follow his best friend. After 18 months, he's ready to return. To this day,

Andrew appreciates how I extended love, honoring his feelings both ways while convincing Wally to shift beyond stale patterns, allowing his son a bit of grace.

In the summer of 2019, Andrew and Kevin marry their sweethearts seven weeks apart, following years of learning, living, and traveling hither and yon. I'm glad they love differently than the way Wally and I dove in. It feels wonderful that Wally coached me to excel as a mom while I coached him to love our sons without an agenda. Consequently, despite our marriage ending after our sons grow up, Andrew and Kevin are wonderful husbands, living into gifts rippling outward from a loving start.

Loving Sunrise Mornings in Slippered Feet

He first notices me from his station behind the Deli counter where I shop, receiving a full-on body buzz (energetic goosebumps that advise him to pay attention). I notice him, as well, as the smiling, tall employee who rushes forward to serve me sliced turkey.

A few weeks later, at the library, I see him enter, heading towards me.

"What are you checking out? I'm Ben; what's your name?"

"A little of this and that. My name is Joy."

Later, when we're dating—

"Joy, I nearly fainted hearing your name. Leading up to the day I saw you in the library, I kept seeing bumper stickers, Don't Postpone Joy."

He writes:

. . .You warm my cold cabin more than any fire, you bring light, shining it into my dark cobwebby corners of self and throw that light upon it with tenderness and laughter. . .

I write:

> *wet dogwood leaves drip*
> *into this cloudy morning*
> *the day brings sun, you*

We move in together, loving one another within sweet routines and road trips north, two poetic souls who love playing with words and sharing presence.

"Over dinner with your sister and her family, Ben, no egoic nonsense niggled; a quiet mind let me be awake to each person and moment, which was amazing."

Ben takes my hand for *walkabouts* in the yard, showing me shadows of new blossoms on tender stalks. We meander forest paths, shell black walnuts, and watch fireflies in the treetops.

Sunrise mornings call me to slip outside in slippered feet. Loving the chill of breathing into unique symphonies of changing light with birdsong, I take photos across our backyard hill, posting online: *To Our Wild and Wondrous Wednesdays! To Our Festive Fridays! To Super Spectacular Saturdays!*

At a conference in Kansas, a CD by Rev. Faerie Elaine Silver rings true to my depths; a month later, I learn she'll sing nearby. Attending the Saturday event, I'm greeted by welcoming, loving souls—*Alliance of Divine Love Ministers*—whose energy invites me to learn more. When we pause for a break, I scoot over to the ADL table for an understanding of this ministry, which feels like a fit. I sign up for the next round of training. https://www.allianceofdivinelove.org/

The Ben bubble bursts when a zippy woman bounces between the conference and my table at a Coptic event, visiting, trying on wares, inviting me for tea.

"Joy, you haven't had a lot of experience with men. What if Wally was *good,* Ben was *better,* and your *best* is yet to come?"

Her words don't jive at first, but driving home, musings stir my paltry pot of partners.

Could someone be better for me than Ben? Hmmm, maybe Liz is right. I haven't had much experience.

When I bring up the topic over pasta, his response surprises me, "I've been feeling it, too."

Neither one of us mentions that we haven't made love in months.

"You can have the master bedroom," Ben says the next day after work, as the aroma of fresh-baked zucchini bread fills our senses. "I'll move to the lower level, and let's continue sharing this house as friends."

"I'll give it a try," I say.

How about that? Though I feel excited to speedily vamoose since our vibrations no longer match, my reply to Ben echoes Wally's replies to try. Well, there you go; I'm not sure if this will work, but we'll experiment. Maybe we can share expenses, kindness, and friendship for a while.

March brings a spate of Netflix nights with Ben in my home office until I awaken feeling bored and restless. Two shakes later, I open to evening potlucks calling me to spread my wings out and about.

"I'm Joy Resor, and I'm writing a book of essays, poems, and questions to inspire joy called *Go In Joy! An Alphabetical Adventure."*

Heading to the parking lot to leave, a short, balding man calls me over.

"My guides told me I'd find joy soon, and here you are. I can't believe it! I'm Dan (not his real name), and these are my housemates; join us Friday night for a gathering. If you give us your number, we'll text the address."

Ever punctual, mine's the first car to arrive. Dan greets me, offering to tweak my frame with chiropractic, which seriously works for me. Next, I skedaddle to my car for the bin of Joy on Your Shoulders (J.O.Y.S) wares in exchange for the impromptu adjustment.

I can't believe Dan selects Joy and Sing; this morning, I circled those words in an angelic devotional. And the synchronicities keep coming. His birthday is the same as Kevin's, he served in the Vietnam war, and Kevin and Anna are traveling at this moment in Vietnam on their nine-month world tour. These signs call me to pay attention, like Ben and his full-on body buzz.

Dan and I begin dating, which leads to hugely unexpected places.

He's good for my esteem, encouraging me to shimmy in ways I earlier didn't. We travel in my vehicle (for he has no car) to Atlanta, where he adjusts clients, and we visit his friend; she's a colonics practitioner who leads me past decades of despair. At an Asheville picnic, a woman invites me to a weekly circle where each soul knows a book I've never heard of, *The Way of Mastery.*

Before returning from a spiritual convention, Ben says Dan's moved in with him and out-of-town me.

What?!

How on earth did this happen? Well, it's water under the bridge. And, yes, Dan and I have an amazing run with the evolution of my needs, though we end a tad past due. (Yes, I'm a slow learner.)

Do you consider boundaries, and how do you manage them?

Do you sometimes stay silent as a kindness? Who does that serve?

"Hey, Ben."

"Hey Joy, welcome home. Today I saw a fresh sign on a new rental down the street."

How about that? It's time to say goodbye to morning sunrises in slippered feet.

Love is Moment to Moment Surprises

Patterns.

How well do we notice the (egoic, habituated) patterns we're living?

Experience teaches me that awakening to patterns lets us live into newness beyond our imaginings.

After dating a trio of post-divorce partners, a knowing enters: I'm living a pattern it's time to release. Soon, a friend tells me about Sue, who reads my soul record (Akashic), giving me an understanding for today.

Really? Thoughts hover near about this being hokey pokey, crazy, and something that won't result in anything. Yet, a deeper part of me believes in my friend's referral for my highest good. I religiously light a candle each morning to read the transliterated Latin prayer out loud, which does release me from the eternal pattern.

Wow!

Thank you!

Yes!

I breathe newly into who I am.

Before long, my energy calls to a dear man who sees me radiating colors in a black and white world.

"Hello, Joy."

"Hello, Michael."

We share *complete* moments of presence Sunday mornings before services at Unity for months into years. He reads *Go In Joy! An Alphabetical Adventure,* the first book through my heart and hands, inviting me to don my author beanie for a book study he leads.

He calls, asking if I'll meet him as friends for lunch, no pressure.

Over soup and salad, I announce, "I don't need a man, though I love being in a relationship."

In time, we lean closer.

"I'd like to start a spiritual practice," he says.

In the morning and evening, I read to Michael on the phone *The Little Prince* and *The Way of Mastery*.

Covid arrives.

I'll invite Michael to shelter in place with me. We've been traveling (I pack The Way of Mastery; he surreptitiously stows kites in the trunk), loving, discovering, and playing in the sandbox together for over two years. I can't imagine breathing into days without him by my side.

After a few months, I extend a new invitation:

"Will you move in with me?"

When our rent climbs in the fall of 2021, I relay the news.

"Let's buy a house," he says.

And we do.

We feel love's presence calling us to buy this house.

We're two humans loving ourselves and one another who've been together for four years so far.

Loving one another enables us to change, grow, and express our authentic selves more than before.

We love to create.

We love to extend the good, the holy, and the beautiful.

We're loved, loving, and lovable.

We love differently than we ever have before.

THE TOOL

Enliven Your Loving

> *. . .It doesn't matter the age of our relations, conventional or unorthodox, we suffer and learn by heart. . .*
>
> ~Terry Tempest Williams

1. Journal to understand your clan:

- Write to separated family, mail a letter afterward
- Forgive yourself and those who didn't love you well
- Lean into extra connecting with goodness
- Appreciate your journey because of your relations
- Slow your pen on the page, revealing mysteries

2. Heal wounds that keep you unhappy:

- Add movement into your day
- Give up practices that aren't healthy
- Consider energy healing for generational issues
- Carve out space to embrace yourself in silence
- Seek solutions beyond band-aids

3. Kick up love for your sweet self:

- Forge a truce with your inner critics
- Honor your needs more fully
- Release what's not working for you
- Rest when you're tired
- Stop racing through your days

4. Enhance your love by working with another

- Pick another's loving heart
- Sign up for spiritual mentoring
- Join a circle that aligns for you
- Start a gathering you'll love
- Call your big or little sibling

Joy is an Alliance of Divine Love Minister and author with a certification in spiritual direction who serves as a mentor, wedding officiant, and joy-bringer to those who suffer. Her experience includes a B.S. in Mass Communications from Miami of Ohio and facilitating classes and workshops for awakening women and inner-city transitional youth when she's not traveling.

Joy lives in western North Carolina, where she writes books and is a frequent guest on podcasts and radio shows. She was born in Brooklyn, New York, but lived most of her life in Ohio, where she and her husband raised two sons before moving south, followed by divorce. She loves her partner Michael, hula hooping in sunbeams, and co-creating evermore to inspire others. After a ride and a half of lessons, Joy loves mystical experiences, aha moments, and guiding others to love life more than before.

https://www.joyonyourshoulders.com
joy@joyonyourshoulders.com
https://www.facebook.com/JoyOnYourShoulders
https://www.instagram.com/joyresor/?hl=en
https://www.linkedin.com/in/joyresor/

CHAPTER 20

SEEKING SOLACE

FINDING HEALING AND JOY IN NATURE

Terri Hawke, Naturalist, Animal Communicator, Energy Healer

MY STORY

Oh my god, who the fuck am I now? A piece of me literally died at that moment.

The frogs nearby are singing loudly, looking for a partner. They will soon fill the ponds and puddles with gelatin-looking egg masses. Robins greet the early morning sun with their dawn chorus, and soaring red-tailed hawks search for food to share with their mate sitting on eggs. Myriad shades of green are starting to emerge in the forest understory filling the air around me with a sweet intoxicating scent. The vibrant magenta of salmonberry and red-flowering currant brighten the longer days. Red alders share their pollen with the whole world, and the woods are full of the pungent earthy scent of skunk cabbage. The air feels fresh on my skin and in my lungs. The evergreen state is coming alive with the promise of new life.

I'm out walking to heal and to find a spot of joy. What brought me here? My son died a few weeks ago, and I'm seeking solace by connecting to the air, earth, water, animals, and plants. I'm alone now and doing what I've done since I was a child, communing with nature.

The call came one Friday evening just after 5 p.m. "Hello." On the other end was my daughter-in-law sobbing, "He's cold." My insides went numb. I asked, "Is he stiff?" "Yes," she replied. My 47-year-old son was gone. He died alone and suffered as his liver poisoned him, no longer able to process the alcohol he depended on to get him through his daily emotional pain—my only child.

Oh my god, who the fuck am I now?

A piece of me literally died at that moment. I drove the 15 minutes to the small trailer he lived in alone. Once there, I sat in the backseat of the Crisis Recovery Counselor's small car while my daughter-in-law sat in the front seat. We discussed what would happen next. At one point, the counselor and the police officer asked, "Do you want to see his body?" *Oh, hell no!*

I answered, "Yes." I knew if I didn't view his body, the disbelief would slow my grieving process. As I stood there looking at my only child's yellowed and jaundiced body, my entire being was knocked to the ground, yet I stood there feeling numb.

On my way back home, I had to stop and release a primal scream and uncontrollable sobbing, unable to see the road. After a few minutes, I was able to continue driving. I slept for three hours that night, tossing and turning as every stage of grief rambled out of control through my mind. Shocked, devastated, broken open: none of these words are strong enough to describe the feeling of losing my only child—the child I brought into this world five days before I turned 17. We grew up together and became close in the last few years.

The next morning, I felt like I wanted to run until I fell flat on my face, kissed the ground, melted into the soil, and just disappeared into the earth's dampness. I wanted to scream until I could no longer swallow and cry until I was shriveled up to nothing but bone.

The numbness lasted for a few weeks, only lifting when I was out in the natural world, touching the earth, hugging the trees, inhaling the newly emerged sweet scents, and basking in bird song. How does anyone survive such sorrow? By falling back on what I always seek—solace in nature. And, in addition, reaching out to friends, reading about others' experiences moving through such traumatic grief, screaming and sobbing without holding back, holding tightly to my sense of purpose and self-worth, and writing prolifically in a journal or through poetry. Writing helps me express the constant barrage of emotional pain running through my mind and body. These healing methods have had a profound impact on my survival. Haiku is a simple way of expressing what I hear, see, or feel.

My son is now gone.

In his death, my heart breaks open.

His light heals my soul.

In my late 20s, I questioned why I seemed to feel things deeper, experience things stronger, and see things differently than most everyone I was around. In my early 50s, the answer appeared while sitting in a waiting room: a drawing on a magazine cover of a woman sitting on top of a large pile of mattresses with a pea buried beneath—a representation of the Hans Christian Andersen fairy tale *The Princess and the Pea*. The tale is about a test to see how sensitive the princess is which would prove she was a princess. This was a feeling I knew only too well. The Psychology Today magazine article (July/August 2011) explained, like 20% of the population, I am a Highly Sensitive Person (HSP)—to me, it's a gift and a curse.

My son was also an HSP which meant the intense bullying he suffered as a child and teenager took a heavier toll on him than anyone realized at the time. No one had the tools to recognize and help him overcome the accompanying anxiety and depression. Since discovering my gift, I have found ways to live happily in this world. But now, I face the greatest challenge. Bearing the unbearable, as one of the book titles I'm reading says.

How did I discover my ease in connecting with nature? On visits to my maternal grandfather's rural backyard I was introduced to a den of hibernating garter snakes by him. "I have a surprise for you, Trixie" (his nickname for me), he said one day. Excitedly I asked, "What, Grandpa?" I marveled at their numbers coiled together, their stripes intertwined in the mass. He taught my mom to notice the birds, which she passed on to me. I grew up on an acre of forest, marsh, stream, and field. Mom pointed out the Canadian robins and flocks of tiny birds flitting around the shrubs when I was a child. I later found out they were varied thrushes and bushtits. I built ground forts and trails and followed banana slugs and millipedes around the forest floor. These are some of my earliest memories of wonder and seeds of connection.

I grew up in a house of turmoil. A misogynistic, narcissistic father, an anxiety-ridden mother, and a developmentally disabled brother made for a difficult childhood. There was little to no support for families back then and plenty of shame. I didn't understand it all, so I disappeared for hours into the woods. I didn't know it then, but I was developing a survival skill, a way of healing. As a troubled, shy, sensitive child, I desperately sought love and acceptance, and as a result, I ended up getting pregnant at 16. I spent a few years experimenting with drugs and alcohol, eventually realizing I had a child and needed to start acting responsibly. I never lost my love or connection to the natural world through those years. By my mid-20s, I was headed to college.

When my son was around six or seven years old, my partner and I noticed these colorful birds in the pink flowers of the backyard hawthorn tree. My partner asked, "do you see those big yellow birds with the white on their wings picking at the flowers?" My son and I looked outside and had no idea what they were. I answered him, "I have no idea, I wish we could see them better!" His dad gifted us a pair of binoculars, and my obsession with birds began. We bought the *Golden Guide to Birds* and identified the birds as evening grosbeaks. I found an easy way to connect again, my son became a birder and naturalist in his own right, and we taught others how to identify birds. Once I connected with birds, I was thoroughly entranced and pulled deeper into the natural world. My life changed, and I pursued a college degree in environmental education to spread the word about understanding our reliance on the natural world and ways to connect to nature. My son, on the other hand, disappeared into his darkness, yet he still observed and loved nature.

So here I am, deeply grieving, walking, talking, and finding my new place in the world. And still, wondering who the fuck I am now without my son. I look to the natural world for my healing and connection to keep me grounded and moving forward. I find little bits of joy in nature—in a bee pollinating a flower, the first emerging butterfly in spring, the songs of the returning migratory birds, the smell of damp earth, the frog and salamander egg masses in the pond, the newly blooming trillium, and the intoxicating sweet scent of fresh cottonwood leaves. My son understood my love of the outdoors, and I know he's free from his pain and probably walking and laughing out there in the forest. That's where we will meet, and that's where I will find the answer to my question of who I am now.

And into the forest, I go, to lose my mind and find my soul.

~John Muir

THE TOOL

This tool has helped me and many others with finding solace in their lives. Awareness of the elements of nature provides opportunities for connecting with nature, restorative writing, and deep healing.

Let's deepen our connection by spending some time communing with nature. You can do this in your backyard, in a city park, or anywhere you can walk in nature. You can also do this walk by sitting down and closing your eyes.

1. Make sure you're ready for your walk. Bring water, a journal, a pen, and anything else you need.

2. If you're sitting, get comfortable. Find your sit spot in a park, backyard, or wherever you feel safe. If you're walking, take it slow.

3. Start by taking three deep, slow breaths—in through your nose and out through your mouth. Relax your body. Imagine roots going from the bottom of your feet deep into the center of the earth. You can always lie on the ground and imagine sinking into the earth and being enveloped in love. If you're walking, think about stopping to sit or lie down for a few moments.

4. Let it all go for a while—thoughts, stress, to-do lists, aches, and pains and be in the moment in this place.

5. Focus inward.

6. Listen. What do you hear? Focus on all of the sounds around you. Now, start eliminating those daily human-centered sounds—vehicles, trains, planes, and so on. Concentrate on the natural sounds. Can you hear your footsteps? Frogs croaking? Birds singing? Water nearby—rushing, gliding, babbling? Is there a gentle breeze or heavy wind? Lightly falling rain? Rustling leaves? Insects?

7. Feel into the moments. What does the air feel like? Hot, humid, dry, cool, warm. Hug a tree and lean into it. Can you sense it breathing? What does the bark feel like? The plant leaves? Is there water nearby? If so, is it warm, icy cold, hot?

8. Breathe deep the fresh air. Inhale the scents. Is it spring, summer, fall, or winter? What is the difference in the seasonal scents? The different habitats you might visit? Can you smell the earth? Does the tree bark have a scent? The leaves? Flowers?

9. Observe. Notice the colors around you. Are there tracks on the ground? Did you find a wildlife trail? Look for the small moss, lichen, fungi, pebbles, and insects. Are there holes in trees for woodpeckers? Holes in the ground? Animal poop? Broken stems? Nibbled plants?

10. Taste. Does the air taste? Can you find edible berries? Are there edible plants in the area?

11. Lie, sit or walk as long as you want. If you're sitting or lying with your eyes closed, open them when you're ready.

Take a few more deep breaths and celebrate your new awareness. Once you feel connected to the area, try writing a Haiku or about what you're feeling in your journal. Writing helps capture the moment, anchors your senses, and keeps this energy available for later. Short poetics like Haiku bring your walk to life and create vivid memories for later when you need connection but can't get outside. You can come back to your writing to feel it all over again. Your mind will take you back to those moments.

A Haiku is a three-line Japanese poem and is written as follows:

Five syllables.

Seven syllables.

Five syllables.

Once you're done with your writing, take another deep breath and enter back into your world feeling more connected, joyful, refreshed, and maybe even a little bit healed by being out in nature and feeling into your little space in the natural world. For Haiku inspiration, look for Matsuo Basho's writings.

I find creativity is sparked and healing inspired through writing. It can be a Haiku but also longer writing exercises. Every day I write my three *morning pages*. The book *The Artist's Way* written by Julia Cameron, suggests enhancing creativity by writing three pages daily, in the morning, of longhand writing as a way to do a brain dump. Mine sometimes say nothing of importance, and other days everything of importance. Since the loss of my son, a whole book idea has developed through processing my grief in this way.

Email your Haiku to me at twdwolf@yahoo.com, and I will add it to my blog. A collection of memories and connections to share with others who will be inspired by all of our writing. You can also order your signed copy of the book there.

Resources:

https://greatergood.berkeley.edu/article/item/what_happens_when_we_reconnect_with_nature

https://www.psychologytoday.com/us/articles/201107/sense-and-sensitivity

The Highly Sensitive Person, by Elaine Aron.

The Artist's Way, by Julia Cameron.

Our Wild Calling, by Richard Louv.

 **Terri Hawke** is incredibly intuitive, an animal communicator and energy healer, Reiki practitioner, naturalist, writer, environmental educator, and an animal guardian to Templeton the pom-chi and Maura the cat. Her mission is to bring humans closer to nature through their companion animals and by discovering ways to create a deeper connection to the natural world, which encourages healing and provides joy.

She makes her home in Washington State, where she grew up. She has spent much of her life observing native birds and wandering around ecosystems all over the US. She enjoys showing others the joys of birds. She spends time camping and exploring. She has always felt safe in the natural world.

She received her BA in Environmental Education from The Evergreen State College in Olympia, Washington. She went on to become an interpretive naturalist ranger at North Cascades National Park, Washington State Parks, Edmonds Parks and Recreation, and City of Seattle Parks and Recreation. She also worked for the North Cascades Institute, teaching people of all ages about the natural world.

She recently retired from 21 plus years as an environmental planner for a local government agency. This allowed her to refine her skills in writing technical documents, delineating wetlands and streams, and conducting wildlife and amphibian monitoring.

She is currently a teacher-trainer with the Communication with All Life University and continues to pursue learning opportunities in other healing techniques to help heal animals and work to achieve the best possible results for their companions and caregivers.

She is working on becoming a published author and writing a children's book about grief over losing a companion animal. She also hopes to create a healing environment for other parents who have lost a child.

You can find her at:
https://twdwolfwoman.wixsite.com/terrihawketalk/my-blog
www.critterchatwterrihawke.com
https://www.facebook.com/TerriHawkeCritterChat
twdwolf@yahoo.com
https://3weekalaskajourney.blogspot.com/

CHAPTER 21

THE POWER
OF YOUR STORIES

A YOGIC PATH FOR WRITING TO HEAL

Rebecca Lyn Gold, E-RYT, Founder of Yogic Writing™

MY STORY

The first time I walked into a yoga class, I was in my early 20s and clueless about what I was doing with my life. I dropped out of college, drove across the country from Vermont to California, took a job waitressing graveyard shift at a coffee shop, and spent a lot of time wandering through my days. One day I wandered into a building with a sign on the door that read: "Yoga and Meditation Center." This was not usual in the early 1980s.

I walked into a room full of men and women dressed in white from head to toe, sitting cross-legged on floor cushions, chanting. A man came up to me and told me to take a seat, close my eyes, and breathe. "Your life will change," he said.

I was immediately reminded of a traumatic experience in my early teens when I was recruited by an *Adidam* leader—one of the many cults that sprang up in the early 1970s. I spent several months with a group of latchkey and troubled teens like myself in a home led by an older man posing as a guitar teacher, whose self-proclaimed calling was to *heal our soul* and did so with drugs, sex, and secrets. That experience left me with a deep-rooted cynicism toward anyone claiming to be a guru or preaching a better way to live. The yoga center in Long Beach, California, brought me back to those days. I turned around and walked out of the building as fast as I could.

Yoga, I decided, was not for me.

Life went on, as it does—a marriage, a baby, a divorce. And then a remarriage, two more babies, and a budding writing career. I wrote and published a handful of technical books, a children's biography, a book about adoption, and a lot of feel-good stories for parenting magazines, children's magazines, adoption listservs, and other outlets.

Life was good.

Then something I hadn't planned on showed up, unannounced.

That *something* was depression.

And not just *having a bad day,* but rather a revisit from the debilitating, near-suicidal depression I suffered during my teens. I was, on the outside, happy and healthier than I had ever been, but damn if that heaviness in my shoulder started to make me slump, causing me to walk a little slower, smile a little less, unable to feel joy. It got to the point that I could barely get out of bed, and when I did, all I wanted to do was crawl back in. I didn't want to be with anyone, including my husband, friends, or even my babies. I just wanted to be alone and escape the world.

I stopped writing, publishing, or even wanting to write. I was shut down.

Eventually, with the help of a therapist and medication, I found my way back to my life, although not back to my writing. That book, so to speak, was closed and put back on the shelf.

One day, my teenage daughter told me, "Mom, you have to go to yoga."

"Been there, done that," I said. "No, thanks."

But she insisted and told me she found an awesome yoga teacher at a nearby gym. Because she kept insisting, I went and watched beautiful young bodies doing handstands and headstands and moving in all sorts of contorted positions with ease while I could barely touch my toes. I loved watching my daughter with her newfound passion but once again decided that yoga was not for me.

Fast forward ten years, we moved from California to Rhode Island, my kids were becoming more independent (a.k.a. needing me less), and my desire to write and publish came back with a vengeance.

Every time I sat down to write, stories from my past would sneak up to the page. And every time that happened, I'd quickly close my journal or my computer. I did not want to go there to write about moments in my life that weren't happy ones.

Instead, I tried to write stories for children and feel-good stories about family life, like I used to publish in years past, but my writing felt stale, unimportant, unauthentic, and uninspiring.

It hadn't occurred to me that I was now living in the town where I grew up, where the trauma of my teenage years took place. Clearly, it was time for me to write my own life stories. But I couldn't get past the first sentence or two.

I heard that Natalie Goldberg was hosting a writers retreat at Kripalu Center for Yoga and Health, a few hours away from where I lived. I devoured her book *Writing Down the Bones,* so I thought that might be just what I needed to get unstuck.

Natalie urged us to try the different yoga and meditation offerings throughout the week, so I did. And, for the first time, I thought yoga was *kind of* interesting. And maybe, just maybe, it wasn't as weird or as difficult as I once thought. And during the week, in between yoga and meditation and sessions with Natalie, I was able to write a little bit, day by day, even stories that were painful. Words were finding their way onto the page.

I was intrigued.

That's all it took for me to dive deep into the research about the science of yoga and meditation and how it could affect my brain and, possibly, my writing. I took multiple workshops and programs, studied with well-renowned yoga teachers, and began a yearlong training with Devarshi Steven Hartman to become a certified Pranotthan yoga and meditation teacher.

One of the most impactful concepts in yogic philosophy I studied was that of the *Pancha kosha.* In Sanskrit (the language of yoga), "Pancha" means five, and "kosha" means layer or sheath. Simply stated, this concept tells us that as human beings, we experience our world through five layers: our physical body (anamaya kosha), our energetic body (pranamaya kosha), our emotional body/mind (manomaya kosha), our intuitive body (vijnanamaya kosha), and our bliss body (anandamaya kosha).

I realized that when I sat down to write, I was connecting with only one layer of experience, that of my thoughts and emotions, my mind. But what about the rest of me? What about the stories that I held in my physical body? My energetic body? My intuitive body?

I became fascinated with this concept and began learning as much as I could about the koshas and practices to ignite each one individually and multiple koshas with each other. Movement for my physical body, breath practices for my energetic body, mudras and mantras for my emotional and intuitive body, and mindful meditation practices to awaken my bliss body.

The more I practiced yoga, meditation, and breathwork, the memories and stories I hid deep within came to the surface.

The pose connected me to the prose.

The breath to the paragraph.

Stories were flowing from my mind through my body to the page. I was creating again. Yoga unleashed me.

My writing practice changed. What used to be a timed ten-minute Natalie Goldberg "Write like your life depends on it" (as Natalie would say) had now evolved into a practice of tuning in to my koshas before I sat down to write, and then I would *write like my kosha depended on it!*

Slowly but surely, my daily practice led me to write my life stories, and with each word, each story that came onto the page, I could feel my body begin to soften, to heal.

This yogic path was inviting me to open up and write my stories. Not just the feel-good happy ones, but *all* of them. The good, the bad, the beautiful, the ugly. Nothing was off-limits.

I wrote stories about my childhood, the breakup of my family home, my experiences in the cult, my divorce, my struggles with infertility, and my path to parenthood. All of it was coming out word by word—story by story. And the more I wrote, the more I felt myself begin to heal, cell by cell.

I call this practice *Yogic Writing*.

The word yoga literally means *union*. The ultimate yogic experience is when we become one with every layer of ourselves and are in alignment with the universe. When this happens, it can feel like we are channeling words onto the page. Our stories write themselves.

I want to share this path I have found from my mat to my memoir with anyone who feels blocked in their creative process and is ready to access and write stories that may be stuck in their mind or body.

I want you to experience the healing power of yogic writing so that you, too, can write your life stories and leave your legacy.

THE TOOL

Use your breath to recall memories and write your stories.

Life stories begin with memory, whether it's an event yesterday or 20 years ago.

Interesting fact: It's impossible for the average human brain to record with total accuracy something that happened just minutes ago. So, of course, remembering events that happened years ago will not be 100% accurate by a long shot.

The good news: What we do remember mostly are the feelings and emotions about the event.

The better news: Feelings and emotions are universal. So even if our reader has never experienced an event similar to what we are writing about, they will connect with the feeling behind it.

The best news: The more you write about a particular memory, the more you can retrieve the details about it, and it can lead to more memories that have been hiding within. So, writing can actually improve memory. How about that!

This practice will take 30 minutes total. You need a timer or your phone and a pen and paper or a journal. It's important that you do the writing by hand because it gets another kosha (your physical body) into the practice. Not only that, but multiple studies have shown that regions of the brain associated with memory are more active when writing by hand as it promotes deep encoding in a way that typing does not.

To get into a space of deep writing and conjure up memories, we can tap into our pranamaya kosha (our energetic body) with a breath practice.

This particular breath practice is called **Alternate Nostril Breathing.** The primary function of Alternate Nostril Breathing is to restore balance in the left and right hemispheres of your brain. It slows down your heart rate, lowers your blood pressure, and is very relaxing and calming. When you are in a state of balance and calmness, your mind can retrieve memories that may have been hidden, stored, or hard to access. It's also a practice suited well for a writing prompt that deals with opposites—as shown in the exercise below.

STEP 1: BREATHE

1. Start by placing your thumb gently on your right nostril and take a deep inhale through your left nostril.

2. Then with your ring finger, close off your left nostril (so both nostrils are closed) and hold your breath for a few counts. Then release your thumb from the right nostril and exhale through your right. Pause.

3. Now inhale through your right nostril, place your thumb back on the right nostril (so both are closed), then release your ring finger from the left nostril and exhale through the left. Pause.

4. Continue this practice for a minimum of ten rounds or five minutes. Inhale/hold/switch/exhale. Repeat.

Feel the breath *(prana)* cleansing both nostril channels and slowing your heart rate down. After ten rounds of this Alternate Nostril Breathing (or when you feel ready), pick up your pen and journal and **smile!** *(Not kidding, it really does help!)*

STEP 2: WRITE

Set your timer for ten minutes and write the prompt: *I remember. . .*

Keep your hand moving and pen on the page—don't worry about spelling or grammar—just keep writing, *I remember. . .I remember. . . I remember. . .* repeatedly until something surfaces. Your brain will eventually kick into gear, and something will emerge. Trust me. Trust yourself.

STEP 3: BACK TO THE BREATH

When your timer goes off, finish your last sentence, and then go back to the alternate nostril breathing for ten more rounds or five minutes.

Inhale left/hold/switch/exhale right.

STEP 4: BACK TO THE PAGE

Set your timer for ten minutes and write the prompt: *I don't remember.*

Keep your hand moving and pen on the page and keep writing, *I don't remember. . .I don't remember. . .I don't remember. . .* until something surfaces.

STEP 5: TRANSCRIBE AND CRAFT!

When your timer goes off (or when you feel complete in your writing practice), look at both writings with compassion, as if someone you love wrote them. In other words, don't invite your inner critic to the party! Now it's time to transcribe what you wrote onto your computer and have fun with editing and crafting and turning it into a life story.

You can use this practice of Alternate Nostril Breathing with opposing prompts such as:

If only I had known; I wish I never knew. . .

Lies I told my parents; Lies my parents told me. . .

The secret that devoured me; The secret that saved me. . .

To learn more about yogic writing and how to incorporate practices to write your life stories, I offer a free three-day yogic writing journey. https://yogicwriting.com/3-day-yogic-writing-journey/

My book: *From Your Mat to Your Memoir: Creating a Yogic Writing Practice to Find and Write Your Life Stories* will be released in the fall of 2022.

Rebecca Lyn Gold is an author, editor, writing coach, and yoga and meditation teacher. She is the founder of YogicWriting.com, a practice that utilizes the philosophies and disciplines of yoga, meditation, and journaling for writers of all levels to break through resistance, uncover memories and write their life stories.

Rebecca has studied with esteemed memoirists, including Natalie Goldberg, Julia Cameron, Dani Shapiro, and Candace Walsh, among others. She received her RYT 200 yoga and meditation teacher certification through the Pranotthan Yoga School in Rhode Island, with an additional certification in Yin yoga. She is also a graduate of the MBSR (Mindfulness Based Stress Reduction) program.

Rebecca served on the board of the Society of Children's Book Writers and Illustrators (SCBWI) and founded the first international region in Argentina and Uruguay. She is the author of *Till There Was You: An Adoption Expectancy Journal*, *A Wizard Called Woz: a biography of Stephen Wozniak*, *How To Write It Funny* with Amy Koko, *That's Why We're Here: Stories from passionate James Taylor fans,* and *From Your Mat to Your Memoir: Creating a yogic writing practice to find and write your life stories.* Rebecca's memoir, *A Friend Named Sunny Skies: A Memoir of Trauma, Healing, and the Music of James Taylor,* will be released in the Spring of 2023.

Rebecca Gold has been teaching and coaching writers of all ages for over two decades. She leads workshops, retreats, and online programs using YogicWriting.com as a tool to find and write life stories.

You can find Rebecca on Facebook (Facebook.com/YogicWriting), Instagram@YogicWriting, or email Rebecca@YogicWriting.com

CHAPTER 22

REBOOT, RESTORE, AND HEAL YOUR BODY

HOW TO DETOX THE RIGHT WAY

Birgit Lueders, MH, CCII

MY STORY

Just as I finished a live TV interview about detoxing, an elderly lady came up to me and asked, "What does food mean to you emotionally?"

I was quite taken aback by this question since I hadn't thought about the emotional value of food for a long time. Most people, especially food lovers, would respond that food is happiness, togetherness, excitement, cultural, and adventurous.

As an herbalist and iridologist, food to me means medicine. I know that ginger helps with digestion, carrots improve eyesight, beets support the liver, and sprouts nourish the adrenals, but at that very moment, I had no idea what food meant to me emotionally.

From early childhood, I was a very picky eater. I loved desserts more than anything else. You could say the quote, *"Life is short, eat dessert first,"* was truly my slogan. My food memories were about my grandmother's German chocolate cake and poppy seed strudel.

The only way my parents could talk me into eating regular food was the promise of having dessert after the meal. I loved everything from ice cream to lollipops, Sunbursts candies to cookies and chocolate. I even went so far as helping my mom with random jobs around the house so I could earn a few coins to buy candy.

I think this obsession started quite early because I had an overly sensitive stomach. For example, after eating regular German cuisine like breaded veal and Schnitzel with potato salad, I would feel nauseous and exhausted. But I never experienced that with desserts and sweets. They always made me feel good.

Meat and heavy creamy sauces created physical pain in my stomach like bloating, cramping, and nausea. Unfortunately, at that time, nobody taught me about digestive enzymes or proper food combinations. I still remember my mother's shock when I announced that from then on, I would only eat side dishes at dinner because eating meat made me feel ill. At that early age, I didn't know that people who didn't eat meat called themselves, vegetarians.

Even with my dessert obsession, I'm happy to say I never developed an eating disorder. I've always understood the value of listening to my body. I ate when hungry, stopped when full, and avoided the foods that made me feel tired.

But my story didn't end there, and unfortunately, life sometimes throws you a curveball. This was mine. Around the fourth grade, I started to have severe stomach pains, and it turned out I had an infected appendix. After surgery, the doctor came into my room and said to my mom, "Everything went well, but we need to keep your daughter for a few more days in the hospital to make sure she will gain some weight back!" I didn't even understand what he meant, but it turns out he suggested intravenous feeding. I thought to myself, *This is going too far.* I turned to my mom, "There is no way you will let him do this to me. You know I have always been on the skinny side. It doesn't matter what I eat!" Gladly she agreed and took me home earlier despite the suggestions of the doctor.

A year later, at my family doctor's office, the discussion about my weight came up again. "Birgit, I think you would be a great candidate for a mini-vacation on top of the mountains," my doctor said. "It is a retreat specifically for children to receive wellness treatments, which might help you gain some weight."

Mind you, at that time, I loved my mother's home-cooked meals. I was happy and completely carefree. I didn't think anything was wrong with me. I was just a little bit on the lighter side. But my mom thought it would be fun for me to meet new friends and have a vacation in the mountains.

Those three weeks away from my family was anything but fun. I was homesick, and I missed my sisters, family, grandmother's chocolate cake, mom's potato salad, and two cats. Even with the mountain air and healthy organic food choices, I came home skinnier and totally upset by the experience.

During that trip, I became depressed, sad, and lonely. I didn't want to make new friends; I had plenty of friends at home. The feelings of isolation and homesickness caused my digestives system to worsen. This clearly shows that we do not only digest food in the stomach, but we also digest our feelings in the gut. No wonder scientists are starting to call the gut the second brain.

After this experience, my mom realized I was thriving just fine with the love of my family and my entire village. Over these last 40 years, I still remind my mom of that horrible vacation experience, at least once a year.

As of today, I still digest all my feelings in my stomach. At times when I feel stressed or anxious, I'm not very hungry. Others might experience the exact opposite; instead of feeling their emotions, they overcome their worries by filling up with more food.

Food truly reflects our emotions more than we give it credit for. My lifelong journey of living with an extremely sensitive digestive system led me to become who I am now, an herbalist and iridologist. I've made it my life's purpose to educate my clients about the healing power of food while adding an occasional detox.

THE TOOL

DETOX

What is a Detox? It's a diet that frees the body of unwanted toxins that have made their way into the cellular system. For example, if you experience unexplained fatigue, allergies, skin rashes, digestive issues, bloating, etc., it might be time for a reboot (more about that later).

This is where it can get a bit confusing. You might wonder if doing a detox means that you should go on a 21-day water fast or that you should swallow a handful of herbal pills every three hours, forcing you to make endless trips to the bathroom all day long.

Have you heard about a cleanse where you only eat durians? Durian is a fruit that smells like your brother's week-old wet, dirty socks! It turns out this fruit is so smelly that the Philippines has banned it in some public places. I wonder if we could be on this diet while commuting on New York's subways?

How about the one about a woman who created customized detox plans, but before giving her clients instructions, they had to sign a waiver stating they would not publicly reveal their customized plan because of confidentiality? Did I mention that her detox advice was a whopping $7,000 and was the same cabbage diet for every single person? No wonder she didn't want the public to know!

New detox and diet books are published every year. The debate about the correct ratios of proteins to carbohydrates and fats will go on forever. I followed a famous self-proclaimed nutritional guru for 25 years. Anytime he published a new book, he discredited his previous one! In his latest bestseller, he tells us to forget about proteins or carbs, that the answer to health is now all in fats.

The Roman poet and philosopher Lucretius once said, "Food for one man may be bitter poison to another." We all have a different genetic makeup. Some of us have ancestors from South America, and some have ancestors from Alaska. Do we think that we all have the same dietary needs just a few hundred years later?

This is where my background as an iridologist has been extremely helpful. For the last 40 years, the field of Iridology has researched the identification of genetic strengths and weaknesses in DNA through specific indicators in the eyes. For example, people who come from the northern part of the World usually have blue eyes. Iridologists studied the health of people with blue eyes and found that they have tendencies towards kidney weakness, lymphatic system stagnation, joint pain, and allergies, to only mention a few.

What about people who come from the southern part of the world? They usually have darker brown eyes, and their weaknesses are associated with blood sugar imbalances, thyroid weaknesses, mineral (iron) deficiencies, cardiovascular risks, etc.

There are many more colors and signs in the eyes, but I don't want to go too deep into the details of Iridology. I only wanted to demonstrate that no diet fits all. Therefore, if you would like to start a detox on your own, you need to know yourself on a deep level.

Here is the good news, the body is quite sophisticated. Through the organs of detoxification, it can eliminate viruses, bacteria, chemical toxins, fungus, etc. As a matter of fact, the medical world does not support the practice of detoxification to stay healthy.

Unfortunately, our organs of elimination aren't capable of detoxing all the pollution that humanity has created over the last hundred years or so. Our water is filled with fluoride, our earth is filled with pesticides, and our air is full of hundreds of different synthetic pollutants.

Honestly, it is a miracle that more people aren't sick. Just think about the industrial food we eat, especially in the cities. I don't know about you, but to understand the ingredients of some of our food demands a chemical degree, not a gardener's knowledge.

The importance of preventive care has never been more important than today. For the last two years, a virus has paralyzed the entire world and taken many lives. The more we studied the virus, the more we realized that the only weapon we have against it is staying free of chronic diseases. Too many people have underlying issues like blood sugar imbalances, cholesterol build-up, joint inflammation, digestive issues, migraines, asthma, and allergies. If the body is already busy fighting inflammation from chronic issues day in and day out, dealing with a virus can have a life-threatening, devastating outcome.

Therefore, we should integrate an occasional detox, preferably during seasonal changes. This can help the body rid itself of some underlying issues, but how to go about it can be daunting and confusing. Here are a few simple tips on how to reboot, restore, and heal your body through the process of detoxification.

REBOOT

I don't know if you have ever had computer issues. If so, you might have had a laptop for quite a while, and then suddenly, nothing worked from one day to the next. The first thing that most experts tell you to do is to unplug and reboot your computer to see if things might go back to normal.

That same scenario could be true with our bodies. We go through life for 30 or 40 years, and suddenly we start to have indigestion, bloating, acid reflux, constipation, etc. So, it makes sense to try the reboot, which means to stop eating altogether and go on a three-day juice fast.

These days, you can easily order fresh-pressed juices online to start your reboot. After your juice detox, you might feel much better because it gave your digestive system a needed break. If we don't eat solid food all day, the body uses the extra energy to digest old metabolic waste, cleanse the liver, and break down old cellular matter.

Most of my clients feel better after a short juice detox, but it shouldn't be done repeatedly or longer than three days. Here is the reason why every time you stop eating, your digestive system's energy slows down. After a juice fast, most people make the mistake of going right back to eating the same foods they ate before, the foods that caused the issues they were experiencing, and the issues they wanted to eliminate.

Imagine, if you will, a fireplace, you throw in a big, huge wooden log before you start a fire, but it simply won't burn or create heat, right? Well, food works the same way, it has to be broken down in the stomach and then used as energy and fuel for the rest of the body. After a juice fast, the energy from your digestive system is diminished, so you need to slowly turn the heat back up.

Instead of jumping head-first into a juice detox, it's important to prepare your body with a four-day vegan diet. Then you can start your three-day juice fast, followed by a three-day vegan soup diet. This will give your digestive system the appropriate preparation and adjustment to heal and restart its energy again.

RESTORE

Let's assume you have done a juice fast, but you still don't feel better. The moment you started to eat again, all your issues like skin rash, bloating, cramping, allergies, constipation, or acid reflux, for example, came right back. If this is the case, you don't need another extreme detox. Rather, you're in need of nourishment. Over the years, our bodies developed deficiencies in certain minerals and vitamins because of certain medications or eating a diet filled with processed food.

Minerals and vitamins play a significant role in our bodies. For example, magnesium relaxes our muscles, iodine keeps our thyroid happy, and the B-vitamins are involved in the production of hydrochloric acid. Without hydrochloric acid, the body won't be able to break down and absorb amino acids from protein which is vital for cellular and muscular tissue repair.

L-tryptophan, one of the nine essential amino acids, is a precursor for serotonin and melatonin. Melatonin regulates our sleep and serotonin our mood. You might think you don't have a mineral deficiency if you're taking a multivitamin pill, but trust me, the primary problem for people, especially as they get older, is that their digestive system doesn't work as well. If you cannot absorb your nutrients from real food, do you honestly think you can absorb the ingredients from a synthetic one-eighth-inch pill?

I use the word restoring in my holistic practice to mean rebuilding your mineral content within your cellular system. Try to replace a negative food with a positive one. A negative food is food that cannot be broken down without using your own mineral storage. For example, your afternoon Venti latte might make you feel more energized, but it robs your body of vital alkaline minerals, lowers your hydrochloric acid, and fatigues your adrenals. And in case you're not one of the few people who can digest cow's milk after the age of eight, you will experience lots of mucus in your throat, lungs, ears, and sinuses due to your inability to break down casein, the dairy protein, after your shot of latte.

Instead of your trip to Starbucks in the afternoon, check out the tea aisle from a local herbal store or even HomeGoods. Yes, I found some amazing herbal teas there lately. Nettle, dandelion, oat straw, raspberry leaf, and holy basil are all herbs with a high mineral and vitamin content. If you are willing to change from a coffee routine to a tea ceremony, make sure you buy loose herbs and soak them in hot water for at least 30 minutes and up to three hours to get the most benefit from them.

HEAL

The last step of detox includes our emotional wellbeing. I have clients who have tried every single diet and detox out there and still can't seem to lose weight or find relief from debilitating migraines. To find healing, these clients need guidance through an emotional detox.

Most of us are aware that stress can create dis-ease in our bodies, but when it happens, we get confused about how and why we feel the way we do. For example, when somebody goes through an emotionally challenging time like a divorce, financial trouble, or job loss, their sympathetic nervous system becomes the dominant system in the body. In the holistic world, we call this the Fight and Flight System. And it does exactly that, it makes us breathe faster, run faster, hide quickly, and scream louder.

For a body to heal and regenerate daily, it needs to function in the parasympathetic nervous system called the Rest and Digest System. This system regulates all the automatic functions within the body, like absorbing, digesting, and eliminating food, regrowing healthy cells, and removing toxins from the liver.

If a body gets stuck in the Fight and Flight System for an extended period of time due to stress, the immune system becomes weaker and eventually ends up with an autoimmune disorder like thyroid issues, heart palpitations, chronic anxiety, adrenal fatigue, extreme allergies, or viral and bacterial infections.

In this case, healing can only come through exposure to therapies that can help release emotional pain (trauma). I usually suggest methods like emotional freedom tapping, brainwave meditation, cut-the-cord meditation, the golden light meditation, talk therapy, walking barefoot in nature, hugging trees, you get the idea. I call this an emotional detox.

The most important thing is to understand that our bodies are not machines. We are a spirit in a human body. True healing can only come through understanding that our bodies have a physical, emotional, and spiritual layer. Nutrition is only one part of the whole. It might not heal your fears, worries, or sadness, but feeding the body with high nutritional, colorful food combined with acknowledging your emotions along with an occasional detox might be the perfect way to guide you in the right direction.

Birgit Lueders is the mother of two wonderful daughters, Emma and Lisa, living in Philadelphia, Pennsylvania. She is a certified Master herbalist, yoga teacher, Iridology instructor, and wellness coach.

Birgit first learned the values of an organic herbal lifestyle in her home country of Austria. Since 2009 she has operated BirgitCare—a business focusing on health, wellness, and natural healing in Philadelphia, Pennsylvania. Through BirgitCare, she offers personalized wellness coaching to support her clients' emotional, physical, and spiritual wellbeing by using modalities like Iridology, herbalism, nutrition, and colorpuncture.

In 2012 Birgit founded the Center for Iridology, where she teaches Iridology courses around the World and annually in major cities in the USA. In 2020, during the pandemic, she adapted her Iridology courses for online certifications and was able to move her wellness coaching program online.

Throughout the past ten years, Birgit has been a known speaker in her field at numerous national and international EXPO's, a best-selling author on Amazon, while being consistently featured on radio and TV. After being a Fellow, a Diplomat, and the Vice-President of the International Iridology Practitioner Association (IIPA), in 2020, Birgit became President of IIPA.

Birgit Lueders, MH, CCII, Diplomate of Iridology

www.birgitcare.com

www.centerforiridology.com

484-844-5710

CHAPTER 23

BALANCED THINKING

HOW TO LOVE UNCONDITIONALLY

Kelly Karius BSW, RSW, Mediator

MY STORY

"Get out!"

I stood in shock, the reverberation of the door slamming through my ears and echoing into my heart.

What did he just say? Have I just been told to go away?

But I'm a professional! How can he say that to me! He's supposed to be a professional too! Maybe I'm not good enough to do this. I'm probably not. Maybe I need to look more professional? Be more professional? I probably don't have enough experience. Have I ruined my career?

It's the year 2000. A new millennium. A new social work degree. A new private practice. A new client. Her daughter is struggling with the relationship between this man as a teacher and her as a student. He is not just her teacher, he's also the principal of the school. He's hard on her, and she doesn't understand why. In my world, communication is key, and he just slammed the door! He kicked me out of his office, and he slammed the door!

My ears feel hot as my footsteps echo inside my head. I walk away from the Principal's office. I walk past the gym and the changing rooms of the school I attended from grades seven to nine. There is where I terrified myself with the bathroom bloody Mary chant. There is the door to the stage I excitedly went through when I played the stepmother in Cinderella and Marilla in Anne of Green Gables. There is where Tracy had a terrible asthma attack. If I keep going straight instead of leaving, I'll find the home economics room where my friend Karri did all my sewing for me, and right next to it, the room where I volunteered to work with people with disabilities. I smell the 20-year-old cookies baking and feel the laughter and angst of my 12-year-old friends rushing around my shoulders. I walk out the door and breathe deeply of the chill fall air, noticing the orange glow of the early sunset. I let the memories fall away. With these steps past my youth and into the fresh, clean air, I launch into the biggest journey of my life.

I am not that child. That is not my principal's office. I have a job to do.

What is this thought? *I am not professional or experienced enough.*

What is true about this thought? *I am young and new to the profession. I started a private practice very early after just a year in child protection. This seems like it will be a very hard issue to tackle.*

What is not true about this thought? *I am a mother to three kids. I was a late starter to university and have a ton of life experience. I am intuitive, smart, a great communicator, have advocated for people many times before, without a degree, and I know how to ask for help.*

What is another way to think about this? *Even though I am a new social worker, and this is a hard issue, I have all the skills and resources I need to manage this situation, step by step. I don't have to know everything and can seek help when necessary. I can just be who I am.*

Over the next year, I have 20 young clients, Grade 6 students who are being mistreated by their principal/teacher. I'm working with their parents, with systems, with the government. There are times the anxiety about what I'm doing hits so hard. My inner child weeps; my outer adult cries. I go without eating, my stomach turning itself into a macrame plant hanger. I create angst in myself, wondering why no one is paying attention. Children, our most precious resource, are being harmed, and those with the power don't seem to care. I dip my paddle back into anxiety and push into the waters of depression, sinking blackly and hopelessly but always grabbing on to my lifesaver, my balanced thinking mantra.

I'm new, and I have all the resources I need—step by step.

Over time, I learn that this man is using abhorrent teaching techniques. He takes homework out of students' desks and makes them dig through the garbage for it in front of the class. His goal is humiliation and subordination. He hands out in-school suspensions like Oprah giving away cars. One child receives a suspension for not bringing back the outer scraps of paper from a picture that was to be cut out. He dresses up as a serial killer with a bloody hunting suit for Halloween. He tells graphically violent stories and creates assignments that are just as bloody.

I live, work, and raise my children in this small town of 5000 people. Some think we are overreacting. Some quietly urge me to keep going, "You are doing good work." Teachers who have long been friends of my family say, "We can't speak out, it's against our ethics to call out another teacher. Don't stop." The school board has three women on it from my church. I believe they will listen to me. When they don't, I'm heartbroken. They follow the superintendent's lead, who doesn't want to hear anything. I remember babysitting their children and attending church with them, watching them move from teaching careers to school board members. These are good people, and my heart can't reconcile why they won't do anything about this situation. I can't understand why they won't help these children.

What is this thought? *They've broken my heart, and I have no respect for them.*

What is true about this thought? *I'm hurt.*

What is not true about this thought? *My heart is not broken; that's melodramatic. I do have respect for them. I babysat some of their children, and they were lovely parents. I attend church with them, and I pray with them. I was taught by some of them. They are community-minded, good people.*

What is another way to think about this? *Even though I am hurt and feel they are not responding to this properly, I do not have to hold anger or hurt. I can extend love and respect for the parts of them that are honorable and examine why they are not responding the way I want them to from this point of view.*

A few weeks later, a camera is now in the classroom. It feels like the powers that be don't believe the parents. This action has been taken to satisfy the parents and prove the board is right. Nothing bad is going on. Parents have 90 minutes at the end of the school day to watch the videos of the full day. All they see is that he keeps his voice down now and does a lot of whispering in children's ears. This does not calm the situation down. We keep speaking out. There is a meeting with the Saskatchewan Teacher's Federation, the school board, the teacher, and the parents. I'm allowed in the meeting, but I'm not allowed to speak or to write. I meet privately with people from the Ministry of Education. They won't overturn decisions made by an elected board, then the Ombudsman, and the children's advocate. They don't have jurisdiction in schools.

It's the end of the school year. I hear a rumor that the teacher will be leaving after this one year in our community. He hasn't been fired but has been told, "These parents aren't going to stop," and it might be more comfortable for him to take a position at another school.

My work on this job is complete, even if the way the system handles poor teachers is terrible.

Now it's summertime, and a counseling client comes to me with a letter from the Chief Psychiatrist. She has PTSD because of being bullied. This is not his only client with issues of bullying from within our community. "Something needs to be done," he says.

My work on this job is not yet complete.

I submit the letter, with client and parent permission, blacking out identifying words, along with a proposal to coordinate a peer mediation program within the school. I have highly underestimated how angry I made the superintendent with my advocacy.

They don't respond to me, but one of the parents is there and calls me immediately after the meeting.

"Are you sitting down? Sit down."

Within days an article appears in the local newspaper; "Tables turn for school advocate." My throat burns with toxic nausea. My muscles begin to shake and twitch. "Melville Public School Division Trustees banned Kelly Karius from its schools except to take part in events involving her children, during a recent meeting."

"[The Director] told the trustees they should reject the proposal because Karius wasn't qualified to set up such a program. And she should be banned from school involvement because Karius attached a doctor's report on a child, which [he] says breaches confidentiality. [He] says that breach of confidence makes it unlikely Karius would be trusted by staff to deal with children other than her own."

I am ruined.

What is the thought? *I am ruined.*

What is true about this? *This is a bad article, and if people believe it, I won't have a career. I won't have their trust.*

What is not true about this? *I didn't breach confidentiality and can easily prove that. I am qualified to do my work and can easily prove that.*

What is another way to think about this? *This is a challenge I didn't ask for, but I have not done anything wrong. I have all the skills and resources I need and can ask for help when I need it—step by step.*

I spend the next year coping with the fallout and pushing back on the school ban, cooperating with my ethics committee. The superintendent ducks the ethics committee, realizing his assumptions are incorrect. In the end, I sue him.

What was wrong in our community? Why was the bullying so bad? Why did I see everyone bullying at times? The kids, the parents, the school board, the superintendent, government employees? Why did I see so many people who couldn't stand up for themselves in a healthy way? Had no one taught the communication skills to move things forward instead of escalating things up?

The question was the answer. No one taught us communication skills to move things forward instead of escalating things. Not only in this community but in pretty much every community. I started building a communication program to be taught in schools. When I finished, I leaned back in my chair, feeling all the accomplishment, knowing this was going to help so many. This sense of triumph lasted all of ten seconds when an electric shock ran through my body, and I knew it wasn't done.

Are you kidding me?

What is the thought? *Are you kidding me? After all these months and years of work, do I have to change it all? I didn't do it right, and now I have wasted so much time.*

What is true about this thought? *I have to change it, and it's going to take more time.*

What is not true about this thought? *I haven't wasted time or done it wrong. These changes are going to improve the work immensely.*

How can I think about this differently? *Even though I must change it, and it's going to take more time, I haven't wasted time or done it wrong. These changes are going to improve the work immensely.*

The electric shock is what I call "My God Voice," and it must be listened to and answered. Information from My God Voice is best used without whining about it too much. I immediately knew what had to change. I was still using the labels 'bully' and 'victim' all through this work. They had to go. The labels don't matter—they box us in and create bad lessons. We all use both bully actions and victim responses at times. One set of skills solves both. It's not just schools that need resources—it's parents too. After years of hard labor, the *No Such Thing as a Bully System* was finally born.

I know that I wouldn't be loving this life that I've created and helping so many people without being able to balance my thinking. I know I wouldn't be able to release anger and the emotions underneath it in a healthy way without this tool. I know that you can use this too to reach your potential, release difficult emotions and love yourself and others unconditionally.

I welcome you to a new lease on life. This tool is at your fingertips, moving you to real change that will last a lifetime.

THE TOOL

You'll have noticed one of the cornerstones of the system throughout this story, a balanced thinking tool. When I was in my 20s, as a young parent going to university, I was diagnosed with depression and anxiety. Unable to shake the negative thoughts that tattooed disgust about myself into my brain and heart, I sought help. The counselor told me I already knew everything I needed to know about anxiety and depression. The psychiatrist gave me pills.

I found my own help, my own way of balanced thinking, and my own way of unconditional love for myself and other people. This balanced thinking tool is one that I continue to use every single day of my life. It is one that I want to share and shout out to the whole world! Whenever you find yourself in a difficult situation, when your thoughts hold you back or allow hatred to grow, this tool is here for you too!

When I find a thought about myself, others, or the world is unhelpful or disturbing to me. I use this tool to think differently about it. Rather than a coach or friend yelling at you to "Be positive!" This tool helps you find your way of balanced thinking. When your thinking is balanced, it's just a sidestep over to positive thinking.

We all have hundreds of inaccurate negative thoughts daily. We don't even notice all of them. If you've ever been happy and suddenly feel sad, an unnoticed, negative automatic thought is likely the culprit. You do not need to accept the inaccurate negative thoughts you have about yourself, others, or the world. Follow them out into the light and change their power.

1. Figure out the thought that is bothering you. When it appears as a question, form it into a sentence.

2. Ask and write down, "What is true about this thought?" Be factual in your response. There are times when you will find nothing true about a negative thought.

3. Ask and write down, "What is not true about this thought?" Answer this like you are your own best friend. If you find this difficult, work with a friend, or ask yourself what you would say to a friend in the same situation.

4. Ask and write down, "What is another way to think about this?" This will be a combination of your answers in two and three. Acknowledging the factual truth of our negative automatic thoughts allows us to release the thought, or if a thought proves itself true, to make a change plan.

You're likely to find that your most unhelpful thoughts repeat themselves. Write down your answers, and when the thought returns, look at what you've written. Eventually, you won't have to look anymore, the answers will become integrated, and you will notice your thoughts changing without needing to write or read what you've already written.

Kelly Karius, RSW, BSW, Mediator

Kelly Karius is an award-winning social worker, mediator, and author. She is the creator of The Key Method of Communication, helping people find their keys through knowledge, empowerment, and you.

Kelly is an expert at quickly finding the root of problems, reframing, and redefining to give you another way of looking at your situation and new tools to stay calm and peaceful within it.

Kelly is highly skilled at showing people that they can reclaim their power and change their relationships with themselves and with others. The No Such Thing as a Bully System is one of the crucial pieces of The Key Method of Communication.

It has long been known that the way we are approaching bullying isn't working. Many bullying organizations recommend removing the labels. Finally, here is the actual tool that does that!

The No Such Thing as a Bully System teaches that all of us, children and adults, use bully actions and victim responses at times in our lives. One set of tools prevents both. The labels do not move the issue of bullying forward but looking at our individual actions does.

Kelly's books include *This is Out of Control! A Practical Guide to Managing Life's Conflicts, Burgerslinger,* and *No Such Thing as a Bully; Shred the Label, Save a Child* for parents, certified facilitators, and schools.

Kelly is well versed in several areas of practice, including First Nations wellness, divorce, custody and access, adoption, and conflict management.

Kelly has won an award for Ethics in Business from The Better Business Bureau and a Government of Alberta Person of Inspiration Award for her work in bullying.

To get a taste of what The No Such Thing as a Bully System can do for you and your family, Kelly invites you to the next No Such Thing as a Bully Live Online Session. Get more information and sign up here! http://nosuchthingasabully.com/nstaab-live

CHAPTER 24

LEADING WITH SOUL

A SIMPLE PRACTICE TO THRIVE IN YOUR DIVINE PURPOSE

Mark Porteous

MY STORY

My stand is for all people to recognize themselves as Divine Beings who have chosen the human experience for a reason and to live in alignment with who they really are.

My stand has taken a lifetime to uncover and years to refine. I did not always know what I stood for or against. It wasn't until 2016 that I officially announced my stand as part of a high-end mastermind I joined to help me amplify my impact through producing and hosting live events.

Steve Jobs said, "You can't connect the dots looking forward, you can only connect them looking backwards."

In reviewing my own life, I can see how each year became the foundation for those who followed and how each new year offered clues about what was to come in the years ahead.

Starting with my birth in the City of Angels, Los Angeles, California, in June of 1970, the dawn of the Age of Aquarius, soulful leadership was in my blood and written in the stars.

When I was six, my dad was a minister for a Dutch Reformed Church in the town where my parents, sisters, and I grew up. After my parents divorced, the church he personally built and led banished him. Feeling deeply hurt, he began his quest for spiritual truth. Unconsciously, that's when I started my search too.

Only in writing my contribution for this book did I recognize the foreshadowing this was for my own story and fear of stepping into soulful leadership. That's one of the transformational gifts I've received from sharing my stories of *Inspired Living* with you.

I lived with my father at his parent's house for one year during second grade. My sisters and I moved into a rental home with both of our divorced parents one year later. They were pioneers of co-parenting in 1977. Unfortunately, it only lasted for one year.

Shortly after I turned nine, my dad remarried. Both of my sisters and I moved in with him, his wife, and her three kids. Our new family was my first exposure to hippie living. They always smelled like patchouli. They were strict vegans and did not watch TV or listen to the radio. They were only allowed to enjoy live music and entertainment. It was a very different lifestyle than we had ever seen before. I could not have imagined I would later choose a similar lifestyle for myself.

My dad's second marriage came to a sudden halt one night when he woke us all up yelling, "Grab your pillow, a blanket, and clothes, then get in the car right now!" We packed enough clothes for one week, and then he took us to a friend's house. Many years later, I learned that my father walked in on his new wife having sex with her former lover, who was spending the night in our living room on his way through town. Although we never saw them again, their divorce proceedings lasted for years, much longer than their two months of marriage.

I was nine years old and heading into fourth grade when my parents tried a second attempt at co-parenting. This time we moved into a larger home, so my father could have his own bedroom on the other side of the house. Soon he was openly dating again.

When I was ten, he remarried again. I moved in with him and my new stepmother in Housatonic, Massachusetts. It was 1980, and I was going into fifth grade at my fifth new school. My sisters stayed with my mom in our hometown, about 40 minutes away, just over the Massachusetts border. I would often visit them on weekends.

At the end of fifth grade, I went to Maine with my mom's best friend Judy and her son. He was two years younger than me, and we had been friends for two years. I returned home to find my father had secretly moved my belongings into my mom's house. I was shocked! I had no idea it was coming. It was such an emotional punch to the gut I blocked out the pain for the next 30 years.

The following year, Judy had another son. I was eleven. My friend, who was an only child for nine years, now had two younger brothers. He was not thrilled. I was. I loved and cared for Jeremiah like he was my son. The following year Judy had a third son, Jaime, who was also like a son to me.

I was twelve years old and had two baby boys who loved me unconditionally. That's when I started thinking about having my own children. I would fantasize about being a parent, thinking, *Someday, I will be the best father a man can be.*

Before long, I started having visions of my children, both during sleep and when I was awake. At first, I allowed these visions to expand and clarify. In my mind, I saw my children being Christ-like. I could see them as young leaders living in a new world that resembled Heaven on Earth.

Over the years, as my love for Jeremiah and Jaime continued to grow, my visions started to fade. I began blocking my thoughts of parenting children who were Christ-like and the images of them living in Heaven on Earth because I feared these visions were somehow sacrilegious.

Who am I to be entrusted with such precious children?

I buried my crazy vision deep in my psyche, where it remained dormant, quietly rooting its way into my heart.

Jeremiah and Jaime were christened in their mom's church when I turned 18, and I was named their Godfather.

Running away from a fierce confrontation with my stepfather shortly after, I moved in with my godsons' family.

By the end of my first year of college, I decided I wanted to be a cruise director on a major cruise line. I learned three ways to get hired in the activities department on a cruise ship; finish my degree, become fluent in at least one other language, or work for Disney for one year.

I chose Disney. I moved to Orlando, Florida, where I was hired as a lifeguard in Disney's Career Start program.

One year later, my mom was diagnosed with breast cancer. I moved back to New York for nine months to be near her during treatment. Then I returned to Orlando.

I was 22 years old and working for Greenpeace International at the Orlando office when my girlfriend brought me to The Spiral Circle bookstore. It was the first time I remember hearing the word metaphysical. It smelled like incense and felt like home.

I read the phrase that changed my life forever: *"We are not human beings having spiritual experiences. We are spiritual beings having human experiences."*

Suddenly everything made sense. Even beliefs conflicting with what I learned from my mom and others I trusted about Christianity.

As soon as I got home from the bookstore, I eagerly called my dad, who had written three books at the time. I remember the anticipation of his adoration for following in his footsteps as an author. Instead, he responded, "Don't expect to make money writing a book. You have to have a business, not just a book."

Not one to be easily discouraged, I quickly adjusted my plan to include what I received from his advice. I'd build a business so I could write for the joy of writing and sharing my beliefs rather than as a path to wealth.

I didn't know at the time that my business could, and perhaps even should be related to my book. My first idea was a holistic wellness center. I quickly realized that would require an enormous investment and ongoing overhead, plus it would take years to build the business.

A friend of mine had been selling hair wraps on Panama City Beach. After a long wait in the growing line to get his daughter a wearable beach souvenir, a Disney executive invited him to open a test location on Disney property. Within months he had dozens of sites all over Disney property. He did over one million in sales in his second year. That was a business model I could replicate.

I started with a single location at Church Street Station in Orlando. Soon, I had my employees at resorts and smaller amusement parks around Orlando. I then partnered with one of the big distributors of souvenir jewelry and beads. We opened four different locations at Kings Island Amusement Park, just outside Cincinnati, Ohio.

In 1999, I had over one hundred employees at parks all over the country. Most of them were teens working summer jobs. A friend convinced one employee to join my team even though she had a full-time job as a medical assistant in a geriatric doctor's office. Renee was 19-years-old and my most responsible employee. There is no way I could have imagined that we would be married just three years later.

I started Unique Ventures, LLC to fund my dream of writing a book in 1994. By 1999, I realized I hadn't written one more word for my book. Over those five years, it took all I had to run a business that I did not enjoy to pursue my passion, which I had no time even to explore, much less follow.

I sold my business and started working for Time Warner, selling cable and internet services. I figured I could make more money in less time and finally have time to finish my book. In my mind, I would have the book done within two years, and then I could decide what to do with the rest of my life.

Ten years later, in April of 2010, our twins were born. I still hadn't made any progress with my book. Instead, I got comfortable in a job that provided a high income and benefits. I knew the next ten years would go by even faster with newborn twins.

A terrible fear came over me. I was clear that if I did not make a change, I'd be teaching my children the deferred lifestyle of putting off following their passions to do what society suggested as the safe and responsible path.

I did not want to teach my children to conform. I was determined to be an example to them of living a life of meaning and joy. I needed to practice—*Inspired Living*.

By the time our twins had their first birthday, my book, *The Human Experience*, was written, and with Renee's help, we self-published through Amazon. After my 41st birthday, we celebrated with a book launch at a favorite local cafe and 70+ of my closest friends.

Then Renee asked me, "Now what? You've wanted to write this book for 18 years. What do you want to do now?"

Renee suggested life coaching. I didn't know much about it. I considered life coaching a new form of therapy for wealthy housewives. Little did I know it was a huge and growing industry.

The first thing we did was research how much money I could make. With a quick Google search, we learned the average life coach in the United States was making under $20,000 per year. After ten years of averaging over $100,000 per year, I knew $20,000 would not provide a lifestyle that we would enjoy.

Then my wife asked me a profound question. "That's what the average life coach earns," she started. "You have never been an average sales rep. Why do you think you would be an average life coach?"

Wow, Renee was already coaching me!

We looked at what the top coaches were earning. Tony Robbins and other elite coaches were making millions, while many more were making over $100,000 per year. I figured if they could do it, I could too. As I researched, I found plenty of people promising that I could quickly make $10,000 per month with ease if I followed their exact steps.

I decided to test it out by taking a coaching certification program. My coach asked me what my niche was going to be. Although I was unfamiliar with niching, I said I wanted to be a spiritual coach. He laughed at me and said, "You won't make any money as a spiritual coach. You can pick any niche you want, as long as it is one of these three. You can choose health, wealth, or love, and then sneak in spirituality like medicine in the dog food."

I bought that lie for my first five years as a business coach and joint venture strategist. I tried to conform to what I thought was expected of me. Even while investing thousands of dollars doing deep spiritual work and supporting clients who were highly successful spiritual coaches, subconsciously, I continued to believe the lie.

Everything changed when I decided to *lead with Soul.*

THE TOOL

After reading *The Untethered Soul,* by Michael Singer, I decided to follow my inner guidance, no matter what. Suddenly everything began to shift. Synchronicities lead to opportunities I could have never expected. I began to experience great joy and ease in my work; clients seemed to be magnetized to me.

I was beginning to live my stand. The more authentic I was being to who I am, the more magical my life became.

I had discovered my own formula for creating magic in my life.

Would you like to make a more significant impact in the world and make more income?

Imagine for just a moment if all you had to do to make a bigger impact and a higher income was to be more of who you really are so that every action you take is inspired, joyful, and in your highest good.

How great will it feel to quickly recognize when you're out of alignment and easily shift back into the soul energy that best supports you at any given moment?

Being able to shift into alignment is the most powerful practice you can master for soul success.

I started experimenting with something I call Alignment Consciousness as a practice to discover for myself if following my soul guidance can positively impact my business and my life.

So what is Alignment Consciousness?

It's making choices for your highest good based solely on alignment with your values, mission, and vision.

There are three steps in the practice of Alignment Consciousness. These three steps are the magic keys to my soul's success in business and life.

1. Commit to a life-long process of self-discovery so that you can be more of your true magnificent self.

   Abraham Maslow talked about your innate, unchanging core values being the essence of who you really are. The more you learn about who you are and how to optimize your presence in this world, the greater your success, happiness, and life effectiveness will be.

2. Make conscious choices using Divine discernment to maintain alignment with who you are. There are many ways to receive guidance.

Here are some common external and internal sources of guidance:

External Guidance:

- God/Allah/Universe
- Gods and goddesses
- Angels and guides
- Friends or family who have crossed over

Internal or Innate Guidance:

- Muscle testing
- Kinesiology
- Pendulum
- Journaling

I practice a method I call *Embodied Intuition*.

Begin by standing with feet shoulder width apart, knees slightly bent, and toes slightly turned in. Slowly breathe into your lower belly. Feel your belly rise more than your chest. Rock front to back slightly to test your balance and find your center of gravity. Take another deep breath into your belly, and as you exhale, tell yourself a truth you believe to be absolute, such as the current day of the week or month of the year.

For example, say, "My name is [insert your name]."

Notice how it feels in your abdomen. How does your balance feel? Did you feel any pull forward or push back? Did you sense heaviness, or was it light?

Now clear that thought. Take another deep breath. This time on the exhale, tell yourself something you believe to be untrue. You could use the earlier example, except state your name incorrectly or use the wrong date or day of the week. Notice how it feels in your abdomen this time. How is it different? How does your balance feel? Did you feel any pull forward or push back? Did you sense heaviness, or was it light?

Try another example with one truth and one lie. Can you feel the connection between how you feel when you state a truth versus an untruth?

This is your intuition speaking to you. You can use this technique to allow your intuition to guide you in many situations. I highly recommend experimenting with this process any chance you get. You will be amazed at how fun it can be and how clear the guidance becomes when you practice listening for it.

What's your process of receiving inner guidance?

And when you receive guidance, what do you do with it?

3. Take Inspired Action in alignment with who you are being, then trust and surrender to the magic of sacred synchronicity.

    Action is the expression of who you are being. As you continue taking inspired action, you will be open to receiving even more guidance.

Einstein said, "There are only two ways to live your life. One is as though nothing is a miracle. The other is as though everything is a miracle."

These three steps of *Alignment Consciousness* are the process of creating your own miracles. It's simple, but not easy. You can do this!

After a lifetime of searching for answers, I am clear there is no other choice for me than to *lead with Soul.*

Known as The Soul Connector, **Mark Porteous** has been married to his wife and business partner Renee since 2002. They are parents of twins, a boy, and a girl, born in 2010. Mark is a Joint Venture "Strategist, Affiliate Concierge, co-founder of the Soul Affiliate Alliance and the #1 Best Selling author of *Soulful Leadership; A Spiritual Path to Health, Wealth and Love.*

Mark connects people to who they are at soul-level, why they are here, and to the people who can help them thrive in their Divine Purpose.

Transformational leaders and inspired influencers hire Mark to reach more people with their message by developing soulful collaborations and alliances, so they can leverage their expertise to make a greater impact in the world while enjoying more freedom, ease, and flow in their own lives.

CHAPTER 25

MAKING FRIENDS WITH THE DARK NIGHT OF THE SOUL

DISCOVERING INNER VOICES TO TRANSFORM DEPRESSION

Denise M. Simpson, MEd

There are times in life when we're challenged to define or redefine who we are, wondering, *what is my purpose? Is this the life I'm supposed to be living? And, what is my place in the world?*

The period of transition is commonly called a midlife crisis, but it can occur at key transformational points throughout life span development: adolescence, early adulthood, middle age, older age, and very old age.

You can recognize these points when you become stuck, feel stagnant, or bored with life. *Is this all there is? There has to be more to life!* rattles through your brain in the wee hours of the night as you toss and turn. For men and women, hormonal changes have an effect on midlife and menopause. It's difficult feeling lonely, sad, or isolated in the midst of a family gathering, work, team, or social event. What's even more difficult is when life feels heavy, dark, pointless, and the connection to Spirit is lost.

Emotionally you may feel powerless watching your parents age and die. Marriages, births, divorces, and deaths cause strain between siblings creating "Forming, Storming, Norming, and Performing" group dynamics as roles shift. As a spiritual seeker, you may be on your path—you are reading this book! Others may not consciously choose to awaken. "He needs therapy," may be true, but you can't force people to change. And it's exhausting trying to control others. I learned a lot about the "Controller" and other voices over the last seven years as an Advanced Certified Facilitator of Evolutionary Mystic Meditation™.

Interacting with others means we share our opinions, feelings, food, or help. When others reject your offer coming from your heart, it impacts your ability to feel safe and vulnerable, so you choose to shut down or withdraw. You may stifle your giving, laughter, and joy—your ability to feel fully, freely, and authentically.

Rejection leaves wounds in your tender heart. The "Wounded Self" takes on all the pain and suppresses it so that the Self can function. Wow! That's a lot, and healing is so scary because, like Pandora's box, it can feel overwhelming to crack the lid on what may be repressed. It's dark in there, but it also takes tremendous psychic and physical energy to keep all the negativity locked up. This becomes heavy, emotional baggage. Decades later, it shows up as pain and illness. It definitely can rob you of feeling playful, free, and flowing.

We depress within ourselves that which truly longs to be expressed. It's a harsh trade-off that leads to physiological changes in the brain's electrochemistry so the body doesn't operate optimally based on the emotions and thoughts.

On the path to maturity throughout life, transformational stages are supposed to happen. Unfortunately, most of us are ill-equipped to sit, breathe, reflect, release the emotions, and gain peace and strength from them. Western medicine relies on science and drugs to diagnose and medicate sleepless nights, anxious feelings, and weight fluctuations. With a major depressive disorder or other co-morbid factors, prescription drugs may be warranted for safety's sake, and selective serotonin re-uptake inhibitors (SSRIs) can work wonders to jumpstart the neurons firing so that self-care actions are doable. Life is meant to be action, not stagnation.

Most often, though, instead of exploring the root causes of the angst, there is suppression or denial, which is longing to be acknowledged, honored, and evolved into maturity.

To cope with these dark feelings, many people turn to what they were taught growing up, addictions or distractions like alcohol, food, shopping, sex, gambling, gaming, chocolate, television, or social media. Emotions can be addicting too like anger, belittling, humor to cover up serious issues, or dysfunctional power dynamics of abuse. A person who feels insecure with a weak ego may bully others so that he feels better, but the boost to his self-esteem may not last. After the event comes a backlash of shame or worse, a strengthening of the "Enforcer:" "My way or the highway."

Contrast these approaches with Eastern, Native, and other cultures which have practiced rituals for centuries to guide the person with reverence and sacred curiosity. Feeling uncertain, adrift, and unsettled is what the "Dark Night of the Soul" is about. Rituals are used to explore, reflect, and navigate the hero's journey from darkness to light. Life transitions are addressed with sacred tools like meditation, journaling, hypnosis, sound healing, drumming, dancing, chanting, breathwork, yoga, Ho' oponopono, or a myriad of other practices. The wisdom of the elders, the Divine Feminine, or universal truths guide the spiritual seeker. The premise is that "This too will pass," and it will.

There is hope beyond taking a pill. Finally, science is catching up to the universal truths of what is truly possible in the mind-body and now the body-heart-mind-soul connections. We are in the fourth wave of psychology, energy psychology, and it's evidence-based. Whew! What a relief this is happening.

What helped me the most and saved my life was learning and becoming certified in the Emotional Freedom Technique and then Evolutionary Mystic Meditation™ incorporating Tapping.

To heal from trauma I learned to trust the safe presence of my coaches. I began to notice body sensations of temperature, pressure, weight, and constriction. Sensations create thoughts which our minds interpret as emotions. Developing the skill of identifying emotions instead of thinking concepts that masquerade as emotions was a revelation, and is a key component of the coaching work I do with clients.

Dropping from overwhelming, spinning thoughts in my mind into my body sounds simple but this was new to me! The mind is full of stories and illusions that appear true, but aren't. Next I learned to harness courage in my heart to actually feel all my emotions—to process, release, and integrate new perspectives and to become whole again.

Identifying emotional patterns is another key. Gaining freedom to be non-reactive yet engaged—the "Witness" is a divine gift. This is a state of true power with the ability to hold your centered awareness with compassion for the other and yourself. Detached observation is a state where there is no need to be swayed by another's opinion. Releasing the need to force your will on another is a skill worth developing!

Before I learned this, I suffered because I held back and squashed down my energy, needs, and desires in my family, work, money, and relationships. Everyone came first, and there was the judgment of being selfish if I made a choice for myself. The judge fears external viewpoints. It is a powerful cast member of the Dark Night of the Soul. My judge has the ability to stop me in my tracks from taking action, hindering my goal accomplishment. Can you identify your judge?

With enough suppression of our energy, depression changes the brain's electrochemistry and neural structures. Tapping is a mind-body energy tool proven to decrease cortisol and norepinephrine and increase the feel-good hormones of endorphins, dopamine, and oxytocin. And tapping is natural, self-administered, and has no chemical side effects like pharmaceuticals. By driving down cortisol levels, the body's fight or flight system of being hyper-vigilant and flooded with adrenaline lessens or stops. The nervous jitters relax so that the body feels lighter, calmer, and the mind more peaceful. Sleep improves, and tapping helps to regulate weight because cortisol interferes with digestion. I lost 40 pounds in one year without focusing on diets because I was focused on healing my emotional baggage. I became lighter as I freed myself from negative, traumatic memories.

The Dark Night of the Soul happens, and it will happen as we cycle through life, but it doesn't have to be a painful struggle once you learn today's energy psychology tools to address underlying root causes and heal trauma.

When you know the truth of your soul qualities and life mission, you become the conductor directing the instruments of your knowledge, time, focus, communication, boundaries, and love within your life, creating harmony in all realms, body-heart-mind, and soul.

MY STORY

Do you ever feel like there was a rule book for living handed out at birth, but that somehow you didn't receive it? I felt that way often, feeling awkward and unsure. And when I did express what I most wanted or thought, it was often met with my parents' responses of, "No, you don't. Do it this way. Don't be a teacher, therapist, or writer; you won't make any money. Go into business instead." It's been a lifelong pattern of having to battle to prove myself. Once I achieved my goal, I received an acknowledgment of, "You did it. I couldn't have done that."

As a highly sensitive child, I was awkward in my body, and my logic-focused dad reprimanded me repeatedly to, "Get your head out of the clouds!" Teasing and my sister beating me up were common, something my father thought was funny until he was dying, and when I finally angrily spoke the truth of how he supported her bullying me. "Builds character," was his response, still not comprehending the damage inflicted.

It hurt and I suppressed the hurt over and over because expressing anger was not allowed. I could never win and that contributes to the "Voice of the Victim."

To be safe and belong in my family of origin, I learned to be the 'good girl,' the 'helper,' and the 'smart one.' Books became my refuge from the chaotic noise of three siblings in a small house. Family holidays included 18 relatives and sometimes it was too much sensory overload. I would suddenly get sick with a respiratory illness and have to stay home instead of attending the fun, but noisy, family holiday gathering. My presents would be delivered later with a rush of cold, wintry air disturbing my cocoon of warmth and quiet on the living room couch.

Since high school, I've been interested in psychology and have spent a lifetime learning. I have also spent a lifetime with depression and then exuberance, discovering my gifts and how my energy system wants to work. Intuitively I've known since high school that I needed to be away from home to grow and develop. Even before earning a Master's degree in Marriage and Family Therapy (while I was separating and getting divorced), I learned about enmeshed families, scapegoating, and learned helplessness with *The Cinderella Complex* book. There were many A-ha moments of discovery and,

Oh, that makes sense. That's why! There is no way I'd have gained awareness from within the family system. It doesn't work that way.

Albert Einstein said, "The world as we have created it is a process of our thinking. It cannot be changed without changing our thinking. We can't solve problems by using the same kind of thinking we used when we created them." This applies to ourselves, the family, the work unit, the community, or the world. During the Dark Night of the Soul, our thinking calls us to become different.

When my mom died in 2007, being the scapegoat was transferred to me; that's my story. But because I'm conscious of family systems and patterns, I fought to establish boundaries and not be persecuted this way. I was a spiritual warrior for transformation. A 16-year battle for survival ensued. And it's not the only battle to stay alive I've fought. It creates my courageous heart.

For decades I worked in corporate America, drifting from job to job when I was younger. Remember the 'people pleaser' morphing into what anyone else wanted me to be or do? I settled into a training career at the world's largest pharmaceutical company, where I turned into a work addict, routinely working 60 hours per week. Like a hero, I saved projects under unrealistic deadlines and won Global Training awards. I trained thousands of employees in the US and abroad. The recognition fed my ego while draining my body.

My crisis came from being switched to women bosses who were younger and less educated than me. Harassment occurred until I quit in 2010 to move to a top-four pharmaceutical company. That worked great until my old boss moved to the new company, and my new boss started bullying me. A hit-and-run accident in January 2012 after my purse was stolen was the breaking point. It was a day of tears and trauma. After landing on the hood of the car, being crucified like Jesus on the cross, I got the message: *Stop being a martyr.*

For the next six months, I worked despite back pain with my goal to save enough money to be able to quit. By June of 2012, I walked away from a six-figure corporate salary. It was freedom! And then, in July 2012, after a massive family argument, I stood in the bathroom with a pile of pills in my hand, ready to check out of life on this planet. What I was offering my family was being rejected. I had no purpose.

The Dark Night of the Soul is a breaking point. What stopped me from swallowing those pills on that beautiful, warm summer day was hearing a voice inside that said: *Denise, it's not your day to die. No one has power over you. Only you get to say whether you live or die, and it's not today.*

So what's my purpose then? I railed at God.

Silence.

It's not your day to die, I heard.

Sigh. I put the pills down and cried myself to sleep. Fourteen hours later, I awoke, challenging God: *Okay, so what's my purpose?*

Silence.

So I got myself out of bed, tapped, and lived that day. And I kept doing that for weeks until it was no longer a battle cry, but an inquiry.

Over the next year, I woke up, tapped, cried, wrote, gardened, and did not work at a job. My job was healing, including acupuncture, meditation, hypnosis, massage, essential oils, and Reiki. I learned about food as medicine and began juicing. The next year I cleared out my medicine cabinet and discarded over-the-counter medications and even my asthma inhaler. I got certified in the Emotional Freedom Technique and Reiki. I shared myself with a whole new group of people who became friends, healers, and soul sisters. That felt wonderful. I was sleeping better, waking up grateful to experience the joy of being alive. Whew! What a shift. tapping cured me of the major depression I had been in for seven years.

The darkness, pain, disconnection, and isolation I experienced were the blackest of my life, but it's also been my greatest gift in that I came to know myself—the core of me, the soul within the physical body, the Divine healer within. I'm grateful and I'm still discovering and excavating the most precious core parts of myself.

I'm convinced that having a purpose and social connection is what keeps one alive. During my *Dark Night of the Soul* I would listen to the wall clock ticking away every second bringing me closer to death; a scene like a macabre Edgar Allan Poe story. I finally pulled that damn clock off the wall. Time is a choice, and we never get it back, but I can choose to live actively now. I know what my purpose is, and that's coaching with love.

Discover Your Dark Night of the Soul Voices

The Dark Night of the Soul is real, and so is the ability to transform. It's the calling of the soul for the human to evolve. Tapping boosts brain chemistry and changes neural patterning so that transformation is possible.

Every person has a plethora of voices in their monkey mind. Work with the voices of the Dark Night of the Soul to acknowledge the pain, honor the protective role the voice plays, discover when it was created, and dialogue with it so that it feels heard, seen, and loved. The voice will evolve from immaturity into skillful means. When the next Dark Night of the Soul occurs, you will gain a greater ability to process, release, and change, making it shorter and less painful. Empowerment is the result. Keep yourself safe and work with a qualified coach if you need support.

Common Voices: The Controller, The Judge, Invisibility, The Wounded Self, The People Pleaser, The Witness, The Courageous Heart as Divine Love

THE TOOL

Here are seven questions to work with these or your own voices of the mind.

Instructions: Set aside some quiet time to explore your answers and journal with sacred curiosity.

1. Who is the voice?

   I am the voice of: Name the voice

2. What is your job?

   Each voice has a job to do, what it controls, and when it comes to the forefront to guide or take over the Self. Reflect on how it interacts with the Self, others, and the world.

3. What are the risks the Self faces?

4. How do you protect the Self?

5. When were you created?

Explore what was happening to the Self as a younger child/person. Was there a danger, fear, trauma, or overwhelm?

6. How are you supporting the Self today?

7. How could you support the Self better?

Denise M. Simpson, MEd, Coach, Healer, Writer, Speaker, is The Courageous Heart Coach helping women entrepreneurs, professionals, and busy moms connect to the courage within their hearts, build confidence, and celebrate success in writing and life. Clients experience love to transform their fears and build their successful team of inner voices to make an impact, create abundance, and leave a legacy.

Denise brings to Courageous Heart Living and Courageous Heart Writing her unique combination of award-winning training, therapy, creativity, intuition, and evolutionary energy psychology tools so that clients gain life-changing shifts sooner than expected for bigger impacts. She holds two Masters of Educations degrees, multiple certifications, and is an Advanced Certified Facilitator of Evolutionary Mystic Meditation™. Denise has authored A Muse Your Self Writing and is a contributing author to multiple publications on Amazon.com

CLOSING

The biggest benefit of reading a collaboration book is the collective energy and community that the book creates.

The wisdom of each expert layers and builds to create a powerful consciousness that is bigger than the individuals.

Did you feel the energy build as you read each chapter and felt the heart of each author?

Could you feel the similarities and honor the differences?

Did anything surprise you with an author's story?

Did a story help you remember an event in your life that needs attention?

I invite you to connect with the authors whose story and/or tool resonates with you.

We are grateful you joined us for this Inspired Living journey and would love to stay connected. Social media is a powerful tool for connection; please see the biographies at the end of each chapter for how to connect with the authors.

You are invited to join us in our Facebook community, Inspired Living: Superpowers, for new ways to connect with the authors and receive the support you need, want and deserve.

We plan a summit in January 2023 and other magic along the way. The community in the Facebook group will be filled with opportunities to learn more about the authors and their brilliance.

https://www.facebook.com/groups/inspiredlivingsuperpowerscommunity/

MY GRATITUDE

I'm blessed to have many teachers and guides along my journey. Learning to feel gratitude for the lessons and growth opportunities moved me into my true essence.

I acknowledge the gift of my family and ex-husband pressuring me to play by the rules and be supportive versus shine, so I could expand into me. Without this pressure, I would have stayed the piece of coal buried in the earth instead of shining my brilliant diamond self for all to see and experience.

I always loved angels, and they were my favorite part of the few times we went to church. Meeting Rev. Elvia Roe at a healing circle opened my connection to spirit and angelic guidance. Her support helped me remember who I was at my soul's level and my true divinity. With her mentorship, I became an Angelic Life Coach, teacher, and minister.

Margaret Lynch Raniere pulled me out of my comfort zone and into the spotlight and stage. I'm forever grateful for her seeing my *Charismatic Leader* instead of my *Knowledgeable Achiever* I hid behind because my family expected it and it was safe. She also modeled the tap and rant EFT style that changed my life and the lives of many of my clients.

Alan Davidson was my mentor, guide, and friend, the big brother I always wanted. His *Evolutionary Mystic Meditation* and foundational centering and grounding work reminded me that I am a spiritual being in a physical body. Being one of five of his advanced certified facilitators deepened my connection to all parts of who I am and allowed deep forgiveness of the aspects that I wasn't comfortable with. It also allowed me to easily guide clients to the same enlightenment and peace.

Joan Ranquet's program validated my animal communication abilities and took my skills even deeper. Her grounded and practical approach to communication and energy healing opened possibilities in all areas of my life. My connection to animals, as well as my intuitive abilities, exploded.

Taking an Intuitive Writing course with Laura DiFranco shifted my ingrained belief that: *I can't be both logical and creative.* Her coaching and invitation to write a chapter for *The Ultimate Guide to Self-Healing Techniques* opened the floodgates which led to this collaboration book.

I'm blessed with family and friends who are like family. I value you all and appreciate the friendship and support. I am greater because of your love and encouragement.

ABOUT CAROLYN MCGEE

Intuition Coach, Teacher, Speaker, Author, TV, Radio, and Podcast host.

Carolyn's purpose is to help women to break lifelong patterns of how they show up in relationships. The relationship to themselves, others, health, money, and spirit. She lost herself and her divine connection and existed for many years. She is passionate about providing short cuts to the pain of not being connected.

Carolyn will recognize the pattern that is keeping you small and stuck to clear the energy that holds you back. You will start to understand how you show up in one area of your life is how you show in all relationships. Learn more at: www.CarolynMcGee.com

Connect with Carolyn:

https://www.instagram.com/carolynmcgee444

https://www.facebook.com/CarolynMcgeeIntuitiveCoach

https://www.youtube.com/channel/UCt4AWvPgZfX4Xbt8vJEjt_g?

https://www.linkedin.com/in/carolynamcgee

https://www.pinterest.com/carolynm444/

https://twitter.com/CarolynMcGee

https://www.facebook.com/groups/EnhanceYourIntuition/

https://www.facebook.com/carolynmcgee444

WHAT IS SACRED HAVEN LIVING?

Sacred Haven Living with Carolyn McGee

SOULFUL HEALING   INTUITIVE GUIDANCE   EMBODIED ACTION

Sacred Haven is a real place, a place where imagination and reality merge to create deep healing and magical possibilities, clearing old patterns and embracing your soul's true mission so that your visions become tangible.

Live in your world filled with magic, mystery and harmony that supports your inner wisdom to make empowered decisions and take inspired action. Learn to clear out old thought patterns and open yourself to new and tangible visions that result in ease and flow.

Access this new energy and world of magic, mystery, and harmony to help you make the empowered and impactful decisions to guide you gracefully and confidently to your heart's desire.

Change your thought patterns and manifest a magical, mysterious, and inspired life.

Allow the wisdom of your soul to guide you confidently and gracefully to your heart's desire. www.CarolynMcGee.com

HIRE CAROLYN TO SPEAK AT YOUR NEXT EVENT

Carolyn McGee 3 minute Intuition excerpt from
Natural Living Expo talk 11-2019
https://youtu.be/8RsIoEBQm5E

CAROLYN IS A SPEAK FROM THE HEART SPEAKER

https://carolynmcgee.com/contact/

GET YOUR SIGNED BOOKS

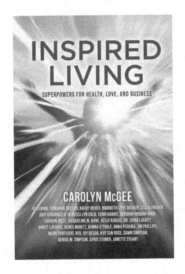

Carolyn has written prayers, poems and chapters in 15+ books. Carolyn has limited copies of books to personalize, sign, and ship for you.

Check out www.CarolynMcgee.com/books for what resonates for you.

This book, *Inspired Living: Superpowers for Health, Love, and Business* will also be available.

Embracing Your Authentic SELF

Chapter Six, page 127

Shedding the "Shoulds"

My "Cinderella" Moment

The Ultimate Guide to Self-Healing Techniques
Chapter Seven
Grounding and Centering
Clarity Through Heart Connection

The Wellness Universe Guide to Complete Self-Care:
25 Tools for Stress Relief
Chapter Fourteen
Tap and Rant
Release Blocked Energy for Empowered Clarity

Soulful Leadership
A Spiritual Path to Health, Wealth, and Love
Chapter Eight
Healing through the Heart
A Gateway to Intuitive Balance and Action

Sacred Medicine, Mystical Practices for Ecstatic Living
Chapter Twenty
Harness Your Home's Energy to Create a Sacred Haven
Amplify Connection, Intuition, and Peace

The Wellness Universe Guide to Compete Self-Care:
25 Tools for Goddesses
Chapter Twenty
Using Voice Dialogue to Tap into your Divine Feminine Power

The Ancestors Within: Volume 3

Chapter Four

A Plant Cutting from Grandma

Energy for Growth, Nurturing and Self-Love

More books, links to blogs and other opportunities are available at:

https://www.amazon.com/author/carolynmcgee

WORKSHOPS

WHAT IS CAROLYN OFFERING?

How can you up-level your life and step into empowerment, grace and clarity?

Check out Carolyn's workshops and classes.

www.CarolynMcGee.com/workshops

TESTIMONIALS

Working with Carolyn gave me more confidence to finally let go of nagging fears. I was tired of reacting to life and wanted to respond easily and grow. I worked through some childhood stuff and went to the next level with getting rid of those beliefs. Each week I learned something, things shifted, and I saw my growth. My confidence in my intuition, my ability to understand myself, and get my own guidance changed from 50% to 100%! My quality of life is better now.

~Joni L

Carolyn's intuitive guidance has accelerated both my personal and business growth over the past year. Clearly an earth angel herself, Carolyn utilizes angelic wisdom and heightened intuitive awareness to provide coaching that is focused and client specific. In just a few sessions, Carolyn helped me break through blockages and old patterns while offering purposeful action steps to ground new behaviors. Carolyn's gentle, compassionate, and non-judgmental demeanor provides the ambiance of safety, security, and love. I highly recommend Carolyn McGee to anyone seeking personal guidance to a happier, healthier life.

~Barbara S

Carolyn McGee is an intuitive coach without precedent. Before working with her, I was feeling a little lost. I've always trusted my intuition and I have used so many tools and strategies in the past. I had to make a decision that was going to impact my business and my life as well. Through our work together, not only did I feel completely held in a sacred way, but also led in a step by step process that allowed me to feel completely empowered, confident, and clear about what to do.

-Laura MG

We each have a superpower and if we don't let it shine then the world is less bright.

~Carolyn McGee

Made in USA - Kendallville, IN
44498_9781954047655
07.13.2022 1329